BLACK BOTTOM STOMP

OTHER BOOKS BY THE AUTHORS

BY DAVID A. JASEN

Recorded Ragtime 1897–1958

Tin Pan Alley

BY DAVID A. JASEN AND GENE JONES

Spreadin' Rhythm Around

That American Rag

BY DAVID A. JASEN AND TREBOR TICHENOR

Rags and Ragtime

BY GENE JONES

Tom Turpin: His Life and Music

The Original Dixieland Jass Band

Fables in Slang: A Ragtime Revue

BLACK BOTTOM STOMP

Eight Masters of Ragtime and Early Jazz

DAVID A. JASEN & GENE JONES

ROUTLEDGE

NEW YORK AND LONDON

Published in 2002 by
Routledge
29 West 35th Street
New York, NY 10001

Published in Great Britain by
Routledge
11 New Fetter Lane
London EC4P 4EE

Copyright © 2002 by Routledge
Routledge is an imprint of the Taylor & Francis Group.

Printed in the United States of America on acid-free paper.

10 9 8 7 6 5 4 3 2 1

Library of Congress Cataloging-in-Publishing Data

Jasen, David A.
    Black bottom stomp: eight masters of ragtime and early jazz / David A. Jasen and Gene Jones.
        p. cm.
    Includes bibliographical references (p.) and index.
    ISBN 0–415–93641–1 (hbk.)
        1. Jazz musicians—United States—Biography. I. Jones, Gene (Gordon Gene) II. Title.

    ML395. J37 2001
    781.65'092'273—dc21   2001031910
    [B]

TO THREE GENERATIONS OF JASENS—
MY MOTHER, GERTRUDE, MY WIFE, SUSAN,
AND OUR SON, RAYMOND

AND

TO ANNIE, JULIE, AND CHRISTOPHER

Five prominent ragtime composer-pianists in one photo! Look for Eubie Blake, Luckey Roberts, James P. Johnson, Joe Jordan, and Jelly Roll Morton.

CONTENTS

LIST OF ILLUSTRATIONS

ACKNOWLEDGMENTS

WE WOULD LIKE TO THANK everyone who helped us prepare this book, beginning with Raymond Jasen, whose idea it was to juxtapose the stories of these giants. Long before we began this project, we had been nourished by the writing and playing of those whose careers we trace here. We hope to present their lives in such a way as to make the reader want to hear what they wrote and played. If our book brings someone to this music for the first time, we are pleased to have launched a discovery. If we spur a return visit to a familiar composer/player, this will please us, too. We are as safe in our recommendations as we would be if we were urging someone to try fresh air or sunshine. The work of the eight artists profiled in this book can be heard on CDs, in historical reissues and in recent interpretations, and many of their published compositions are back in print. Give them a try; none of our subjects will let you down.

As collectors of sheet music and recordings, we are grateful to the dealers in so-called ephemera for their role in preserving America's greatest cultural treasure, its music. Wayland Bunnell, Beverly Hamer, Joel Markowitz, and Paul Riseman are outstanding music dealers who have for years helped countless collectors, including us, find and save what would have not have been found and saved without them.

We thank Ralph and Penny Gossard, longtime friends from Baton Rouge, who answered our questions about Louisiana's "Black Codes" and who supplied the *New Orleans Times-Picayune* articles that are the basis of the last story in the Louis Armstrong chapter.

Lois Battle, a good writer and a good friend, put her keen editorial eye to the early chapters and gave us perceptive comments as well as encouragement.

Three biographers have been especially important to the making of this book. They are, of course, named in our bibliography, but we must express appreciation to Edward Berlin (Scott Joplin), Laurence Bergreen (Louis Armstrong), and Scott E. Brown (James P. Johnson). Their skill and diligence have added immeasurably to our understanding of their subjects. Also, we came to a renewed admiration for the two New Orleans books by Al Rose. We believe them to be definitive in their treatments of the city's wicked past and of its music. And grateful mention must be made of the exceptional research done by Lawrence Gushee in tracking Jelly Roll Morton's lost years in vaudeville.

Ann Steele has graciously and generously helped us make this book. With great good humor, she has—for the third time—led two Luddites through the formatting and preparation of a presentable manuscript. She loves this music as we do, and she wants our book to represent it well.

And—again, for the third time—a tip of the Hatlo hat to our fighting editor, Richard Carlin, and to our first-class copy editor, Norma McLemore.

David A. Jasen

Gene Jones

PRELUDE

THIS BOOK IS ABOUT EIGHT unique, creative musicians who contributed much to the development of ragtime and early jazz. Ragtime and jazz have been treated as mutually exclusive topics for a long time now, so it is unusual to consider musicians from these two styles together in one book. Jazz historians have written *off* ragtime more than they have written *of* it. When it is remembered at all, it is usually portrayed as a quaint precursor of jazz, a stab at free expression that was shackled to the printed page. However, ragtime playing began as jazz playing did, with musicians fooling around, departing from written-out hymns, marches, and pop songs to pump some excitement into their performances. But Scott Joplin and his followers knew that there was something beyond the decorating and embellishing of "Ta-Ra-Ra-Boom-De-Ay" and "Golden Slippers" every night. Joplin saw that decorations and embellishments could be used to make original compositions. Because he published his experiments—and because one of these, "Maple Leaf Rag," was sold and heard everywhere—most Americans made their first acquaintance with ragtime as a *composed* music, with the form, style, and sound of Joplin and company. Early ragtime was not straining to *become* something, it *was* something.

Jazz, from its beginning, was a *way of playing* various kinds of pop music, including ragtime. In fact, ragtime was the foundation, the departure point, from which the earliest jazz bands constructed their improvisations. Among many examples of rag-based jazz was the Original Dixieland Jazz Band's first hit, "Original Dixieland One-Step." The melody of its third strain comes from Joe Jordan's 1909 "That Teasing Rag." Purists thought that the ODJB's treatment of Jordan's theme was a desecration, but the band actually smoothed out the lumps in the tune to make a more listenable—and danceable—number. Later in the evolution of jazz, largely because of Jelly Roll Morton's pioneering work, there would be jazz *composition*. The rhythmic liberation of ragtime—written out for all to see—opened the gate for melodic and harmonic liberation that would follow. As there had to be cubism before there was Dada (and rock before there was rap), so there had to be ragtime before there was jazz.

From the late 1890s through the late 1920s, many new musical styles came and went. Some musicians could not adopt the new sounds; seemingly frozen in time, they would continue to create in styles long outmoded through their entire musical careers. The subjects of this book, however, were professionals who wanted to achieve and to hold onto mainstream, commercial success. They took notice of new styles as they appeared and tried them on to see if they fit. When they rejected sounds and forms, they at least knew what they were rejecting. None of them stayed home or stood still.

Because they had broad and original musical minds, our subjects went at the problem of keeping up in highly individual ways, and each of them took sides (and sometimes changed sides) in a thirty-year tug-of-war between composed and improvised music. Ragtime was the rage when they were young men, and it drew each of them to music as a livelihood. They all began their careers hearing it and playing it, but none of them stayed with ragtime for life. (Even Scott Joplin, ragtime's founding father, although he did not abandon his compositional style in his late rags, became obsessed with other kinds of music.) Eubie Blake and

Luckey Roberts evolved highly personal, supertheatrical ragtime styles, and each had his biggest commercial success as a songwriter. James P. Johnson, Willie Smith, and Fats Waller took their ragtime playing to dizzy technical heights, and spewed such a flood of improvisatory ideas that they forever smudged the line between ragtime and jazz. Jelly Roll Morton decided that all of popular music, including ragtime, needed an overhaul, and he supervised the job himself. Louis Armstrong grew up with the lazy, clattering ragtime of New Orleans bands, laid down a few tantalizing samples of it in his early recordings, then went on to become the one-man embodiment of instrumental and vocal jazz.

Each of our subjects was black, and, because of his race, each had to make his way in a generally hostile world. They made their ways very well. They were among the most original musical minds of their time, and they redrew the map of popular music and rearranged its landscape. Because of them, we do not make music—nor dance nor sing nor pat our feet—in the way that our great-grandparents did. Their lives, personalities, and opinions were as diverse as the music they made. Their journeys were epic, and their destinations are landmarks in American music.

Introduction

TOM TURPIN AND THE
BIRTH OF RAGTIME

I F THE MUSIC THAT WE CALL "classic" ragtime could be said to have
had a home address, it was 2220-2222 Market Street, in St. Louis:
the site of Tom Turpin's Rosebud Bar. The music settled there when
it was young, and it lived there for six formative years. The tall, barrel-
chested Turpin was literally and figuratively the biggest man in ragtime
at this crucial stage in its development. He was the first major composer
of rags, and he was the original patron of the syncopated arts. As mentor, friend, and employer to the handful of young black men who wrote
and played the best early ragtime, he nurtured the music by nurturing
them. Among the beneficiaries of his largesse were Scott Hayden,
Arthur Marshall, Joe Jordan, Louis Chauvin, Charlie Thompson, and
Artie Matthews. With Turpin to encourage them and Scott Joplin to
inspire them, they became ragtime fiends. And in centering their aimless
lives on ragtime, this band of musical delinquents melded into the first
"school" of American popular composers.

Thomas Million Turpin was born in Savannah, Georgia, in 1873, and he came to St. Louis with his family in 1887. His father, known as "Honest John," had been a slave, and he had resolved never to work for another man after Emancipation. The move to St. Louis let him realize his dream of independence. John Turpin bought a stable and opened a small saloon, called the Silver Dollar, next door, at 425 South Twelfth Street. His step toward entrepreneurship was perfectly timed, and his choices of enterprise and location were just right. By 1890 the senior Turpin was a major player in the booming vice industry that had sprung up in the middle of the city, along Chestnut and Market streets. Tom's life in the saloon world began in the early '90s when he took a job as pianist in the city's most notorious sporting house, Madam Babe Connors's "Castle," at 210 South Sixth Street.

As St. Louis houses went, the Castle was a high-class place. It was a three-story white brick building near the elegant Southern Hotel, and its merchandise was a roster of eight or ten "Creole" girls, guaranteed to be authentic Louisianans. Madam Connors was a plump, bronze-complexioned woman who bedecked herself in diamonds before she made her entrance down a chandelier-lit stairway to welcome her callers. On slow nights, her girls could be coaxed into performing the house "specialty" dance: attired in long skirts (but sans underwear), they capered on a mir-rored floor to the accompaniment of Tom Turpin's piano.

But the Castle's real star was fat, coal-black Mama Lou. Bustling about the parlor in her comic maid's costume of calico dress, gingham apron, and red bandanna, she hurled mock insults at customers and girls alike, pausing occasionally to bellow obscene songs. In his book *The Time of Our Lives*, Orrick Johns tells of the evening that his father, George S. Johns, editor of the St. Louis *Post-Dispatch*, escorted the renowned con-cert pianist Ignace Paderewski to the Castle. Mama Lou was singing a piece of homemade bawdry called "Ta-Ra-Ra-Boom-De-Ay" that night, and Paderewski loved it. He ran to the piano and asked her to sing it again. She sang it over and over until the maestro had learned to play it. (Two other songs that were lifted from Mama Lou's repertoire and san-itized for Tin Pan Alley consumption were May Irwin's "Bully Song" and "There'll Be a Hot Time in the Old Town Tonight.") In 1897, thor-oughly trained for the hospitality business, Tom left Babe Connors to open his own place, Turpin's Saloon, at 9 Targee Street (near the barroom where the real-life prototypes of Frankie and Johnny made their violent leap into folklore a few years earlier).

In December 1897, Tom Turpin became the first black composer to publish a ragtime composition. Only a few rags—none of them remarkable, and all of them probably unknown to Turpin—preceded his into the marketplace. Turpin's "Harlem Rag" stands as the first good rag as well as the first important one. It is good because it has that alchemy of inevitability and surprise that makes listeners want to hear a piece of music—or see a painting or a film or a play—again and again. It is important because it was authentic—not secondhand—and it was real ragtime's crossover from folklore into print. There they were—visible at last—the rhythmic and melodic tricks that pianists had been pulling for ages, the tricks in which Turpin and his young piano-playing friends specialized. To Turpin, these eccentricities weren't merely decorations with which to adorn well-known tunes. In "Harlem Rag" they were building blocks for original melodies. The melodies had form; the forms made a structure. Turpin's rag was the road map that showed where syncopated playing would go.

"Harlem Rag" was issued in such small numbers that it was hardly known beyond central St. Louis, but it made a big impression on those who were most susceptible to it: the young players around Turpin. It legitimized ragtime for them, and it made many of those who were playing it want to write it. If a black saloonkeeper could get published, maybe they could, too. When Scott Joplin's "Maple Leaf Rag" appeared two years later, their dreams seemed even more attainable. One of their own—a black itinerant piano player—had put a rag on the music racks of pianos all over the Midwest. It had his name on it (and the second edition had his photo on it), he received a penny for every copy sold, and pianists of all colors and of both sexes wanted to play it. The sports were triumphant: Yo, de Koven! Ragtime rules!

◆

"How Dry I Am"—four words sung to four melody notes that sit precisely atop four beats—succinctly illustrates the barrenness of unsyncopated song. In fact, there can be nothing musically plainer. Its melody and beat maintain a perfect lockstep in their progression through time. Such deadpan tunes may have a lilt ("Casey would waltz with a strawberry blonde. . ."), or a stateliness ("Praise God from whom all blessings flow. . ."), or even a dash of energy ("Old MacDonald had a farm. . .")—but American taste has always run to something less square and more interesting, from "Camptown Races" to rap. In the mid-nineteenth century, when the writing and selling of popular music became a business, pop composers began to pry melody and beat apart and to fill the spaces in between with extra notes, extra words, or extra silence. By the late nineteenth century, pop music in general had at least a strong pulse—the dotted eighth note—if not yet a kick. The misplaced accent of minstrel songs and cakewalks found its way into music of various kinds. However, ragtime composers took it even further. They could imagine several kinds of syncopation at once, and could use them in pleasing melodic forms to make music that was *all syncopation, all the time.* In conceiving three or four fully syncopated melodies per rag, they used syncopation to a degree that was previously unthinkable.

In trying to describe these ceaseless schisms between melody and beat, writers used the words "ragged time"—soon contracted to "ragtime," then to "ragtime"—to suggest this new music's constant surprises. The "raggedness" (unevenness) came from the incessant shifting of accents from the listener's most basic expectation—a conjunction of melody and rhythm—to what is unexpected: the melodic stressing of what would ordinarily be "weaker" beats played against a predictable rhythm. This new American "ragged time" became the basis of the most complex—and most influential because it was the most enjoyable— popular music the world had ever known.

In its published form, "Harlem Rag" has four melodies of sixteen measures each, the first in C major and the succeeding three in the brighter key of G major. (The four-theme rag is thought of as classic ragtime form, but it is really a St. Louis convention. Composers from other places seldom used more than three melodies per rag.) There are echoes of older music in "Harlem Rag"—country fiddles and the call-and-response of field hollers—but it mostly suggests the bustle of a busy city, full of people out for good times. It is a highly pianistic, self-assured piece.

"Harlem Rag" is unique among early rags because it features (in its original printing) written-out variations on its themes. As a composer, Turpin thought like a performer, and "Harlem Rag," more than any other early rag, shows the amateur player how to put excitement into ragtime playing. Instead of the usual repeat-as-written markings at the ends of themes, "Harlem" provides written-out repeats of its second, third, and fourth strains, each of which is trickier—and showier—than the original statement of the melody. The repeat of the second strain is ushered in by a whirling chromatic figure (in measures 15 and 16) that foreshadows the two-bar "break" common to early jazz. When the second strain melody is repeated, it is more densely chorded and more highly syncopated than before. The syncopations of the third and fourth melodies are also complicated in their repeats, and the excitement of each is literally heightened by raising the variation an octave. Simply by playing "Harlem Rag" as written, the living-room pianist could sound something like a professional.

The second of the five rags Turpin published in his lifetime came in 1899, when Robert De Yong, a white St. Louis lawyer and dilettante publisher who had issued "Harlem Rag," sent "Bowery Buck" to music stores in the St. Louis area. Also that year, Joseph W. Stern & Company bought the rights to reissue "Harlem Rag." Stern's arranger, a black bandleader named William H. Tyers, so bowdlerized it that it is unrecognizable as Turpin's work. Nonetheless, this deformed version of ragtime's first masterpiece was the first rag to be published in New York City.

Just as De Yong was a part-time publisher, so was Turpin a part-time composer. The three Turpin-De Yong rags had only small print runs (probably no more than one hundred to two hundred copies each) and received only haphazard local distribution. Turpin was best known in the St. Louis underworld not as a composer of fine ragtime, but as owner-operator-host of Market Street's largest good-time establishment, the Rosebud Bar, which he opened in 1900. The Rosebud occupied most of a city block, and its chambers—barrooms, dining rooms, gambling rooms, and "hotel" rooms upstairs—held diversions of all sorts. Turpin himself was most often found in the wine room, where he had installed a piano on giant wooden blocks so that he could play while standing up. The Rosebud was filled with ragtime, performed by the host and by the young piano sharks who gathered there to emulate him. Turpin organized piano contests for them—and often entered himself—with money and medals as prizes.

The Rosebud flourished for six years, and during that time three more Turpin rags saw publication: "Ragtime Nightmare" (1900); the

First Edition Cover.

melodic "St. Louis Rag" (1903, recorded for Victor by the Arthur Pryor Band in 1904); and "Buffalo Rag" (1904, which got a hit recording by banjoist Vess Ossman in 1905). Turpin's protégés began to publish, too, and their work in this time (along with that of Scott Joplin, another Rosebud regular) is the gold in the golden age of classic rags. As America caught on to ragtime, opportunities grew for its practitioners. The young players around Turpin's bar itched to try their luck in the wider world, and they began to drift away, most of them to Chicago. Their leaving diminished the St. Louis ragtime scene, and in 1906 Turpin closed his bar.

Another event of 1906 more clearly foretold the end of the classic era. This was the publication of ragtime's first runaway bestseller, "Dill Pickles," composed by Charles L. Johnson and published by Carl Hoffman in Kansas City. Johnson's rag had little in common with the rich rags from St. Louis. It was shorter, for one thing, with three melodies rather than four. Its tunes were slight and offhand-sounding, and its harmonies hardly existed. If "Dill Pickles" was weak in the melody and harmony departments, it was strong on hooks. It was a "riff" rag, the first in which a rhythmic melodic figure—not the tonal melody itself—was the ingratiating feature. The hook lay in the shifting accents of a three-over-four pattern, a configuration that would tantalize America again later in "Twelfth Street Rag" and "In the Mood." "Dill Pickles," though it seemed to be made of only thin air and good nature, thrilled amateur pianists. It was noisy, easy, and great fun to play fast.

A year after its publication in Missouri, "Dill Pickles" was bought and reissued by Remick in New York, and it quickly became that company's first million-selling rag. As Joplin's work defined the sound of classic ragtime, "Dill Pickles" was commercial ragtime personified. It awakened Tin Pan Alley to the sales potential of rags, and its breezy, toddling cousins—"Black and White Rag," "Wild Cherries," "Ragging the Scale," and "Twelfth Street Rag," among many others—dominated the rag market throughout the teens.

Tom Turpin was not in ragtime for the money, so perhaps he did not realize the degree to which commercial ragtime was displacing his kind of writing and piano playing. He was back in the bar business by 1910, as proprietor of a little joint called the Eureka Club, at 2208 Chestnut Street, proudly presenting the still-young but already old-fashioned

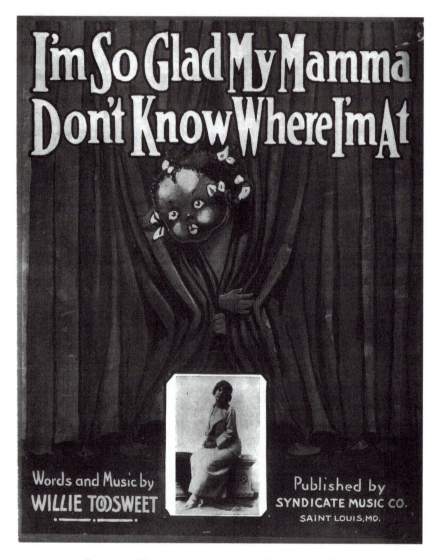

SYNDICATE MUSIC WAS A SUBSIDIARY OF JOHN STARK & SON.

Arthur Marshall as his house pianist. Tom (with his brother Charles) ventured into vaudeville by opening the Booker T. Washington Airdome, a tent theater at 2323 Market Street. It was here that Tom, as music director, surely noticed the next big musical enthusiasm, the blues.

W. C. Handy's "Memphis Blues," issued in September 1912, was the warning shot, and his "St. Louis Blues," published exactly two years later, was the bombshell. By the midteens the blues pervaded every popular music medium: disc recordings, song sheets, piano rolls, vaudeville. To many classic ragtimers the blues represented another dumbing-down of the sweet intricacies of syncopation. Turpin's star comics at the Booker T. Washington, Franklin "Baby" Seals and Willie Too Sweet, wrote and sang their own signature blues, and both men had their songs published in St. Louis.

The death knell for classic ragtime came in 1917. In the spring of that year, the first recordings by the Original Dixieland Jazz Band were released on the Victor label. And in the way that we often embrace notorious music, America went mad for them. This was syncopation all right—and the tunes were firmly rooted in ragtime—but it was syncopation gone wild. It was the first recorded instrumental improvisation, five guys agreeing on a key and taking off. The music didn't come from sheets, and it didn't come from memory—it just came. It was blazing hot, danceable, and slightly scandalous. Only the most fanatic devotees could stay with classic ragtime professionally after the ODJB shook up the pop world.

Turpin continued to work in local show business, but he was no longer the nabob he had been in the early century. In the late teens, he left the Booker T. Washington, and his last city directory listing, in 1920, gives his occupation as "Manager, Jazzland Dance Hall." When he died of peritonitis, on August 13, 1922, there were not many local ragtimers left to mourn him.

In the twenty-five years from the publication of "Harlem Rag" until his death in 1922, Tom Turpin saw musical fads come thick and fast. He was not a professional musician or composer, so he didn't have to understand and absorb them all. Except for a vaudevillish World War I song, he seems never to have tried to write anything trendier than the pastoral rags of his youth. Turpin's work defined a genre, but he never looked beyond it.

Chapter 1

SCOTT JOPLIN

SCOTT JOPLIN WAS *in* the netherworld of itinerant black pianists of his day, but he was not *of* it. He was somehow different from his compatriots, and everyone who knew him thought so. Even as he was scrounging for a living in midwestern saloons, as his friends were doing, and selling his work for the same paltry fees that they were getting, Joplin stood apart. He was quiet, intense, cool. He seemed to know something, to want something, to have his eye on something that his contemporaries could not see.

What Joplin knew was that ragtime, despite its seedy origins and the frivolous uses to which it was put, was important. While most black pianists of the mid-1890s saw the music solely as a way of making a living, Joplin saw it as a new American art. What he wanted was respect: for his music, for himself, and for his race. He envisioned a music that could erase the lines between high and low culture, that used all of what

America had to offer. He was willing to extend himself to realize this vision, to learn as well as to teach.

Joplin was a serious musician and a serious person, but he was not a crank, a martinet, or a martyr. He never wrote down to his audience, and, even more important, he never sacrificed the joy of ragtime on the altar of "art." There are "serious" Joplin rags, but there are no gloomy or self-indulgent ones. His thirty-eight published rags are beacons that cut through the gaslight of his era to illuminate many kinds of music that came after them. Since the publication of "Maple Leaf Rag," Joplin's mastery has been unassailable. He had the greatest command of syncopated melody, and he produced more great rags than anyone else.

Scott Joplin was born on November 24, 1868, in Bowie County, in the northeast corner of Texas. His father, Giles Joplin, had been a slave, and at the time of Scott's birth, Giles was trying to scratch out a living as a backwoods farmer. Giles and Florence Joplin moved their family to Texarkana, Arkansas, a town of about three thousand that had lately sprung up to straddle the line between the two states implicit in its name. Giles got a job there as a laborer on the Texas & Pacific Railroad line, and Florence worked as a laundress and cleaned houses.

Their Texarkana neighbors remembered the entire Joplin family (with four sons and two daughters by then) as being musical. Giles played the fiddle, as he had for plantation dances in North Carolina, and Florence sang and accompanied herself on the banjo. All the children sang too, and Giles and Florence taught them fingerings on the fiddle, banjo, and guitar. Such portable—and sometimes homemade—instruments were usually the only ones that rural black children of the early Reconstruction era could obtain, but when Scott was about seven, he made a marvelous discovery. He went with his mother to clean the house of a white lawyer, W. G. Cook, and there he saw, and was allowed to play, a piano.

Joplin took to it at once, and he showed enough aptitude to prompt his parents to scrimp a bit to pay for lessons. He studied with several Texarkana teachers, but his main teacher was a German immigrant named Julius Weiss. Weiss, a tutor for a white family's children, gave young Scott free lessons and introduced him to the European classics. Giles Joplin left his family in the early 1880s, but Florence, with her household income pinched by her husband's departure, managed to put aside enough money to buy Scott a secondhand piano.

When he was about sixteen, Scott Joplin organized a vocal quartet—himself, his brother Will, and two neighbor boys—to sing at church socials and parties in Texarkana and surrounding towns. Then, with only the experience of playing for his neighbors and singing for northeast Texas and southwest Arkansas churchgoers, Scott Joplin left home to become a professional musician.

His wanderings cannot be precisely tracked through these early years. Like dozens of other young black men starting out in music then, Joplin played where he could. We can pinpoint him only occasionally, in announcements from small-town newspapers and through the recollections of his friends. And it is obvious from these glimpses of him—a brief appearance with a Texarkana minstrel troupe in 1891, a stint at "Honest John" Turpin's Silver Dollar Saloon in St. Louis—that he was, like all the rest, improvising a career. Joplin was based at the Silver Dollar for several years in the late '80s and early '90s, but he worked out from St. Louis, too, all over the Mississippi Valley.

In 1893 the Columbian Exposition, which everyone called the "World's Fair," opened in Chicago. (It was organized to celebrate the four-hundredth anniversary of Columbus's voyage to America, but it was a year late in preparation.) The fair drew many black singers, pianists, and bands to Chicago, all of them hoping for work in the saloons and houses that fringed its grounds. Brun Campbell, a white ragtimer who studied under Joplin, said that his teacher was among the wandering musicians who went to Chicago then. Joplin supposedly organized a small band there and played in several places around the city, but there is no evidence that he (or any other rag player) performed at the fair itself. It is interesting to speculate about what Joplin may have played and whom he may have heard there, but, like most of his early professional life, his months in Chicago are lost to us.

By 1894 Joplin was back in St. Louis, once again a mainstay at the Silver Dollar. It was around this time that he met John Turpin's sons, Charlie and Tom, who had recently returned from a year or so of mining in the West. Although their playing styles were poles apart, the bombastic Tom Turpin and the introspective Joplin became good friends. This friendship would sustain Joplin a few years later, during the most difficult period in his life.

For some reason, Joplin chose to settle in Sedalia, Missouri, in the mid-'90s. This west-central town was much smaller than St. Louis, and its size may have suited Joplin better. For a small town, Sedalia had an active musical life, which also could have attracted him. There were about three dozen saloons, as well as dancehalls, whorehouses, and gambling rooms, strung along Main Street, and there were several semiprofessional concert and choral groups in town, black and white. There was also a newly opened school for blacks, George R. Smith College, which probably played a role in luring Joplin to the town. At first Sedalia was just another temporary base for Joplin, a place to work out of and return to, but he would soon become an integral part of the town's musical scene.

Scott Joplin organized a singing group in Sedalia, called the Texas Medley Quartet (actually an octet of male voices), in late 1894 or early 1895. There is no record of the group's touring schedule, but it may be assumed that their travels took them as far as New York and Texas, because Joplin's first published music came from these states during this time. First there were two songs, issued in Syracuse, New York, in 1895; then three instrumentals (two marches and a waltz), published in Temple, Texas, in 1896. There is no hint of brilliance in these early works. The songs are sentimental period pieces, no more musically interesting than a hundred others of their kind. Joplin's first instrumental, "The Crush Collision March," is a curious piece of program music, depicting two trains crashing into each other. The score is noted as describing "noise of the trains while running at the rate of sixty miles per hour," the "whistle before the collision," and the collision itself.

Back in Sedalia after the octet's tours, Joplin became a sometime member of the town's Queen City Cornet Band, but he left this band to form his own. He added to his income by giving piano lessons. One of his students was Arthur Marshall, the teenage son of the family with whom Joplin was boarding. Another was a young man named Scott Hayden. Both of these students would become their teacher's friends and collaborators. Although the college records are lost, it is believed that both Joplin and Arthur Marshall attended Smith College for a year or so in 1896 or 1897. At any rate, Joplin was becoming a Sedalian.

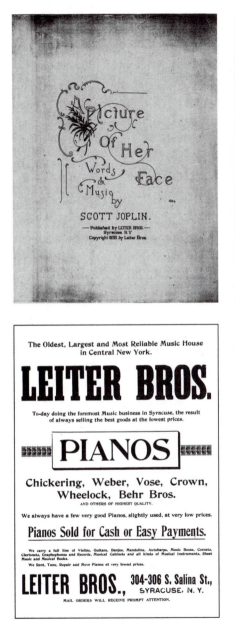

A Picture Of Her Face

Words & Music by

SCOTT JOPLIN.

Published by LEITER BROS.
Syracuse N.Y.
Copyright 1895 by Leiter Bros

Late in 1898 The Maple Leaf Club, a new social club for blacks, opened in a second-floor room at 121 East Main Street. Scott Joplin was the "house man" there, and he was billed on the club's business card simply as "The Entertainer." The Maple Leaf Club was not as raunchy as most of its Main Street neighbors, but it was noisy enough for local black pastors to disapprove of it (they called it a "loafing place" in an open letter of protest sent to the Sedalia papers).

As a result of his new job, Joplin was becoming a specialist in ragtime. He wrote a handful of rags (perhaps including the one that would become known as "Maple Leaf Rag") and showed them at the office of A. W. Perry & Sons, a Sedalia publisher. When Perry passed on them, he took them to the Carl Hoffman Music Company in Kansas City. Hoffman's clerk and arranger, Charles N. Daniels, liked one of the pieces, and in March 1899 Hoffman issued Joplin's "Original Rags." Although it was Joplin's first published rag, it is the work of a composer who knew precisely what he was doing. "Original Rags" is effortlessly melodic, and it is highly sophisticated in its use of syncopations.

In the summer of 1899, John Stark, a white man who owned a Sedalia music store, heard "Maple Leaf Rag" and decided to publish it. Arthur Marshall said that Stark dropped into the Maple Leaf for a beer and heard Joplin playing it; Stark's son and partner, Will, said that Joplin demonstrated the rag for Stark at their music store. Will's version seems more likely, but, however it happened, Stark bought the rag and issued it in September. Each was new at the game, so Joplin had the temerity to ask for a penny-a-copy royalty agreement, and Stark knew no better than to give it to him. Because of this dual investment in the work, the success of "Maple Leaf Rag" would change the lives of its composer and its publisher.

The first buyers of "Maple Leaf Rag" were, of course, people in the Sedalia area who had heard Joplin play it. This was always the way with regional publications, and the story usually ended there. There would be a few dozen local sales—rarely more than a hundred or so—and then nothing. "Maple Leaf Rag" reversed the pattern by selling more and more as time went on. After many of the initial printing of four hundred copies were destroyed by a fire in the Stark storeroom in October 1899, Stark's perpetual series of reprints began. By 1905, it was selling three thousand copies a month, and it was well on its way to becoming the world's most popular rag, the one that would stay in print and be recorded in every decade after its publication.

"Maple Leaf" is an exhilaration to play as well as to hear. It is extraordinarily pianistic, masterful in its structure and rhythmic invention, and loaded with devices to make the listener smile and tap the feet. The first of its four sixteen-measure strains is a short course in ragtime all by itself. Forgoing the conventional four- or eight-bar introduction, a one-note pickup begins the piece. Syncopation leaps out from the very first measure, and a parade of raggy rhythms is under way. Measure 9 begins with a marchlike, on-the-beat figure that can't wait for measure 10 (DA-DA-DA-da-DAA), and this pounce across the bar line moves American music from old-fashioned to newfangled in the blink of an eye. The second strain bubbles with joy, and the third builds excitement with a two-note Charlestonlike figure that is raised by a tone when it recurs. The fourth strain has a strutting, "going home" feel that is enormously satisfying. "Maple Leaf" became the rag that every player wanted to learn, and it has remained the one that listeners have never tired of hearing.

John Stark, at age fifty-eight, found himself the surprised owner of the hottest copyright in ragtime. The adrenaline produced by the sales of "Maple Leaf Rag" flew through its composer and his publisher. Although he was completely unmusical, John Stark honestly loved ragtime, and he decided to commit himself to this new music, to specialize in its publication. In a daring leap, he moved his company and his family to St. Louis in the summer of 1900, eager to swim in the larger pond of commercial music there. Scott Joplin, seeing a bit of financial security in the offing, asked the widowed sister-in-law of his student Scott Hayden to marry him. Belle Hayden accepted the proposal, and the Joplins, joined by Scott Hayden and his wife, Nora, followed Stark out of Sedalia to St. Louis. The two couples shared a rented house at 2658A Morgan Street (now Delmar Boulevard), on the northwest edge of Chestnut Valley.

Joplin returned to St. Louis to find the city aroar with ragtime, and to find himself, as the composer of "Maple Leaf," a local hero. Tom Turpin's new Rosebud Bar was the center of the action, and piano play-

Joplin's St. Louis home.

ing was a blood sport there. Day and night Louis Chauvin, Sam Patterson, and Joe Jordan spelled each other at the Turpin piano, in ferocious displays of noise and speed. Joplin knew better than to compete in such company. He had earned his living at the piano for years, but this kind of fierce, show-off playing was beyond him. Others could embellish his "Maple Leaf," play it hotter and faster, but he was the one who had composed it. The young players of St. Louis venerated him.

Although he had only the small royalties from "Maple Leaf" coming in, along with the fees he received from his handful of other publications, Joplin became choosy about his projects, and he chose to get off the treadmill of bar jobs. He wanted to write and to encourage the young talents around him to write. The first two Joplin rags published by Stark in St. Louis (Joplin's first ragtime works after "Maple Leaf") were collaborations with his Sedalia students: "Swipesy," written with Arthur Marshall in 1900; and "Sunflower Slow Drag," written with Scott Hayden in 1901. Joplin's own "Peacherine Rag" came next, also published in 1901. If Joplin's admirers were expecting a romping follow-up to "Maple Leaf," "Peacherine" must have shocked them with its simplicity. It is a strolling rag, serene and sunny, with a rustic air about it, nothing like Joplin's rambunctious hit. (After Joplin acquired some of the professional pop writer's acumen, he would rework "Maple Leaf"'s devices in later rags, such as "Leola," "Gladiolus," and "Sugar Cane.")

Soon after moving to St. Louis, Joplin felt ready to try something beyond the four-theme rag form, but, to his chagrin, he found that Stark wasn't ready to publish his experiments. The dissension centered on one of Joplin's pet projects, a sort of syncopated ballet that he called "The Ragtime Dance." Joplin had conceived the piece early in 1899 and had staged it for a single performance at Wood's Opera House in Sedalia in the fall of that year. In "The Ragtime Dance," a singing narrator called off figures as couples demonstrated steps that were popular in Main Street's black pavilions at that time: the ragtime dance, clean-up dance, Jennie Cooler dance, backstep prance, dude walk, Sedidus walk, slow drag, World's Fair dance, town talk, and stop time. Arthur Marshall wrote out orchestra parts for the Sedalia performance, and Joplin's brother Will sang the role of the narrator. Joplin himself conducted the orchestra and played the piano part. (Marshall and Scott Hayden filled out the evening with piano solos, making this event the first ragtime concert.)

Joplin wanted Stark to publish "The Ragtime Dance," all eight strains of it, complete with instructions for doing the dance steps. Stark balked. As much as the old man loved ragtime, this was something else. It seemed esoteric and risky to him, twice as long as most rags and twice as expensive to produce, making it twice as costly to the buyer. To give his case its due, Joplin was undoubtedly right in recognizing a white interest in black culture. The summer of 1900 saw the height of the cakewalk craze, after all, and Ben Harney's faux-black rag songs had been selling well since 1896. Why not give white players at home a taste of the real thing? But Stark also had a point when he questioned the likelihood of Dad and the children reading the instructions to do the dude walk around the family piano as Mother played their accompaniment. "The Ragtime Dance" was meant for the stage, not the living room.

Joplin kept urging the matter, but his publisher held firm. Stark finally compromised by issuing a simplified, nine-page song version of "The Ragtime Dance" (with lyrics by Joplin) in 1902. (The Stark publication bears the note that Joplin himself had separately published instructions for doing the steps mentioned in the number, and that they "can be obtained wherever this piece is for sale." If Joplin actually issued such an addendum to the Stark song, no copy has ever been found.) It was a commercial failure. The yearlong wrangle over "The Ragtime Dance," ending in mutual dissatisfaction, did not split up Joplin and Stark, but it was enough to send Joplin to other publishers from time to time. It also planted the idea in Joplin that he might be his own publisher. He self-published his "The Easy Winners" in October 1901.

Besides his worry over Stark's recalcitrance, there was also a strain on Joplin's marriage during this time. Scott and Belle Joplin had moved a few blocks from Morgan Street to occupy a thirteen-room house at 2117 Lucas Street. As Belle looked after the boarders in her charge and Joplin worked on his music, they grew apart. The death of their infant daughter was more than the marriage could bear. Belle left him. Joplin asked Marshall and Hayden to intervene, to plead with her for a reconciliation, but there was no use. Belle vanished from his life.

As ragtime flourished in St. Louis, it began to emanate from other cities as well. By the end of 1900, Chicago, Nashville, Detroit, Kansas City, Philadelphia, and New York had all seen the publication of locally written rags. But Joplin's work held its preeminence. In 1902-03 he produced "Elite Syncopations," "The Entertainer," "Something Doing," "Weeping Willow," and "Palm Leaf Rag," all energetic, lyrical, and richly harmonic. These works show Joplin at the top of his form.

Joplin was even getting attention in the white press. The *St. Louis Globe-Democrat* reported in a February 1901 article that Alfred Ernst, the director of the St. Louis Choral Symphony Society, was an admirer of Joplin's rags. Ernst said he planned to take some of them with him to Germany the following summer to educate that nation "into an appreciation of the real American ragtime melodies." Ernst also expressed his belief that Joplin could "do something fine in composition of a higher class." A June 1903 story in the *Globe-Democrat* said that Joplin was "assiduously toiling upon an opera."

This was *A Guest of Honor*, a phantom work that has tantalized and frustrated Joplin scholars for decades. Joplin's copyright application for his opera was duly filed in the Library of Congress, dated February 18, 1903. But the form includes a notation: "Copies never received." No rehearsal copies, orchestrations, or reviews of *A Guest of Honor* have ever been found. Joplin referred to it as a "ragtime opera," but we have no idea of its libretto or of what it sounded like.

Joplin produced a touring version of *A Guest of Honor* that zigzagged through the Midwest in the autumn of 1903. The company of about thirty singers and musicians took on an erratically booked schedule of one-night stands in small cities, including Webb City, Missouri; Parsons, Kansas; Mason City, Iowa; and Fremont, Nebraska. Early in the tour, in Springfield, Illinois, the company treasurer skipped town with the receipts. The company, probably with an infusion of Joplin's own money, straggled on for a few weeks before disbanding. The final performances, scheduled for mid-October, were canceled.

When Joplin returned from his debacle on the road, St. Louis was bustling with preparations for hosting the World's Fair, set to open at

Forest Park in April 1904. There were several rags written to commemorate the fair, but Joplin's "The Cascades" (issued by Stark in August 1904) was easily the best of them. It is a winding and gracefully syncopated impression of the majestic watercourse of pools and fountains that lined the midway.

Early in 1904, while visiting relatives in Arkansas, Joplin met a nineteen-year-old girl named Freddie Alexander. Their friendship quickly turned to courtship, and the first edition of "The Chrysanthemum: An Afro-American Intermezzo" (issued by Stark in April 1904) was dedicated to her. They were married on June 14, at the home of her parents in Little Rock. After the wedding, they went to Sedalia, where Joplin had work lined up for the summer. (Joplin's returning there would seem to indicate an uneasiness with St. Louis's professional milieu. At the height of the World's Fair hoopla in St. Louis, with the sporting district booming, Joplin chose to play at picnics and dances in and around Sedalia.)

Freddie did not go with him to his jobs that summer because she was suffering from a severe cold. In August she developed pneumonia, and on September 10, three months into their marriage, she died. Joplin was bereft. He returned to St. Louis because there was nowhere else to go, and, because there was nothing else to do, he went to work. His next publication after the joyful "Cascades" was a melancholy syncopated waltz, "Bethena."

As Joplin mourned Freddie, there was little comfort to be had from his colleagues at the Rosebud. A restlessness had set in among them, prompted by rumors of wonderful opportunities in Chicago's sporting district, known as the Levee, and one by one, they began to disperse. In the summer of 1905, John Stark, still ambitious at sixty-four, relocated his publishing offices to New York. Joplin also nursed ambitions, but he was too depressed to act on them. For more than two years, he drifted— to Chicago, back to St. Louis, back to Chicago—not going anywhere, just going.

During his visits to Chicago, Joplin made a few perfunctory calls on publishers. He placed his "Eugenia" with the Will Rossiter company (which issued it in February 1906), but it is not a "Chicago rag." This lovely piece, with its flowing, long-line melodies, is named for the street running behind the Rosebud Bar. It evokes simpler times in St. Louis rather than the rowdy doings in Chicago's Levee.

Joplin kept in touch with his St. Louis friends who had immigrated to Chicago, and he was often the houseguest of Arthur Marshall and his wife, Julia. Marshall was working occasionally as a wine room pianist in the Levee, and he was still writing. (Stark issued five of his rags between 1906 and 1908.) Joe Jordan was doing well as music director of the New Pekin Theatre and was already making professional forays into New York.

Scott Hayden's career was a different story. He was the first of the Rosebud players to go to Chicago, but he never quite got on his feet there. He remarried after his first wife died in 1902, but, by the time of Joplin's first visit in 1906, Hayden had long since given up his musical hopes. In 1903 he had taken a job as an elevator operator at Cook County Hospital, where he would work until his death from tuberculosis in 1915.

Louis Chauvin was an even sadder case. He was playing in Chicago's sporting district, but his health was failing, and he was dazed by alcohol and opium. Joplin went to see him and suggested that they write something together. He set down two of Chauvin's rag themes, to which he added two of his own to make the poignant "Heliotrope Bouquet." Chauvin died of multiple sclerosis six months after the September 1907 publication of "Heliotrope," the only rag to bear his name.

Even while his own career was faltering, Joplin provided encouragement and help to another young ragtimer. James Scott had grown up in Carthage, Missouri, and he worked at the Dumars Music Company there. He had immersed himself in ragtime, especially the works of Joplin, and three of his rags had been published by Dumars. In mid-1906, when he heard that his idol was back in St. Louis, Scott traveled to Chestnut Valley and sought out the writer who had inspired him. Joplin heard several of the young man's pieces, and he advised Stark to publish them. At Joplin's insistence, Stark issued Scott's "Frog Legs Rag" in December 1906. It would be Stark's second-best seller after "Maple Leaf," and James Scott would publish twenty-four more rags with Stark over the next sixteen years.

Just as the Marshalls provided Joplin a home in Chicago during this rootless time, so did the Turpins in St. Louis. In acknowledgment of the saloonkeeper's kindness to him, Joplin's "Rose-bud March" (issued by Stark in 1905) bore the legend: "Respectfully dedicated to my friend Tom Turpin." Scott Joplin's last St. Louis rag was "Leola," published by

American Music Syndicate late in 1905, and it was the first of his rags to carry the famous admonition: "Notice! Don't play this piece fast. It is never right to play 'rag-time' fast. Author." Joplin was not asking that his work be played slowly, only warning against the obliteration of its musicality in a blur of speed. But he was symbolically moving away from the "hot piano" mentality of the Rosebud, and he would soon be leaving St. Louis for good.

◆

Scott Joplin's name was known somewhat in New York by the time he moved there, in the summer of 1907. Several of his rags had appeared on mechanically cut piano rolls, and his first hit was in the repertoires of many New York pianists. "Maple Leaf Rag" had also been recorded three times: first by the U.S. Marine Band in October 1906; and twice by banjoist Vess Ossman, in March and May 1907. (There would be a total of six recordings of "Maple Leaf" done during Joplin's lifetime. Oddly, there was not a piano recording made of this rag until Willie Eckstein's in 1923.)

But, at nearly forty years old, Scott Joplin was new to the New York publishing scene. He had to introduce himself, make some calls, meet some people, find out how it was done there. For a few years, he prospered before becoming consumed by the project that was beyond imagining by Tin Pan Alley, his opera *Treemonisha*.

Joplin took a room in a boardinghouse, the Rosalline, at 128 West Twenty-ninth Street, then he began making the rounds. He met with Ed Marks at the Joseph W. Stern Company, a publisher that had had hits with the works of black writers since the mid-'90s. Marks took two of Joplin's rags, "Searchlight" and "Gladiolus," and issued them soon after buying them. Joplin took Arthur Marshall's "Lily Queen" around to the W. W. Stuart Company and allowed Stuart to publish it with his own name appended as co-composer. (Joplin knew his name would help sell the rag, but he took none of Marshall's profit from it.) And either by mail or in person, he placed his "Rose Leaf Rag" with the Joseph M. Daly Company of Boston.

And, of course, he had to see John Stark. Their relationship had been strained since "The Ragtime Dance," but there had not been a year without a Stark publication of a Joplin piece since 1899. Stark had been in New York for two years, with offices at 127 East Twenty-third Street, but during this time, he had not discovered a single new ragtime writer of any promise. His best publications of the 1905-07 period were compositions by Joplin, Marshall, and James Scott that he had bought by mail.

Although Stark was not the ragtime avatar in New York that he had been in St. Louis, Joplin made his call. Stark bought two rags, "The Nonpareil" and the Joplin-Chauvin "Heliotrope Bouquet," and issued them both late in 1907. Another purchase was the masterful "Fig Leaf Rag," which Stark published in February 1908. This piece is subtitled "A High Class Rag," and indeed, after "Maple Leaf," it is Joplin's best. The harmonic ideas in "Fig Leaf" are far ahead of their time, lending it emotional shifts from the playful to the majestic.

As Joplin's mastery held, so did his eye for young ragtime talent. He successfully urged Stark to publish "Sensation," by a white New Jerseyan, Joseph F. Lamb. Its appearance late in 1908 began one of the most important writer-publisher relationships of ragtime's classic era.

In January 1908 Scott Joplin published his own "School of Ragtime," a three-page collection of six exercises for the amateur pianist.

In prefaces to the four-measure exercises, he repeatedly warns against "careless" playing. He advises "giving each note its proper time" and playing "slowly *until you catch the swing* [italics added]." In a short introduction, he defended his form and explained his aim:

> Syncopations are no indication of light or trashy music, and to shy bricks at "hateful ragtime" no longer passes for musical culture. To assist amateur players in giving the "Joplin rags" that weird and intoxicating effect intended by the composer is the object of this work.

Also in 1908, Joplin established ties to Seminary Music, the firm that would issue six of his rags and be his most important New York publisher. The Seminary publications include "Pine Apple Rag," the high-spirited "Wall Street," and the etudelike "Euphonic Sounds"—masterpieces all—as well as the sensuous tango "Solace." "Wall Street Rag" was recorded in a peppy arrangement by the Zonophone Concert Orchestra, released in March 1910. The quality and quantity of the Joplin rags of 1909-10 were very high. He was working hard and working well.

Joplin was also putting his personal life back together. Although not naturally gregarious, he was making friends in New York. Ed Marks remembered Joplin's socializing with other writers in the Stern offices, and Joe Lamb visited him occasionally at his boardinghouse. He frequented the theater and became acquainted with several performers, among them the vaudevillian William Spiller and the actor/manager Bob Slater. He hosted parties. He joined the Colored Vaudeville Benevolent Association, and he even played the piano at a small CVBA dinner.

Sometime around 1911 or 1912, Joplin met Lottie Stokes. Late in her life, she always spoke of their relationship as a marriage, although there is no record that they were legally wed. But they would remain together until Joplin's death. They moved into a house at 252 West Forty-seventh Street, where Lottie took in boarders and Joplin composed and taught. Joplin had a few pupils, at fifty cents a lesson, but his teaching soon fell away as he became rapt in the project that would engulf him.

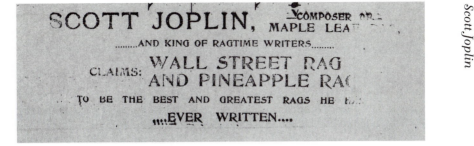

SCOTT JOPLIN, COMPOSER OF MAPLE LEAF
........AND KING OF RAGTIME WRITERS........
CLAIMS: WALL STREET RAG
AND PINEAPPLE RAG
TO BE THE BEST AND GREATEST RAGS HE HAS
....EVER WRITTEN....

MUSIC DEALER'S STAMP, 1910.

◆

In March 1908, a *New York Age* article reported that Scott Joplin was "writing grand opera and expected to have his scores finished by summer." Somehow, over the next two years—when he was writing more ragtime than ever before—Joplin managed to finish it. Before 1910 was out, he was showing *Treemonisha* to publishers. John Stark, who had moved back to St. Louis in the spring, passed on it immediately. And neither Seminary nor Stern would risk investment in its publication. These rejections did not deter Joplin, because he knew that *Treemonisha*'s time would come soon. He published the entire 230-page score himself in May 1911, not in desperation but as a show of confidence in his work.

Joplin was trying to snare a producer to place *Treemonisha* on the stage, and he baited his trap with publicity. He planted items in the *New York Age* about the completion of his masterwork and about a party given for him to celebrate its publication. He took a copy of the score to the editor of the *American Musician and Art Journal*. As Joplin hoped it would, the *Journal* gave a glowing "review" to the still-unperformed work.

But, because of its subject matter, there were built-in reasons for both black and white producers to reject *Treemonisha*. White producers dismissed out of hand the idea of an opera-length work by a black writer, simply because there was no commercial precedent for it. Black producers, preferring to show the progress of their race, would not stage a work that depicted the low estate of their people in Reconstruction Arkansas. Even the devotees of Joplin's rags would have had their doubts.

Treemonisha is not a "ragtime opera"; it is as high-class as Joplin could make it.

Treemonisha is part folktale, part preachment, set in 1884 in a dirt-poor farming community "somewhere in the state of Arkansas, Northeast of the Town of Texarkana and three or four miles from the Red River." Years before the action of the play begins, a girl-child was found under a tree there. She was adopted by a hardworking couple, who named her Treemonisha, and she was taken by them to a white woman teacher. As the opera opens, Treemonisha is eighteen. She realizes that, as the only educated person in her community, it is her duty to lead her people out of the morass of superstition and ignorance represented by a trio of conjurers who prey on the settlement by selling their spells and "bags of luck." When Treemonisha begins to speak against the conjurers, they threaten to throw her into a wasp's nest. She is rescued by a neighbor named Remus, and through her moral leadership and intelligence, she breaks the power of the evil men. After the people elect her their leader, Treemonisha forgives her tormentors in a magnanimous gesture, and they all celebrate by dancing to "A Real Slow Drag," a sensual syncopated march.

Treemonisha has its light moments: the barbershop harmonizing of four laborers, the act 2 finale, "Aunt Dinah Has Blowed de Horn," and the celebratory "A Real Slow Drag." And there is a bizarre scene in which eight bears dance to an eerie waltz. But there is no mistaking *Treemonisha* for a light work. Its theme was Joplin's credo: education is the key to black progress. Not only is learning more powerful than superstition, it is more practical than the pieties sung by the windbag preacher Parson Alltalk.

Late in 1911, Joplin thought he had found someone willing to risk staging the work. Thomas Johnson, a black producer, announced that he would present *Treemonisha*, with eleven principal singers and a chorus of forty, in Atlantic City in early November. When Johnson withdrew from the project during rehearsals, Joplin was distraught. In desperation he decided to stage a backer's audition of *Treemonisha* in a rehearsal hall in Harlem, using the singers from the defunct New Jersey production. It was a bare-bones affair, without costumes or scenery. There was no money for an orchestra, so Joplin himself accompanied the singers and conducted them from the piano. The meager showcase drew but a handful of people. It was the only time Joplin would ever see his opera on a stage.

In his scramble to launch *Treemonisha,* Joplin had neglected the writing and teaching that were the bases of his income. In 1912 Joseph Stern issued the exotic "Scott Joplin's New Rag," the composer's only publication of that year. But instead of concentrating on more commercial composition, Joplin threw himself into extensive revisions of *Treemonisha.* Of necessity, he began to ransack the opera's score to extract pieces to issue as single publications. He published "A Real Slow Drag" and "Prelude to Act 3" in 1913, and he would self-publish "Frolic of the Bears" two years later.

In July 1914 he self-published his haunting "Magnetic Rag," the last Joplin rag to be issued in his lifetime. It is the ragtime equivalent of Prospero's breaking his staff, not a renouncement of his powers but a farewell to them. The first section is a jaunty, folksy strain, with a call-and-response in its last eight bars. The B section is minor-keyed, and the C section is downright blue, with upward, trombonelike slurs worked into its bittersweet harmonies. The fourth strain is rueful and pensive sounding, but Joplin knew that, even though he has led the listener into melancholy, it is not where he must leave him. He returns to the swingy A section, and, after a smiling little coda, "Magnetic Rag" is gone. Joplin's final rag is as serious as ragtime gets, but it is not somber.

Late in 1914 Joplin and Lottie moved to Harlem, taking a row house at 133 West 138th Street. Lottie hoped for boarders and Joplin hoped for piano students, and somehow enough of each materialized to keep some money coming in. Living was hard, and it increasingly became Lottie's job to keep them going. By 1915 Joplin was selling his music by mail order, "six piano copies of any of his compositions" for a dollar.

Eubie Blake recalled hearing Joplin play during the mid-teens, and he was shocked at the pathetic performance: "So pitiful. He was so far gone with the dog [syphilis] and he sounded like a little child trying to pick out a tune." The "professor's disease" had indeed struck Joplin. His coordination was already gone; dementia and death lay ahead. And about this time, in a ghastly irony, Joplin received an offer—his first—to cut hand-played piano rolls.

He was in great need of money now, so he had to accept. He made seven rolls: a "Maple Leaf Rag" for Uni-Record and six more for the Connorized Company. The Uni-Record roll is not edited, and it is awful, full of uneven rhythms and flubbed notes. The Connorized rolls (five of which have been found) were edited to the point of blandness, and, perhaps mercifully, they do not accurately reflect his playing. In their different ways, they are sad testimony to Joplin's decline.

Even in the last nightmare year of his life, Joplin tried to write, but he destroyed his work in fits of depression. Finally he became unmanageable. Lottie couldn't bear any more of his torment, and she committed him to Bellevue Hospital in late January 1917. A few days later he was taken to Manhattan State Hospital on Ward's Island, where he died on April 1. Years earlier, Joplin had predicted that posterity would be kind to him, but at the time of his death, could even Lottie have believed it would come to pass?

Decades elapsed before his achievement got its due, but Joplin's vindication was total. His vision of a music without boundaries—cross-pollinated by styles and forms, high and low, from every era, written by black as well as white composers—came to be generally accepted, one composition at a time, by highbrows and lowbrows alike. Works by W. C. Handy, George Gershwin, James P. Johnson, Duke Ellington, Harold Arlen, Billy Strayhorn, Mark Blitzstein, Jerome Moross, and Leonard Bernstein paraded across the years, and each work in its turn added to the realization of Joplin's dream. Reversing the usual order of such things, the crossbred compositions of these men opened the door for their predecessors: *Treemonisha*, "The Ragtime Dance," and the vault of Joplin's near-forgotten syncopated masterpieces. In the 1970s, the cultural establishment gave Joplin its respect, as it never did in his lifetime, and the music business treated him as a hot property again. The ragtime revival of that time was, at its core, a Joplin revival, because he had written the rags that mattered most.

Joplin's complete works came back into print, and "The Entertainer" spent twelve weeks on the pop charts in 1974, thanks to the use of its theme in the popular film *The Sting*. *Treemonisha* finally had its first performance, on January 28, 1972, at the Atlanta Memorial Arts Center. In October 1975 *Treemonisha* began a sixty-four-performance run on

Broadway, and the following year Scott Joplin received a Pulitzer Prize in Music. Joplin rags were used in film scores and as ballet accompaniments, and albums of his work could be found in both the popular and classical bins of record stores. On June 9, 1983, the day the U.S. Postal Service issued a stamp in Joplin's honor, Sedalia, Missouri, presented the first of its annual ragtime festivals bearing his name.

Other kinds of ragtime arose during the long wait for Joplin's rediscovery, but none of them, no matter how flashy, made "Maple Leaf" seem old-fashioned. Even after hundreds of hearings, that leap from its first note to its second starts a tingle in the spine, and long before the "drive it home" finale, the tingle blossoms into a smile.

Chapter 2

EUBIE BLAKE

EARLY RAGTIME was an underground activity, with no show business infrastructure to support it. Each player acted as his own booking agent, manager, and publicist, going from saloon to saloon, house to house, city to city—wherever the grapevine said there was work. The first ragtimers peddled a single commodity: hot playing. They had to be good enough to beat out the competition for jobs and entertaining enough to hold jobs once they had them. Every player had a repertoire of tricks (always including a few borrowed from others) to command attention in noisy rooms. Professional survival depended on the material chosen and the assortment of pianistic devices used to put it over.

The sound of this saloon Darwinism is mostly the stuff of folklore. Only a handful of these dawn-of-time rag players wrote anything down—music or memoirs—and even fewer made recordings of their work. We generally had to take it on faith that the playing of the pioneers was wonderful. But one first-generation player, Eubie Blake, lived long enough to prove that *his* playing, at least, *was* wonderful. Through him, we were given a glimpse into the lost world of saloons and whorehouses that sustained pianists before the turn of the century. His memory was remarkable, his string of anecdotes was charming, and, best of all, his playing was astonishing. Here was a giant, left over from an age of giants, living evidence that the golden age was golden after all. To those raised on the piano albums of Floyd Cramer and Roger Williams, Eubie was a revelation, a literal blast from the past.

Like Turpin and Joplin, Blake composed a ragtime masterpiece before 1900, and, also like them, he stepped away from ragtime after his early success with it. As vaudevillian, theater composer, recording artist, bandleader, and arranger, he wove a distinguished career. He was a consummate showman, hell-bent not to go out of style because ragtime was going out of style. And when the ragtime revival brought him yet another career, he seized it. He realized that his new audience was not interested in his interim lives, but in his first one, so he became Mr. Ragtime. After a forty-year hiatus from ragtime playing, he embraced the music again. He wrote new rags, dusted off old ones, and made new recordings and new piano rolls. Ragtime would support him in the last thirty years of his life, as it had for the first thirty.

The belated attention pleased him so much that, beginning in the 1960s, Blake picked up where he had left off decades earlier. He was not a nostalgia machine but a vital creator of ragtime. Well into his eighties, he came into his own as a composer, devising several of his best (and most progressive) rags. The playing of popular pianists usually becomes sparer as they age, but Blake's playing became denser, slathered with thick harmonies and rococo ornamentation. Amazingly, he kept his formidable technique into his tenth decade. And he was a funny and salty talker. He gave scores of interviews, joking about his age, recalling long-dead cronies, and never boasting of his own playing, but praising players whose names only he could remember. He became what the Japanese call a "living treasure," our dapper *griot* of ragtime.

James Hubert Blake was born on February 7, 1883, at his parents' house on Forrest Street, in Baltimore, Maryland. He was the eleventh (and the only surviving) child of John Sumner Blake, a stevedore, and Emily Johnston Blake, a laundress. Both his parents had been slaves in

Virginia, and Eubie never forgot the whip scars on his father's back nor the story of John Blake's first pair of leather shoes, given to him when he joined a Union army regiment.

At the age of six, while on a shopping expedition with his mother, Eubie wandered into a music store. When Emily Blake found him, he was sitting at an organ, pecking away at the keys. Sensing a chance to sell an instrument, the store manager proclaimed the boy a genius and recommended that his mother buy a $75 pump organ for him to practice on. Terms were arranged at $1 down and twenty-five cents a week, and a Weaver organ was carted to the Blake home.

Emily Blake liked only the respectable kind of music, so she arranged for Eubie to take lessons from Mrs. Margaret Marshall, a neighbor who played the organ at Waters' Chapel Methodist Church. Eubie sawed out his Czerny exercises under Mrs. Marshall's tutelage, but he began to notice other kinds of music around him on Forrest Street. On errands for his mother, he eavesdropped at the doors of barrelhouses to hear the rollicking piano inside. He attended strangers' funerals to hear the bands in processions to and from the cemetery. When he tried to play what he heard, Emily Blake, at the first hint of syncopation, swooped down on him with her ritual cry, "Take that ragtime out of my house!"

Eubie knew that there was money to be made by playing nonrespectable music, and at age fifteen, just such an opportunity came along. Basil Chase, a pianist in a neighborhood whorehouse, needed some time off because of a death in his family, and he passed the job along to Eubie. The house was run by a white madam named Aggie Shelton, whose *prix fixe* was $5 a throw. She guaranteed Eubie a minimum of $3 per night if he didn't make at least that much in tips. She never had to pay him.

The job had to be hidden from his parents, of course, but the work hours (10 P.M. until dawn) made it possible to keep the secret for a little while. As soon as the elder Blakes fell asleep, Eubie would sneak out. He headed for a poolroom, where he could rent a pair of long pants from the proprietor; then, dressed like a grownup, he went to Aggie Shelton's. After six or seven hours of playing ballads and ragging some pop songs, he would gather his tips, return the rented pants, and go home. He banked his money under his bed.

The system worked for about a week, until a neighbor lady told Emily Blake that she had heard Eubie's wobble-wobble bass emanating from a bawdy house. His mother confronted him and predicted dire punishment when his father got home. John Blake took his son upstairs, and Eubie admitted to working at Aggie Shelton's. Then the boy brought out his cache and gave it to his father. There was nearly $100, more than ten times John Blake's salary for six days a week of hard labor. Clearly, the matter had to be rethought. His parents tolerated Eubie's disreputable job for nearly three years.

Whether because of his parents' nagging or simply a longing for travel and adventure, Eubie left the Shelton parlor in 1901 to join a medicine show. The show was organized by Dr. Frazier, a Baltimore veterinarian who sold homemade remedies—for humans, rather than animals—from the back of a wagon. One of five boys in the troupe, Eubie played the pump organ and did a little buck dancing to entertain the crowds before the doctor made his pitch. After a few days, Eubie and two of his friends became dissatisfied and gave notice in Fairfield, Pennsylvania. Of course, Frazier withheld their salaries, so they walked the thirty-five miles back to Baltimore.

Eubie's next show job, in 1902, took him all the way to New York. He joined one of the three companies of *In Old Kentucky*, a "plantation revue." The show stayed three days at the Academy of Music on Fourteenth Street, and the performance schedule was so heavy that Eubie saw nothing of the city and heard no music there. Back in Baltimore, he found work at Greenfeld's, a low-class saloon, and at Annie Gilly's, a dollar-an-hour whorehouse.

Blake's professional status rose in 1905, when he began to work in Atlantic City. The old resort town was becoming a fashionable summer place, and a cluster of clubs and hotels catering to blacks had grown up along Baltic and Mediterranean avenues. A bar called the Middle Section Club hired Eubie and a Baltimore schoolmate, Hughie Woolford, to share its piano duties. Eubie saw that a musician needed more to offer than a nightly star turn at the piano. He worked at becoming a "utility man," learning to transpose, to play in any key, to accompany singers, and to fit in with any band.

One of the habitués of the Middle Section was the distinguished black composer-conductor Will Marion Cook. One evening in 1906 Cook was struck by something that Blake was playing, and he asked what it was called. Blake said that it was a rag he had worked up in 1899 and that he had never named it. Cook gave it a title—"Sounds of Africa"—and urged Blake to come to New York to seek its publication. A few days later, Blake arrived in the city and found Cook, who told him that they were going to the G. Schirmer Music Company to sell the rag. (Cook's idea to try Schirmer was odd; Schirmer was a publisher of classical music and, it would seem, the least likely company in New York to want "Sounds of Africa.") Cook ushered Blake into the Schirmer offices and introduced him to the manager, Kurt Schindler. Schindler asked to hear his piece, and Blake played it several times. The amazed manager offered him a $100 advance and a contract to publish it, but while the contract was being prepared, he casually questioned a key change in the rag. Cook exploded, berating him for his ignorance in criticizing Blake's artistry and demanding that he apologize. Instead of apologizing, Schindler withdrew the offer.

The world would have to wait another eleven years to hear "Sounds of Africa," the number that would become internationally known as "The Charleston Rag." First, Eubie made it as a hand-played piano roll for Ampico in 1917. In July 1921, he made a disc of it for Emerson Records, under Cook's "Sounds of Africa" title. Eubie's "Charleston Rag" stands with "Maple Leaf Rag," "The Lily Rag," and "Pork and Beans" as one of the most original conceptions in ragtime. It was the first truly urban rag, so sophisticated in its syncopated ideas that it would have been startling had it been written thirty years later.

Comparison must be made to "Maple Leaf," the other landmark rag of 1899. Both are lively, but they are lively in different ways. Joplin's rag gallops, but Blake's rag hustles. "Maple Leaf" has a sunny, open disposition, while the minor-keyed and edgy "Charleston Rag" seems to be looking for a fight. It is lightning-fast, dark, and dangerous sounding, and it is packed with Blake's trademarks: the wobble-wobble, backwards-walking bass (a sort of boogie-woogie figure in reverse), his flickering, octavewide grace notes, and a nervous, broken-handed syncopation. It is far beyond any other ragtime thinking or writing that was going on in 1899.

◆

Atlantic City attracted the best East Coast pianists, and Eubie Blake heard and absorbed them all. Among them were men who had rocked regional saloons for years: Slew Foot Nelson, William Turk, No Legs Casey, Jess Pickett, and Big Head Wilbur. Eubie's favorite among these warhorses was One-Leg Willie Joseph, whose specialties included "Poet and Peasant Overture," as well as a ragtime version of "The Star-Spangled Banner." Joseph had had some conservatory training in Boston, and his dramatic, textured playing was a great influence on Eubie's style. Among his contemporaries, Eubie was most impressed by Luckey Roberts, Willie the Lion Smith, and James P. Johnson.

From 1907 to 1910, Eubie Blake held the job that every player in Baltimore wanted: that of house pianist at the Goldfield Hotel, at the corner of Chestnut and Lexington streets. The hotel was an island of elegance in the middle of the city's "district," built and owned by the pride of black Baltimore, the lightweight champion Joe Gans. In September 1906, in a brutal forty-four rounds fought outdoors in the sweltering heat of Goldfield, Nevada, Gans had wrested his title from Battling Nelson. He brought the $11,000 purse back to his hometown, where he erected the hotel named for the site of his victory. Gans's gourmet restaurant and well-stocked bar drew celebrities, black and white, to taste their delights. George M. Cohan, Jack Johnson, and Eddie Foy were among the visitors who heard Eubie earn his $55 a week at the Goldfield.

It was during his years at the hotel that Blake began to take his composing seriously. (Because he didn't learn to notate music until the late teens, Eubie always made a distinction between his "composed" and his "written" music.) "Tricky Fingers," "Troublesome Ivories," "Poor Katie Redd," "The Baltimore Todolo," and "Kitchen Tom" were among the Blake rags "composed" to impress customers at the Goldfield. "Tricky Fingers" and "Troublesome Ivories" are especially difficult pieces, devised solely to show off the skill of their composer, one of the very few pianists who could play them. (These early rags would not see publication until the 1970s.)

Having attained a solid reputation and a prestigious job, Eubie Blake decided, at age twenty-seven, to marry. He proposed to Avis Lee, a Baltimore beauty from a wealthy family who owned a fleet of oyster boats, and they were married in July 1910. Within a month of the wedding, Joe Gans died (from tuberculosis and the injuries sustained in two bloody rematches that he lost to Battling Nelson), and his death derailed the newlyweds' dream of a stable life in their hometown. The Goldfield faltered under incompetent new management and the loss of its star greeter, and it soon closed its doors.

Eubie teamed with a singer named Madison Reed and went back to the bipolar club circuit of Atlantic City and Baltimore. There was more "composing" during this time, but no "writing," copyrighting, or publishing. "Chevy Chase," "Fizz Water," "Brittwood Rag" (named for a club in Harlem), and the daunting "Troublesome Ivories" were among the weapons Eubie used to defend his turf around 1911.

In 1914 another admirer tried to help Blake get published. Luckey Roberts, Eubie's closest friend among the Harlem pianists, arranged for a hearing of his work at the Joseph Stern Company, which had published Roberts's first two rags. Stern accepted two Blake numbers—"Chevy Chase" and "Fizz Water"—and issued them in 1914. No amateur could play these rags as Blake had conceived them, of course, so the Stern arrangements were simplified for the benefit of Woolworth's demonstrators and home players. In their published versions these pieces became fox-trots with dollops of ragtime in them. Stern would also issue a similarly diluted "Bugle Call Rag" (written with Carey Morgan) in 1916. It was the last—and the blandest—of Blake's three rags published during the ragtime era.

In May 1915 Blake booked a job with Joe Porter's band at Baltimore's Riverview Park. The last person to arrive for the gig was a mustachioed young man from Indianapolis who was to begin a summer of singing with Porter. When the leader introduced the preppy-looking Noble Sissle to the band members, Blake thought he remembered having seen Sissle's name on a song sheet. He tersely recalled their meeting for his biographer, Al Rose:

> I said, "Do you write lyrics?"
> He says he writes lyrics. . .
> I said, "I need a lyricist. I've been looking for one."

In the passing of these few words with a stranger, Blake's life changed forever.

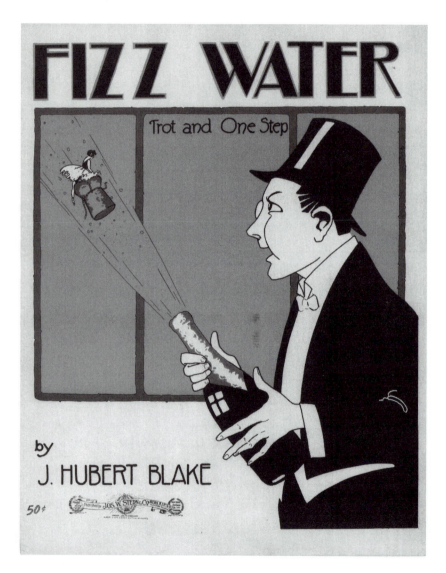

◆

Sissle and Blake's first writing session produced their first song, a ballad called "It's All Your Fault" (with Eddie Nelson as co-lyricist). Sissle couldn't wait to get it to Sophie Tucker, who was headlining at the Maryland Theatre. With Blake in tow, Sissle elbowed his way backstage after a Monday matinee and pressed Tucker to hear the number. She liked it and asked for Blake's piano copy. By Thursday, Tucker was singing "It's All Your Fault" in her act, and the writing team of Sissle and Blake was launched.

Noble Sissle did not yet have his eye on Broadway, but he certainly did not intend to spend his life in Baltimore clubs. He wanted to establish himself and his partner in New York, and toward that end he went to the city early in 1916 to meet the black bandleader James Reese Europe. Europe ran a large and complex enterprise called Europe's Society Orchestras, and he hired musicians literally by the dozens, supplying everything from combos to full orchestras for nightly dances and parties given by the city's white elite. Surely Europe could use a handsome singer, and surely the need would arise for an excellent pianist. Europe took Sissle on, and soon after, at Sissle's urging, he sent for Blake.

Sissle and Blake became indispensable to Europe, as administrators as well as performers. Blake did arranging and rehearsed the various bands. Sissle ran the office, juggling a busy calendar of parties and dances and hiring players for them. The young men idolized their boss and worked hard for him. Because of Europe's trust in them, they had entered New York's music scene at the highest level.

When Jim Europe enlisted in the Fifteenth Infantry Regiment (Colored) of the National Guard in September 1916, Sissle (who would follow him anywhere) enlisted, too. Blake (who would follow him *almost* anywhere) stayed in New York to run the Society Orchestras while they were away. Europe trained as a machine gunner, but the colonel who commanded the Fifteenth had other ideas about his duties in service. He asked Europe to create "the best band in the U.S. Army," and, with Sissle's help, he did. From January 1, 1918, the day the Fifteenth landed in France, until they returned to New York thirteen months later, the "Hellfighters" bandsmen were as honored for their valor as for their

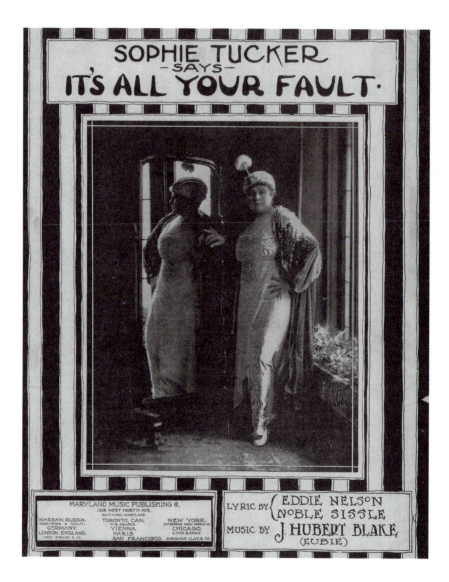

morale-boosting music. When he reentered civilian life, there was no more admired musician in America than James Reese Europe. His professional horizons—and those of his aides—seemed boundless. But, in May 1919, while on tour with members of his military band, during the intermission of a concert in Boston, Jim Europe was fatally stabbed by one of his drummers. His death shattered his empire, and it left Sissle and Blake at a crossroads.

Europe's agent, Pat Casey, had an idea. He knew of Sissle and Blake's success with the Society Orchestras, and he saw in them the makings of a "class act" for the vaudeville stage. With Casey's help, they built an act featuring their own songs, and they polished it to perfection. Within a few weeks of their debut in New Haven, Casey got them booked at the Palace Theatre in New York.

As they launched their career in vaudeville, the duo remained in demand for private parties in New York's wealthiest homes. Since their repertoire had to match their settings, Blake's scrappy, saloon-based ragtime fell into disuse. There were flashes of it in the instrumental breaks between Sissle's vocals, but what had wowed them at the Middle Section would not do at the Wanamaker mansion. Eubie's ragtime was put aside, and his playing became song-centered. The loss of Blake's specialty did not bother Sissle. He told Al Rose: "When they wanted ragtime, I sang ragtime. Not that I ever enjoyed it particularly."

In 1919 Blake was recognized by a stranger on a train while passing through Meriden, Connecticut. The man offered him $500 to make six piano rolls for the Artrio-Angelus Company, based in Meriden. (This was an enormous sum for piano-roll work at the time. In 1916 George Gershwin received $25 for making six rolls.) The man said that Blake could play anything he liked, and his choices indicate how far he had strayed from his original passion. The six titles for Artrio included "Chinese Lullaby" and a *Ziegfeld Follies* medley, but they did not include a rag. In fact, there is only one rag among the thirty piano rolls that Blake made from 1917 to 1921 ("Charleston Rag," his first roll), and only one rag (again, "Charleston," recorded in 1921) among his dozens of discs made before 1931. (A 1917 Pathé recording of "Hungarian Rag" bore his name, but Blake denied that it was his playing.) After the 1921 version of his masterpiece, which was the first ragtime piano disc made by an

African American, Blake would not make another commercial ragtime recording for thirty-seven years. One of the world's great rag players simply gave up the habit.

◆

Because we are tracking Eubie Blake's life in ragtime, we must fast-forward over his forty years of work in other kinds of music. But his accomplishments during this middle lifetime are so remarkable that we must at least note them. The Sissle-Blake team attained international vaudeville stardom, and they wrote four Broadway musicals together, beginning with the decade's most successful black show, *Shuffle Along*, in 1921, followed by *Elsie* (1923), *The Chocolate Dandies* (1924), and *Shuffle Along of 1933*. Blake wrote three other theater scores: two with Andy Razaf, *Blackbirds of 1930* and *Tan Manhattan* (1941); and *Swing It*, a Works Progress Administration production, in 1937. He made more than fifty recordings with Sissle before the end of their performing partnership in 1927, and more than a dozen thereafter as leader of his own orchestra. A segment of the Sissle-Blake vaudeville act was captured on one of the earliest sound-on-film shorts in 1923. As a bandleader, Blake was featured in another short, "Pie, Pie, Blackbird," in 1932, and in an all-black feature, *Harlem Is Heaven*, that same year. Throughout the 1920s, major publishers issued his songs and show music, and royalties from two of his standards, "I'm Just Wild about Harry" and "Memories of You," kept him going during the lean '30s.

In 1946, after nearly fifty years as a working musician, Eubie Blake retired. He had spent the war years leading a USO band that toured military hospitals, and he was exhausted. His second wife, Marion Gant Tyler, examined his financial situation, and she found that they could live comfortably in her Brooklyn brownstone on the income from his two hits. Eubie was ready to "sit on his ASCAP," as the guys in the Brill Building used to say.

But a few weeks into his golden years, Blake grew restless, so he enrolled in the music department of New York University. He chose NYU in order to study with Professor Rudolph Schramm, a leading exponent of the Schillinger system of composition. Joseph Schillinger, a theorist greatly admired by Arnold Schoenberg and other modernists, viewed composition as a series of problems to be solved by the mathematical variation of "master patterns." This chart-and-graph approach to music writing had proved helpful to George Gershwin, Glenn Miller, Oscar Levant, and Benny Goodman, and Eubie was intrigued by it. Blake sincerely wanted to learn the Schillinger method, but he was an obstinate student, as he had been in Baltimore decades earlier. He told Al Rose about a run-in with Professor Schramm:

> He really pressed me for my opinion of Stravinsky's music, and I said I thought it was lousy. It bothered him because I was so much older than the rest of the class and because I was a well-known composer. He thought I might prejudice them against modern music. I hope I did. I told him, "You asked for my opinion and that's my opinion."

Eubie received his degree in music from NYU in 1950. He always spoke highly of his teacher and said that he found the Schillinger approach to be practical and sound. His thesis composition, "Dicty's on Seventh Avenue," was published in 1971. ("Blue Rag in Twelve Keys" is another example of his "Schillinger work.") The June graduate had no immediate plans to reenter the workplace, but later in the year of his graduation, the Alfred A. Knopf Company issued a book that sparked a new national interest in ragtime. As the music's elder statesman, Blake became the living centerpiece of this revival, and it would keep him busy for the rest of his life.

The book was Rudi Blesh and Harriet Janis's *They All Played Ragtime*, and among the information in it was the startling fact that Eubie Blake was still alive. No one in the music world had thought of him, much less heard him play, for years, but there now seemed to be an historical obligation to invite him to do a few numbers at benefits and at small jazz festivals. Flattered to be remembered, even in such an offhand way, Blake accepted the invitations. The nostalgia merchants got more than they bargained for when he took the stage. He was an historical figure all right, but he was no fragile relic. He was still capable of taking the roof off with his piano playing, and stories of his thunder-and-lightning performances spread through the new ragtime underground. (He even got a chance to give an unsuspecting classical audience the shivers, at Music Inn in Tanglewood in 1955.)

Blake still had the stuff, all right, but no record company was ready to commit to an album yet. Finally, in 1958 and again in 1959, he was asked to record for 20th Century Fox. He made two LPs for the company—one of ragtime, one of marches—backed by a small combo. There was no doubting his ability after the Fox recordings. His fireworks had been caught on vinyl, and his personal revival was under way.

In 1960, "Ragtime Bob" Darch, a tough-talking saloon pianist and proselytizer for ragtime, decided that it was time for an all-Blake event. After two days of cajoling by Darch, Blake was persuaded, at age seventy-seven, to make his first club appearance as a solo pianist in forty-five years. Darch arranged for Eubie to be the featured player for a week at Toronto's Club 76 in July 1960. It was the first of many such events honoring Blake, and it proved that not only did he play like a demon, but that he could play like a demon all night, every night.

After his triumph in Toronto, Blake was featured in every conceivable setting: outdoors, concert halls, TV studios, riverboats. He became a familiar sight to concertgoers, a natty little man walking deliberately to the piano, as stage lights glinted off his bald head and thick glasses. He sat gingerly on the piano bench, then he tore into "Charleston Rag," his hands a blur of veins and bones as his long fingers flew over the keys. After a final flourish, he congratulated himself prizefighter style, clasping his hands over his head as audiences went wild. He often threw in a smattering of firsthand history and deadpan jokes (mostly about his age), to complement the playing that was the envy of performers fifty years younger.

Blake had to practice to stay sharp for his bookings, and he worked at it several hours a day. He found that he needed more material, so he brushed up rags he had written in the early part of the century, and he wrote eleven new ones. In 1969 Columbia Records issued a two-LP set called *The Eighty-Six Years of Eubie Blake*. It was recorded in three sessions (the first on December 26, 1968, followed by two more on February 6 and March 12, 1969), and it shows a marvelous mix of music in his fingers. There is Jesse Pickett's ancient "Dream Rag" (known in the ragtime era as "The Bull Dyke's Dream"), as well as pieces by Joplin and

REUNION IN RAGTIME

3 OF THE GREATEST COMPOSERS AND PIANISTS
OF RAGTIME PLAYING TOGETHER AGAIN...
AFTER FIFTY YEARS!

First in a New
RAGTIME SERIES

Presented by
"RAGTIME BOB" DARCH
the leading young authority,
collector and player of ragtime

C 1900

NEW COMPATIBLE STEREO
PLAYS ON ANY PHONOGRAPH
PLAYS STEREO ON STEREO EQUIPMENT OR HI-FI
(MONAURAL) ON HI-FI EQUIPMENT

THRILL TO THE WONDERFUL MUSIC THAT INSPIRED ALL AMERICA'S
COMPOSERS AS IT WAS ORIGINALLY WRITTEN AND PLAYED....THE
FORERUNNER OF BLUES, JAZZ AND ALL MODERN SYNCOPATED MUSIC
PLAYED BY THE MEN WHO WROTE IT!

EUBIE BLAKE   JOE JORDAN   CHARLES THOMPSON

John Philip Sousa. Noble Sissle joins him for a *Shuffle Along* medley. There are two pieces by Cole and Johnson, three by James P. Johnson, and a tango by Luckey Roberts. Best of all, there are ten of Eubie's own rags, from his 1899 masterpiece to the brand-new "Blue Rag in Twelve Keys." The album clinched his reputation as ragtime's living master.

In 1972, with the help of record producer/engineer Carl Seltzer, he formed Eubie Blake Music Company (EBM), which would issue ten LPs of Blakiana, ranging from original '20s recordings with Sissle to recent ones made in his Brooklyn living room. The first EBM album featured debut recordings of three Blake rags: "Dicty's on Seventh Avenue," "Novelty Rag," and his latest, "Melodic Rag." Later releases brought "Eubie's Classical Rag" and "Rhapsody in Ragtime," along with some non-rags such as "Rain Drops," "Corner Chestnut and Low," "Capricious Harlem," and "Eubie Dubie" (composed with Johnny Guarnieri). The only one of his early rags that he didn't care to revisit in his old age was "Bugle Call Rag."

The playing that was recorded in Blake's living room, like his playing on the stage, was carefully calculated to please an audience. It is alive with theatrical effects—thundering chords that vanish to a whisper, shifts in tempos as well as rhythms on repeated strains, pell-mell octave runs—all done with absolute control and authority. Blake also made several albums featuring singer friends (notably Ivan Harold Browning and Edith Wilson), in which he showed great sensitivity as an accompanist.

In May 1973 Blake made his first airplane flight, to Buffalo to cut five piano rolls for the QRS company; two months later he flew to Europe for concerts in Scandinavia. His music company issued a folio of his rags (*Sincerely, Eubie Blake*) in 1975 and a collection of his waltzes in 1978. Well into his nineties, he performed tirelessly, and he was in constant demand as a talk show guest. He gave interviews to newsmagazines, campus newspapers, ragtime researchers, *Penthouse, Women's Wear Daily*. He addressed students at Yale and Princeton; he received honorary doctorates from Rutgers, New England Conservatory of Music, and Dartmouth. *Eubie!*—a Broadway revue of his work—opened in September 1978, and he was a frequent (nonpaying) customer. No ragtimer had ever received so much attention, and Eubie gave as good as he got. He talked—and played—wonderfully.

The engine of the Eubie Blake bandwagon was his wife, Marion, the overseer of his money, his health, his travel, his contracts, and his visitors. He required personal regulation, too. He was a lifelong smoker, a garrulous and stalwart host, a night owl, a man who made dinner of desserts. Marion spent thirty-seven years controlling and channeling his enthusiasms, and it was only when she died in the summer of 1982, at age eighty-six, that Eubie's grip on life began to loosen.

The calendar of his centennial year was studded with tributes planned for him, including a Kennedy Center celebration, an all-star birthday salute at New York's Shubert Theatre, and a twenty-four-hour marathon of music at St. Peter's Lutheran Church in Manhattan. His wife's death took the wind out of him, and he was too weak to attend any of these events. But he willed himself to live until his one-hundredth birthday. Then, five days later, on February 12, 1983, the human chain that linked the computer age to the hand-played piano roll was broken.

Chapter 3

LUCKEY ROBERTS

FROM ABOUT 1915 UNTIL ABOUT 1930, popular piano playing in New York City held a standard of brilliance never known before or since. During this time, there were two dozen or so piano masters, white and black, writing, recording, and playing in the city. Their writing was impressive, but theirs was essentially a performer's art. Their musicianship can still amaze us when we hear their piano rolls and records. James P. Johnson told an interviewer in 1953:

> The other sections of the country never developed the piano as far as the New York boys did. . . . The reason the New York boys became such high-class musicians was because the New York piano was developed by the European method, system and style. The people in New York were used to hearing good piano played in concerts and cafes. The ragtime player had to live up to that standard. They had to get orchestral effects,

sound harmonies, chords and all the techniques of European concert pianists who were playing their music all over the city. New York developed the orchestral piano—full, round, big, widespread chords and tenths—a heavy bass moving against the right hand. . . . When you heard the biggest ragtime specialists play, you would hear fine harmony, exciting touch and tone and all the themes developed.

The first major Harlem rag player and composer was Luckey Roberts. By 1910 he was a comer in a lively lot of pianists; by 1915 he was generally thought of as the best of them. In 1913 he became the first of the "Harlem school" to publish a rag. Like Eubie Blake, he would leave ragtime, and, also like Blake, he would make a set of valedictory recordings long after the ragtime era was over. But there are no Roberts recordings from his heyday. (He made two sides that went unreleased by Columbia in 1916.) And there are only five known Roberts piano rolls, compared to Fats Waller's twenty-four, Blake's thirty, and James P. Johnson's fifty-four. Only five of his seven rags were published. His contemporaries, who were in awe of him, would eventually overshadow him with the amount and permanence of their work. Time has muted the impact of the Roberts rags, which, in their day, rocked Harlem with their power and energy.

Charles Luckeyth Roberts was born in Philadelphia on August 7, 1887. Although his parents, William L. and Elizabeth Roberts, were Quakers, they were not averse to young Luckey's going on the stage. He was singing, dancing, and tumbling with a vaudeville troupe called Gus Seeke's Pickaninnies by age five. There was Quaker modesty in William Roberts, however. He once yanked his boy off the stage of the Bijou Theatre in Philadelphia when he strutted out wearing only a grass skirt in Gus Seeke's idea of a "tropical" number.

Luckey became interested in the piano around age six or seven, during the time he was touring with Mayme Remington and Her Black Buster Brownie Ethiopian Prodigies. Remington was an exponent of the "pick act," a vogue of white performers who featured black children in their shows. (Several other Remington Prodigies, including Bill Robinson and Eddie Rector, also went on to major careers.) The vaudevillian Coot Grant remembered his old boss: "She was a former French burlesque dancer and her specialty was a Hawaiian dance, which sure looked like what they call the Shake in Birmingham." Remington's act was successful enough to get international bookings, and Roberts claimed to have gone to Europe with her three times by age ten. He was given $1.25 a week—plus board and tutoring—as a Prodigy, and his father was sent $5 weekly during Luckey's employment.

The hard trouping life was brightened by Luckey's explorations at hotel and boardinghouse pianos. Seeing the hint of a musical gift, his father arranged for him to meet Lonnie Hicks, a pioneer Philadelphia ragtimer. Hicks encouraged the boy and prescribed constant practice. While waiting out the daytime hours before his show began, Luckey heeded his advice, practicing every chance he could, wherever he could.

In August 1901 a photo of the teenage Charles Roberts appeared in the (Philadelphia) *North American*. His headshot is last in the line of boys in the Wissahickon Sextette, called by the paper "Lively Little Negroes . . . Who Made Wissahickon Ring With Song." Roberts made the occasional foray into the suburbs with the Sextette, but his steady job during this time was playing piano and (occasionally) accompanying singers in Philadelphia's Green Dragon saloon for $25 a week. (He could play only on the black keys then, and this limitation thwarted any singer who couldn't belt out a number in F-sharp.) It must have been early in the century when, a friend wrote, Roberts joined "a drum corps of youngsters" and left Philadelphia for New York.

Like most other young piano-playing sports, Roberts was rootless. He drifted through the Tenderloin neighborhood, just west of midtown Manhattan, haunting saloons there, listening more than he played. But he played often enough to acquire a New York fan, a young classical pianist named Ernest Green, who urged him to learn to read music and who recommended teachers to him. Luckey studied in Harlem with Eloise Smith and Melville Charlton when he could afford lessons. He also made a point to get to Baltimore to hear a pianist whom everyone raved about, Eubie Blake. Their meeting at the Goldfield Hotel began an enduring friendship.

By 1910 Luckey Roberts had a regular job at Barron Wilkins's Little Savoy Club, on Thirty-fifth Street near Eighth Avenue, and the word was getting around that he was a powerhouse. Everyone who remembered him from this time used the word "strong" to describe him. He was only four feet, ten inches tall, but "wide," Blake recalled—solidly built and capable of seismic attack at the piano. Like Eubie's, his fingers could span a fourteenth on the keyboard.

In the winter of 1911, Roberts met a New York showgirl named Lena Stanford. They became close during their rehearsals of Leubrie Hill's *My Friend from Dixie*, and they were married on December 28. The show's regional tour was their honeymoon trip.

Like his rivals in the club world, Luckey knew he needed material all his own, preferably material so difficult that only he could play it. His signature piece during this time was a torrent of notes called "Nothin'" (written around 1908 and probably his first ragtime composition). Roberts never copyrighted or published it, since it was devised solely to settle matters in cutting contests. However, he finally recorded "Nothin'" in 1958, and his performance of it can still make pianists gasp. His hands are spread as far apart as the width of a keyboard will allow, and both are in perpetual motion. "Nothin'" has a marchlike bass line, but it is a rag, suggesting a parade gone berserk, taken at breakneck tempo, with bursts of syncopated interaction between the hands. The third strain sounds like a squabble between a piccolo and a trombone. It is the kind of performance that a rival did not follow with "Dill Pickles."

In 1913 the Joseph Stern company took two of Roberts's rags to water down for publication, and they were his first to see print. "Junk Man Rag" was issued in May, and it quickly became a popular number for dancing the one-step. It got a big send-off with a performance by James Europe's Clef Club Orchestra at its semiannual concert at the Manhattan Casino in Harlem. Some four thousand people attended the event and proclaimed Roberts's rag the hit of the evening, along with a demonstration of the Texas Tommy dance. Fred Van Eps made a banjo recording of it in September for Columbia, and this was followed by the Victor Military Band's disc in November. (It finally received a piano recording, by Lionel Belasco, on Victor in 1915.) "Junk Man" is a cheerful, aggressive rag, and the instrumental version sold well enough for Stern to reissue it as a song, with lyrics by Chris Smith and Ferd Mierisch. A two-bar break prompted the line: "The dance is bound to win you, Puts a lot of ginger in you."

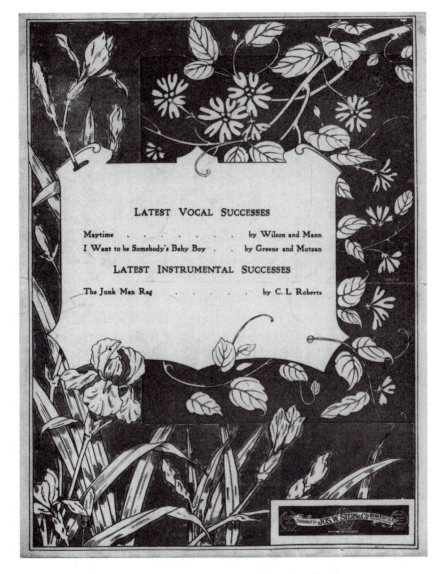

First edition sheet music cover of "Junk Man Rag," 1913.

One month after "Junk Man"'s appearance, Stern issued Roberts's "Pork and Beans" (named for the poor man's sandwich filling), his best rag. Its A strain is propelled by a stabbing three-note melody figure, shifting constantly between major and minor modes. The second strain barrels along, major and minor still flirting with each other. The finish is a joyous shout that was built for Luckey's legendary tremolo playing. The published version begs to be embellished, but the piece is so solidly constructed that embellishment is not necessary to enjoy it. "Pork and Beans" is the Rosetta Stone of Harlem ragtime. It encodes everything that had come before it, and it hints at the stride style just over the horizon.

Stern published Luckey's flirtatious, medium-tempo "Music Box Rag" in 1914 and, in the same year, issued his raggy fox-trot "Palm Beach." But other Roberts compositions were deemed unpublishable because they were unplayable by the amateurs who might buy them. One of these was the triplet-laden, impossibly fast "Ripples of the Nile." Roberts could toss it off, but even his most promising students couldn't master it. (James P. Johnson and George Gershwin were both stumped by "Ripples of the Nile." Gershwin, who came to Roberts for private coaching, was particularly obsessed with the number. His only rag, "Rialto Ripples," echoes his fascination with the "Ripples" of Luckey Roberts.) Roberts would finally record "Ripples of the Nile" in 1946.

The hallmark of Roberts's playing was sheer physical power. His contemporaries recalled his shattering tremolos, as well as the drumming effect he got by the rat-a-tat playing of one note with two or three fingers (of either hand), and the blinding, pianowide chromatic runs. (All these devices are heard in Robert's 1946 recording of "Music Box Rag.") In contrast to the bombast coming from his piano, his physical appearance was elegant, even graceful. And there was his showmanship, which impressed the teenage Duke Ellington when he first saw Roberts at Washington's Howard Theatre. Ellington said, "He had a flashy style and a trick of throwing his hands away from the piano. It occurred to me then that I might try doing what he did."

Roberts's Quaker upbringing kept him from the temptations of alcohol and drugs, but he was not a model of honesty and forbearance. The traditional hobby of pianists was shooting pool, and Roberts was a shark. Eubie Blake began to worry when Luckey started to use his pool playing as a professional sideline. Roberts was an exponent of "lemon pool," of intentionally losing games until the bets got high, then wiping out an opponent. He ran the lemon pool scam on underworld characters, white and black, in the roughest joints in Baltimore and New York. Eubie told him "he was gonna get himself killed fooling around like that. Some of the places he'd go in and pull that! But he always got away with it." Roberts never had to fight his way out of a poolroom, but Pops Foster remembered a pugnacity in him that went beyond self-defense: "One night a couple of guys tried to hold him up. He grabbed them and knocked their heads together and then started whipping them something awful. By the time the police arrived, the two robbers were hollering for the cops, Luckey was beating them up so bad."

The 1915 Ricordi publications of "Shy and Sly" and "Bon Ton" (a reworking of "Junk Man") complete the list of Roberts's five published rags. His characteristic ferocity is absent from these two publications, and their hummable melodies suggest that theater writing was beckoning to him.

In 1917 Roberts was hired by the Tutt-Whitney company, producers of black touring shows, to write the score for *My People*. He followed this first effort with two more for the producers, the 1918 edition of their *Smart Set* revue and *Darkest Americans* in 1919. There were only three publications from his Tutt-Whitney shows, including "Irresistible Blues" in 1918. However, these scores marked a career transition for Luckey Roberts.

Roberts was firmly set on the path toward theater when he formed a partnership with Alex Rogers, one of the most respected lyricists of the time. Rogers had written the best of the Bert Williams songs, and he had spent the last few years writing and producing shows for the Negro Players company in Philadelphia. The Rogers-Roberts collaboration was not an exclusive one for either man, but they would write songs and shows together for more than ten years. Harms published their first song, "The Robin and the Red, Red Rose," in 1915, and their 1917 "Rockaway" was adopted by Sophie Tucker. During his theater period, Luckey was the "house man" at Barron Wilkins's new club in Harlem, and he was still hanging out with the ticklers at Lottie Joplin's boardinghouse at 163 West 131st Street. But, even as he worked at show scores, yet another new world lay on the horizon.

Song Hits From

The SMARTER SET

By

J. HOMER TUTT & C. "LUCKY" ROBERTS

Little Boy – Soldier Boy
· The Irresistible Blues
Keep On Smiling

ROBERTS and TUTT PUB'G CO.
2329 Seventh Ave., New York, N.Y.

Rogers and Roberts's handful of successful songs led to their being hired by the Quality Amusement Company, a Philadelphia-based organization that controlled the major black theaters in the East—New York's Lafayette, Philadelphia's Dunbar, Washington's Howard, Chicago's Avenue, Pittsburgh's Pershing, and Brooklyn's Putnam—and produced its own shows to tour on its wheel. For Quality they wrote a revue called *This and That* and a book show called *Baby Blues*, both produced in 1919. Roberts served as music director as well as composer, and his wife, Lena, was in both casts.

Coming off the Quality Amusement shows, the team started the Rogers and Roberts Company, based at 386 Cumberland Street in Brooklyn, to publish and promote their songs. (Their fancy letterhead announced that two songs from *Baby Blues* were available on piano rolls.) In June 1920 they sent copies of their songs to the Edison Company in West Orange, New Jersey, hoping to get recordings of them.

But Luckey was having more success from casual collaborations with other lyricists than with his full-time partner. His 1920 "Railroad Blues" (lyrics by Haven Gillespie and Howard Washington) got several recordings, and his 1921 "Tallahassee" (lyrics by B. G. DeSylva) was featured in the Al Jolson show *Bombo*. Roberts was also writing with Sam Lewis and Joe Young, two veterans of Tin Pan Alley ("Goo Googily Goo" and "I Want a Good Baby Bad").

Rogers and Roberts kept writing together, however, and in 1923 their persistence paid off. John Cort, who had produced Sissle and Blake's *Shuffle Along* in 1921, hired them to write scores for two (white) shows at Daly's Theatre on Sixty-third Street in New York. The first was *Go-Go*, which opened in March 1923; the second was *Sharlee*, which opened in November. *Go-Go* ran several weeks and then toured, but *Sharlee* lasted barely a month. Shapiro-Bernstein published numbers from both shows, and two of *Go-Go*'s songs received fine recordings: Zez Confrey and his orchestra made a disc of "Rosetime and You," and Roberts made his best piano roll when he cut "Mo'Lasses" for the QRS company. In 1924 Rogers and Roberts tried another show without much success when they wrote, produced, and starred in a touring revue called *Steppin' Time*.

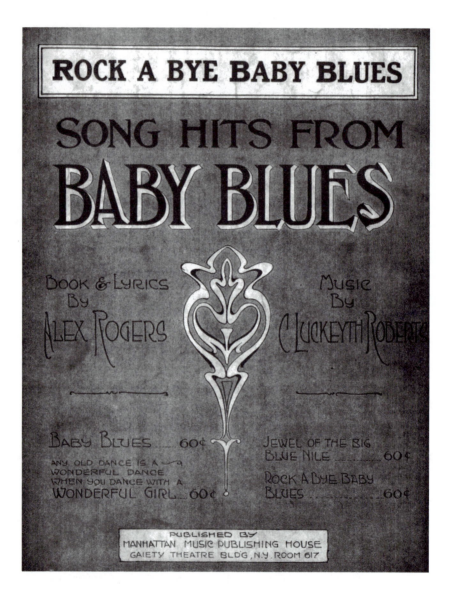

Luckey Roberts was making a good living with his songs and theater work, but late in 1924 he stepped into the ranks of America's best-
paid entertainers. It all started with a single booking to play at the
Everglades Club, in Palm Beach. The snowbirds of New York society,
who wintered there, heard him at the club and wanted more. They began
to hire Roberts for Florida parties and social events. Sometimes the
request was for solo performing; sometimes a small combo was required,
sometimes a large dance orchestra. As James Reese Europe had done
before him, Luckey Roberts became the musical guru to America's rich-
est families. He played at debutante balls, weddings, birthdays, and
receptions for DuPonts, Goulds, Vanderbilts, Hearsts, Harrimans, and
Biddles. There was a bit of ragtime in his one-hour sets at the Everglade
Club, but when he was out in society, he kept his saloon origins hidden
behind the broad planes of his dinner jacket.

The elite loved Roberts, and they couldn't wait until the next winter
in Palm Beach to hear him again. When the Florida season was over,
they sent for him to play at their Newport estates, Park Avenue parties,
and Fifth Avenue holiday balls. His asking price was $1,500 for two
hours of music, and it was happily paid. And for a few hundred dollars
per extra man, he could supply larger bands, as needed. (He once assembled a forty-five-piece dance orchestra.)

And of course, he had his annual invitation to Palm Beach. He
would spend seven winters there, teaching dowagers the Charleston in
1926 and playing nine consecutive evenings at the request of the duke of
Windsor during his visit in 1927. (Roberts helped the duke select jazz
records for his collection well into the 1930s.)

There was one more Broadway show, *My Magnolia*, written with
Alex Rogers and presented at the Mansfield Theatre in 1926. Luckey
and Lena Roberts appeared in the cast, as did Rogers. But *My Magnolia*
did not interrupt its composer's society work for long. It ran for only
three days.

In the late 1920s, Rogers and Roberts spent a few months writing
for Moran and Mack's radio show on WABC. They took occasional roles
on the blackface team's broadcasts, and Luckey's piano was the mean-
dering background music for the comedy recordings of the "Two Black
Crows." But breeding was the ticket that permitted one to hear Roberts

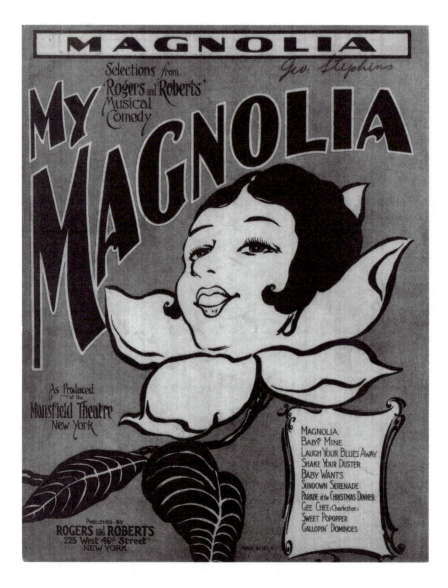

at his best. He withdrew from the Harlem piano scene, and he left his Tin Pan Alley career when *My Magnolia* failed to produce hits. He was going nowhere musically, but he was getting rich in the process.

His society period lasted about ten years. The Depression didn't stop the high life, but even Luckey's millionaire friends began to see the thirty-piece dance orchestra as an unnecessary expense. As European political tensions added to the unease of the late 1930s, the smart set— now calling itself "cafe society"—became openly cautious with its money. They cut back on elaborate entertaining at home and began to frequent small nightclubs, where someone else paid for the music.

As his society jobs ebbed, Roberts began to experiment with symphonic writing. He was the soloist when his "Whistlin' Pete—a Miniature Syncopated Rhapsody for Piano and Orchestra" was performed at Philadelphia's Robin Hood Dell in 1939. On August 30 of that year, he presented a concert of his "legitimate" music at Carnegie Hall. Eleanor Roosevelt, a Roberts fan from his days of playing for Roosevelt weddings, was there for his big night. Roberts finished his three-part *Spanish Suite* around this time, but it was not published or performed. (Eubie Blake played one of the parts, "Spanish Venus," on his *Eighty-Six Years* album.)

On July 1, 1940, Luckey Roberts was nearly killed in an automobile accident. His ankles and jawbone were broken, and both of his hands were crushed. His friends despaired of his ever being able to play again, but he amazed them with his recuperative powers and by getting his playing back. He showed off his recovery by performing with nearly undiminished skill at a Town Hall concert in New York on May 28, 1941.

In 1942 Luckey Roberts got a draught of the pop composer's best tonic: a hit song. The A section of his unpublished "Ripples of the Nile" was slowed to a crawl and turned into a ballad. Kim Gannon wrote a lyric for the tune and renamed it "Moonlight Cocktail." It was introduced by the Casa Loma Orchestra late in 1941, but the 1942 Glenn Miller recording, with vocals by Ray Eberle and the Modernaires, was the big one. "Moonlight Cocktail" stayed on the *Billboard* charts for nineteen weeks in the Miller version, and it was also successfully recorded by Bing Crosby, Horace Heidt, and Dolly Dawn. Another Roberts song that got multiple recordings in 1942 was "Massachusetts," with lyrics by Andy Razaf. It was not as popular as "Moonlight Cocktail," but the Johnny Long record sold well, and the Gene Krupa–Anita O'Day version did even better.

With the income from "Moonlight" and "Massachusetts," Roberts bought a small Harlem bar, which he named Luckey's Rendezvous, at 773 St. Nicholas Avenue. The affable host often played the piano there, and his waiters were known for their singing—ranging from opera to the blues—which they did for extra tips. Willie the Lion Smith often visited the place and remembered that "[Luckey] was too generous to make a good businessman. . . . His trouble was that when business was poor, he still was dishing out too many free drinks." The Rendezvous was a popular spot with Harlem's show crowd during the twelve years of Luckey's management.

In 1946 Luckey Roberts finally made his first piano solo recordings, in a session arranged by ragtime aficionado Rudi Blesh for the small Circle Records label. There were six Circle sides: "Railroad Blues," "Ripples of the Nile" (with a section taken at "Moonlight Cocktail" tempo), "Pork and Beans," "Junk Man Rag," "Music Box Rag," and "Shy and Sly." Despite his age (and his career sidetracks), Roberts's playing was clean, dexterous, and still powerful. The general public was hardly aware of these three 78s, but Blesh's recording had at least caught the essential Roberts for the first time.

In 1953 Roberts, Clarence Williams, Willie the Lion Smith, and Ethel Waters organized and appeared in a Town Hall benefit for James P. Johnson. (Johnson had suffered a stroke in 1951 and needed help with his medical bills.) This tribute to his friend would be Luckey's last concert appearance.

In March 1958 Nat Hentoff brought Roberts (at age seventy-one) into a studio to record for the Good Time Jazz label. Roberts shared an LP with Willie the Lion Smith—one side each, no duets—and he did impressive treatments of "Nothin'," "Railroad Blues," and a syncopated waltz, "Inner Space." The six Good Time Jazz sides doubled (and completed) Roberts's recorded output. Later that year, Roberts suffered the stroke that would incapacitate him for the rest of his life. He died in New York on February 5, 1968.

Luckey Roberts hit the mark that all saloon players aimed at: a truly personal sound. His rags don't have the theatrical nuances of Eubie Blake's; they are not as harmonically rich as Johnson's and Smith's; they do not joke like Waller's. Like Tom Turpin, the composer-host of the previous generation, Luckey was about power: not the power to beat hell out of a piano, but to *play* hell out of it, to use every inch of it for making ragtime.

James P. Johnson
1921

Chapter 4

JAMES P. JOHNSON

IN THE LATE TEENS, amateur players—who had always been the most fanatic of ragtime's fans—began to notice that mastering a rag came harder than it used to. Those who instinctively bought anything in the music store with the word "Rag" in its title took their purchases home to find that some serious woodshedding lay ahead before they could show off to their friends. The simplified (published) rags of Artie Matthews, Eubie Blake, and Luckey Roberts were harder to play than the undiluted rags of a decade earlier had been. The home players were confronted with brisk one-step tempo markings, complex syncopations, chord clusters, and unpredictable breaks. And even harder syncopated homework was around the corner. When novelty ragtime became popular in the early 1920s, more players were cowed into giving up playing than were inspired to practice.

The aim of the novelty player was to sound like a piano roll: to become the mechanical piano, to do its impossible tricks in live performance. (Zez Confrey's "Nickel in the Slot" is a literal imitation of an automated piano, complete with breakdowns and erratic tempos.) The titles of novelty rags suggested antic music: "Dizzy Fingers," "Loose Elbows," and "Hot Hands" were set to "Teasing the Ivories" or "Bluin' the Black Keys" to make "Piano Phun," "Sunshine Capers," or a "Lotta Trix." When novelty pianists made rolls—their two hands sounding like four—the magic of doctored enhancement (through cutting extra holes in the roll) was often added to their own, giving the impression of a "fifth hand" or even a "sixth hand" darting about the keyboard. There is a hardness in their hilarity, and, for the amateurs, there is discouragement in it, too. They know that they may enjoy such music only at a distance. No matter how much they practice, they will never play that way, any more than they will someday sing like the Mormon Tabernacle Choir.

As Confrey and his (white) followers worked at sounding nonhuman, the Harlem players worked at sounding superhuman, in the stride style exemplified by James P. Johnson. Like novelty ragtime, stride requires great dexterity and instantaneous mind-hand coordination. But stride takes syncopation even further than novelty ragtime does—takes it, in fact, to its human limit—by freeing the left hand to syncopate with the right. It is the most sophisticated of all popular piano playing, and Johnson was the one who carried its high-octane performance devices into composition.

Although Johnson wrote and recorded the flashiest pieces in the stride repertoire, he wasn't flashy himself. In his milieu of loud talkers, cutups, and sharp dressers, Johnson was singular in his ordinariness. He was a quiet man—with Joplinesque "classical" ambitions—sleepy eyed and slow moving, but in his playing, he showed the most adventurous ragtime mind of the 1920s.

James Price Johnson was born on February 1, 1894, in his parents' home at 6 City Alley, in New Brunswick, New Jersey. He was the youngest of William H. and Josephine Harrison Johnson's five children. His father was a mechanic; his mother was a maid. When James was about four, Josephine bought a piano for herself and her daughter Belle, although neither of them knew how to play. Josephine could soon pick out a few Methodist hymns and popular songs, but Belle was bored by the piano. James was fascinated, however, and he quickly taught himself to copy his mother's rendition of "Little Brown Jug."

The Johnsons were serious about their churchgoing, but their religion did not crimp their social life. Josephine, a native Virginian, knew many other transplanted southerners living in New Brunswick, and she often invited them to her home for covered-dish suppers and dancing. Young James watched from the top of the stairs for the moment when, after a sumptuous meal, the guitars, mandolins, and Jew's harps would be unpacked. Then the fun really got going, as old-time square dance figures were called out and executed in the crowded parlor. Next the dancers might try some of the patterned cotillion steps that they had seen as servants at long-ago plantation balls. Best of all were the ring-shouts, the dances from West Africa that were transmuted from the holy to the secular after the conversion of the slaves in the early nineteenth century. The ring-shout dancers moved counterclockwise in a circle, their feet close to the floor, snapping out intricate syncopations with their heels. A couple in the center of the ring did fancy struts and turns, urged on by call-and-response chanting, hand clapping, and rhythmic shuffling all around them. Johnson loved to watch these country dances, and he used their rhythms in many of his compositions.

In 1902 the Johnsons moved to Monmouth Street in Jersey City, where James first heard the sound that captured his imagination even more than Josephine's party music had done: the ragged playing of pop songs that came from nearby saloons and bawdy houses. James wanted to play ragtime, and his attempts at it were overheard by a neighborhood businesswoman, who approached the boy one day and asked him if he would like to earn a quarter. When he said yes, she led him into her parlor and seated him at a piano. She faced him firmly toward the wall and gave him his only instruction: "Don't turn around." At age eight, Johnson had unwittingly made his whorehouse debut.

Through a friend of his brother's, James began to get free tickets to symphony concerts in New York. He liked the experience so much that he was delighted when his family moved to the city in 1908. They lived in the "San Juan Hill" area—a neighborhood so tough that it was nicknamed for a battle—just north and west of Columbus Circle, where Lincoln Center now stands. James kept up his symphony attendance, and his new friend, a pianist named Charlie Cherry, began to teach him what Johnson called "real ragtime," the music of Scott Joplin.

In 1911, the Johnsons moved again, this time uptown to Ninety-ninth Street, where James's professional life began. He acquired the typical journeyman's experience: a first job at a nearby Irish Society hall; a few weeks at a cabaret and crib-house in Far Rockaway; accompanying singers in a Tenderloin dive for $11 a week; a stint at the Nickelette (a silent movie house in Hell's Kitchen), and another at Jim Allan's, a club near James's old San Juan Hill address.

In the spring of 1913 James was hired to play one night a week at Drake's Dancing Class, which was really a club—known as "The Jungles Casino" by its patrons—at Sixty-first Street and Tenth Avenue. (The club called itself a dancing school because an "educational" license was easier to get than was one for a dancehall.) At the Jungles, Johnson furnished the music for San Juan Hill's ex-southerners to dance to. They did the same country steps that James had seen in his mother's New Brunswick parlor, as well as some that were new to him: the mule walk, the gut stomp, and "in the alley." A contingent from South Carolina had a favorite step that called for a particular rhythmic pattern from the piano. They wanted four heavily accented beats, followed by four lightly accented ones. Johnson would eventually compose eight of these "Charlestons" to accompany their dancing at the Jungles Casino. One of the eight would make cultural history.

During his "dancing class" period, Johnson attended his first rent party, held at an apartment on West Sixty-first Street, and he knew he had found his element. A rent party was a private, semicommercial enterprise—sometimes called a parlor social or a chitlin' strut—which allowed paying guests to dance, eat, and drink in a neighbor's home. The piano was the nucleus of the socializing, and if players kept the music coming, an evening party often lasted into the following day. Pianists weren't booked, they just appeared, drawn by the sound of laughter and the smell of home cooking in quantity. Cutting contests erupted among players, and a newcomer could make a name for himself by displacing a neighborhood champion. The pay wasn't much (Johnson made $1.50 at his first one), but pianists could eat and drink free. In the 1920s, when rent parties roared in Harlem brownstones at all hours, a good player could go for days without buying a meal. Johnson became the parties' fiercest competitor, the cutter who could not be cut. (The mild-mannered

Johnson kept a streak of the killer in him. When he was living in Queens, years into his marriage, if he received a call from a friend telling him that a new hotshot was making waves at a parlor social, he would rouse himself from sleep and dash to Harlem to defend his reputation.)

Johnson began to move among the rakish elite of his profession. He met Eubie Blake first, in the summer of 1914, and Willie Smith a few months later. Ernest Green, the young player who had befriended Luckey Roberts, suggested to Johnson that he get some classical training. Green's mother worked as a maid for a teacher named Bruto Giannini, and she arranged for Johnson to meet her employer. For four years in the midteens Johnson studied with him, learning harmony and counterpoint, as well as acquiring the ability to play in any key. Giannini was a stickler for correct fingering, and thanks to him, Johnson's stride pieces on hand-played rolls are all the more dazzling, taken at whirlwind tempos in difficult keys (A, E, and F-sharp).

In 1917 several career "firsts" for Johnson widened his fame far beyond the Harlem party circuit. His first theater experience came that year when he teamed with a young black lyricist named Will Farrell to write songs for touring revues. He served as music director of the Smart Set's *My People* (with a score by Luckey Roberts). And he briefly shared a vaudeville bill with Ben Harney, the white Kentuckian who had introduced ragtime playing and singing to the variety stage in New York in 1896. Harney was at the tag end of his celebrity—doing a two-piano stunt, playing one with each hand—while James P. Johnson was beginning to imagine a kind of ragtime beyond Harney's wildest dreams.

In 1917, Johnson's name appeared on music sheets for the first time. He and Will Farrell placed three of their songs with the F. B. Haviland company; the first to be issued was "Mama's Blues." The team sold the three songs for $25 each (no royalties), and Johnson used his share to make a deposit toward the purchase of a baby grand piano. After some close calls with his draft board, he took a "safe" job in a Quartermaster Corps warehouse to avoid military service during World War I. He kept up his musical activities at night, organizing combos to fill engagements booked through James Reese Europe's Clef Club organization. Secure in the knowledge that he would not be sent to fight, Johnson got married to a singer named Lillie Mae Wright, whom he had met three years earlier.

Also in 1917, Johnson made a remarkable debut as a piano-roll artist, cutting seventeen hand-played rolls (of eleven tunes, ten of them his own compositions). The first was a piano duet played with Will Farrell of their song "After Tonight," made for the Universal company in May. He made four different versions of "Mama's Blues"—for four different companies—as well as romping rolls of his songs "Monkey Hunch" and "Stop It." This work forced Johnson to sharpen his skills at notating his pieces, because "master" (written) copies were needed to edit and correct the rolls.

There were five rags by Johnson among his 1917 rolls: "Caprice Rag" (made twice that year), "Steeplechase Rag" (which would be called "Over the Bars" when Clarence Williams published it in 1939 and Johnson rerecorded it in 1944), "Daintiness Rag," "Innovation," and "Twilight Rag." All of these are bright numbers in the current New York ragtime mode, but none is conceived as a stride piece. There is a lightness in them, and they are looser than the Luckey Roberts rags, but levitation is not yet there. Johnson would later rework and rerecord four of them (not "Innovation"), transforming them into showpieces of stride.

The concept of stride piano is usually explained by describing the "striding" movement of the left hand in an octave-chord, oom-pah bass pattern. The trouble with this explanation is that it also describes the left-hand playing of every other kind of ragtime, from Tom Turpin's to Zez Confrey's. The hallmark of stride is the *alternation* of syncopations between the hands. The left hand is often relieved of its duty as metronome, set free to jam with the right, to provide syncopated countermelodies, and to produce unexpected accents to contrast with those in the upper octaves. Stride literally doubles the possibilities for syncopations, and its playing requires great concentration and control. Rhythmically, stride piano has a loose, middle-ground feel, with neither the lyricism of classic ragtime nor the crispness of novelties. It may be played fast, of course, but it needs room to breathe, space in which two-handed interplay can swing. And it is always rollicking. Even when it is minor-keyed, stride is never sad.

Johnson's development from "straight" ragtime to stride happened after February 1918 and before May 1921. The crossover cannot be pinpointed any closer, because between those dates, he made no recordings or piano rolls, nor did he publish any instrumental works. But during this twenty-seven-month hiatus in his piano-roll career, the change happened. The evidence can be heard in two rolls that Johnson made of "Carolina Shout," the rag that is considered his masterpiece.

As written, "Carolina Shout" is a jaunty number comprising four melodic strains. The first of its melodies is a four-note figure that scampers lightly down from the upper registers; the second strain gets a rocking effect by putting a half-note melody in the left hand and letting the right answer each melody note with a three-note fillip; the third is a call-and-response tradeoff of two-bar patterns; and the fourth is built on octave leaps that suggest fiddles at a barn dance. It is a masterfully constructed piece, building excitement by getting funkier as it goes. "Carolina Shout" is solid, advanced ragtime, and this is the way Johnson presents it on the first roll he made of it, for Artempo in February 1918. The playing is "on the beat," with a firm and steady left hand.

By the time Johnson made his second roll of "Carolina Shout"—for QRS in May 1921—he was thinking and playing stride. His left hand is peripatetic, keeping a rock-solid beat as it had done before, but also jabbing notes into odd places, making a darting response to the call of the right in the third strain. There is a distinct difference in his right hand, too. He is now harmonizing the melody in thirds, giving a chimelike effect to the playing. The QRS roll is alive with syncopation, but it also has a relaxed feel. Johnson had by then not only conceived stride playing, he had mastered it. He made the near-impossible sound easy.

Johnson's 1921 roll shattered the other Harlem pianists. They had never heard such busy-ness—and such calm—in the playing of ragtime. Everyone wanted to learn "Carolina Shout," needed to learn it, in fact, as it quickly became the test piece for East Coast players, the way to bare one's fangs at a cutting contest. "Carolina Shout" was still unpublished, so the way to learn it was to slow down Johnson's roll and watch his placement of notes. Fats Waller and Duke Ellington worked it up that way, and it served each of them well.

In August 1921—one month after Eubie Blake recorded "Sounds of Africa"—Johnson made the first phonograph recording of a stride piece, his "Harlem Strut," for the Black Swan label. On October 18 he made a recording of "Carolina Shout" for OKeh. It was his third performance of

"Carolina Shout" to be captured, counting his two piano rolls, and he tweaked the syncopated interplay even more than he had on the QRS roll. But it was the QRS roll that mattered most. By the time the OKeh recording appeared in stores, Johnson's devotees were already hurling "Carolina Shout"'s at each other like hand grenades.

Johnson's refusal to let perfection alone in his remakes of "Carolina Shout" is typical of his approach to composition. (He would rethink "Carolina Shout"—and complicate his variations on it—yet again in a 1944 Decca recording.) Like Jelly Roll Morton, Johnson composed ragtime but performed his numbers as jazz. He kept an open mind about his works, even his classics, and never set ultimate arrangements of them to stick with for life.

Of all the popular pianists, only Johnson and Morton kept growing within their styles throughout their careers. Neither changed anything to accommodate pop fads, but each rethought his tunes as he matured musically. Like Jelly's, Johnson's late recordings show him still improvising to enrich and expand his original conceptions. His ideas were large enough to have it both ways: to conceive well-structured pieces, then to improve on them in performance. This composing/playing mind-set is at the core of jazz arranging and composition, and the works of Johnson and Morton exemplify it.

In 1923, on his recording of a pop song called "You Can't Do What My Last Man Did," Johnson applied his stride ideas to non-rag material for the first time. The tune is ordinary, but Johnson gives "You Can't Do" a potent swing, and there is a jazz feel to his playing for the first time on record. He would never abandon stride, but he submerged it, using its effects to flavor many kinds of music. The recordings that he made from the mid-'20s on irrevocably blurred the line between the ragtime and jazz of his era. When his renaissance came in the late 1930s, Johnson would be hailed as a jazz pianist rather than as a masterful creator of ragtime.

◆

As his stride rolls and recordings poured out, James P. Johnson didn't have mere admirers, he collected acolytes. Willie Smith had been his companion and protégé since 1914, during the pre-stride years, and

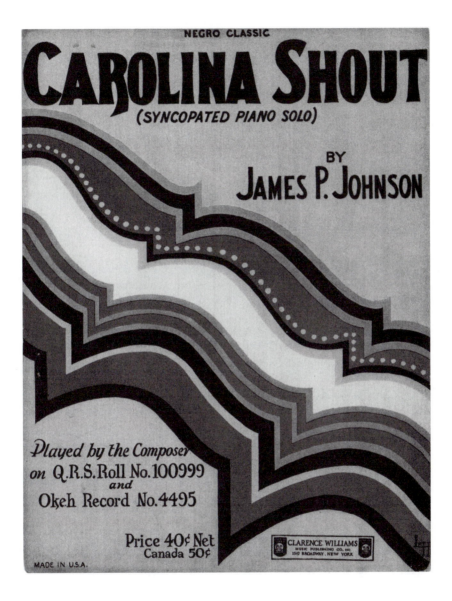

Johnson's progression swept Willie along with it. Smith worked hard at sounding like Johnson, because—it was undeniable by the early 1920s—Johnson sounded better than anybody else. In 1921, seventeen-year-old Fats Waller practically moved into the Johnson home on West 140th Street to live in the house of stride. (Lillie Johnson indulged their near-permanent guest, providing him a bed and tolerating his 4 A.M. practice sessions.) George Gershwin went looking for Johnson at Harlem rent parties, where he sat transfixed as the master played. Johnson's followers acquired followers, and the stride school was under way.

A Harlem pianist named Raymond "Lippy" Boyette became Johnson's factotum and unofficial "agent." Boyette would steer his idol—and his entourage of hangers-on—through a nightly crawl of rent parties, get him in, get him to the piano, and get him out and on his way to the next. If there were no party on a particular evening, Lippy could conjure one. Duke Ellington recalled:

> Lippy would walk up to any man's house at any time of night. He'd ring the doorbell. Finally somebody would wake up and holler out the window about who was it making all the disturbance. Lippy would answer, "It's Lippy, and James P. is here with me." These magic words opened anybody's door, and we would sit and play all night long.

In the '20s and '30s, the work of Johnson and his followers was available in every medium: on piano rolls, recordings, and radio, and in films and print. Their artistry and technical skills were hardly secret, but as had always been the case where popular music was concerned, the musical establishment was literally looking the other way, toward Europe, where it had always sought genius.

In July 1924, *Etude* magazine published an article titled "Pianistic Talent and Race" by Rudolf M. Breithaupt, identified as a "Distinguished European Pedagog." The professor says, "The talent for playing an instrument is primarily a question of race, that is, it is more a matter of blood, heredity and disposition . . . than of general physical organization, training and education, atmosphere and culture." The "two races which manifest extraordinary adaptation for playing on instruments" are "the Semitic and Slavic, and the mixture of them with other races." He gives several recipes for breeding good pianists: "Rumanian father with Polish Jew mother, pure Pole with Russian Jew mother," and so on. There is no American pianist, white or black, listed among his dozens of examples of good players, almost all of whom would have been unknown to the general public of 1924. Then he ranks the American regions according to where the best musicians might someday grow. Of Johnson's native state, he says, "The pure New Jersey man shares the fate of the pure Englishman. This branch gives only sour wine." But he saw hope for America:

> The whole complex of the States, with its vivid mixture of peoples, needs only good schools and the Old World tradition and cultivation to achieve perfection. But the day is not far distant, when this land of technic . . . will make itself entirely independent of foreign importations, and when its own art centers and schools will bring forth material quite equal to that of the old mother countries—if not even better material.

◆

In the early 1920s the career of James P. Johnson became a juggling act. He signed on as an exclusive QRS piano-roll artist in 1921, and he turned out fine rolls of tunes by Spencer Williams, Eubie Blake, Perry Bradford, and W. C. Handy, as well as his own rags and songs. In 1922 he reentered the pop market (he had published no pop songs since 1917), issuing "Desperate Blues" and "Ivy." Neither was a hit, but each got a recording, the latter by the Original Memphis Five. Johnson's first recordings, made for Arto in August 1921 as leader of Jimmy Johnson's Jazz Boys, were accompaniments for blues singer Alice Leslie Carter. And he was becoming serious about writing for the musical theater. He would keep juggling, throughout the decade.

There was not much money to be made from publishing stride pieces, because hardly any amateurs and only a few professionals could play them. Nonetheless, five of James P. Johnson's eight published rags saw print in the mid-'20s. Clarence Williams issued his "Carolina Shout" in 1925, and Perry Bradford brought out "Scoutin' Around" and "Toddlin'" the same year. "Jingles" and "Keep Off the Grass" appeared in

Clarence Williams's editions in 1926. ("Jingles" is a rare example of a novelty rag by a black writer.) In 1927, Perry Bradford published his "Snowy Morning Blues." Johnson's 1927 Columbia recording of his sexy—and bluesiest—blues was his biggest-selling record.

Theater became the axis of Johnson's various musical activities. He served as music director for *Plantation Days*, a touring show, in 1922, and for *Raisin' Cain* at Harlem's Lafayette Theatre in the summer of 1923. In October 1923 producer George White (of *Scandals* fame) presented a black show called *Runnin' Wild* at the Colonial Theatre on Broadway. The score, by James P. Johnson and lyricist Cecil Mack, and the show's frenetic dancing made *Runnin' Wild* one of the season's major hits. Harms published six songs from *Runnin' Wild*, and two of them became standards: the soulful, hymn-like "Old Fashioned Love," and the dance number that would become the biggest of the decade, the "Charleston."

Johnson's next Broadway opportunity came in 1928 with *Keep Shufflin'*, for which he and lyricist Henry Creamer shared songwriting duties with Fats Waller and Andy Razaf. Johnson and Waller shared piano-playing chores in the revue's pit band, but their nightly stride duets could not sustain the show. *Keep Shufflin'* ran a bit above breakeven for 104 performances.

Johnson's luck on Broadway declined with his 1929 show, *Messin' Around* (33 performances) and got worse with his 1931 effort, *Sugar Hill* (11 performances). He hit bottom with his last Broadway show, *The Policy Kings*, which presented its three performances in late December 1938. His theater writing had yielded only two hits ("Charleston" and "Old Fashioned Love"), but they were huge. These songs, along with the royalties from his and Henry Creamer's 1926 pop song, "If I Could Be with You," saw him through the Depression years.

As Johnson had turned to theater music to subsidize his ragtime career, he began to depend on recording fees to supplement his declining theater income in the late '20s. As pianist and in various band combinations, he accompanied an array of singers on records, including Ethel Waters, Eva Taylor, and Rosa Henderson. In February 1927 he went into Columbia's studios to make his first records with Bessie Smith. They would make a total of fourteen sides together, and he would be her favorite of all the pianists to play for her. Johnson also recorded with topnotch jazzmen: King Oliver, Jabbo Smith, Louis Armstrong, and Buster

Bailey. There were piano duets with Fats Waller in 1928, and in 1930 he recorded a classic duet (with dialogue) of "How Can I Be Blue?" with Clarence Williams.

In 1927 Johnson tried his hand at an extended composition, a concert work called "Yamekraw," which he subtitled "A Negro Rhapsody." "Yamekraw" was given its first performance (with Fats Waller as piano soloist) when W. C. Handy presented it in a concert of African-American music at Carnegie Hall on April 27, 1928. Johnson's "Rhapsody" was well received, and it would be programmed by orchestras for ten years or so. (Johnson recorded excerpts of the work for the piano in 1944.) Johnson was so pleased by the response to "Yamekraw" that, around 1930, to his economic detriment, he threw himself into symphonic writing. His *Harlem Symphony* was completed in 1932, and his "Jassamine Concerto" and "American Symphonic Suite" followed in 1934. Johnson got a few performances and even some scattered publications of his orchestral work, but by the late '30s he was off his course. He remained active in recording studios, most often as a sideman in other people's bands.

Johnson's reputation as writer and performer was restored by John Hammond's "Spirituals to Swing" concert on December 23, 1938, at Carnegie Hall. Johnson's two piano solos, "Mule Walk" and "Carolina Shout," were striking reminders of the rhythmic revolution that he had brought to piano playing. The following day, he played and talked through an extensive interview with Alan Lomax for the Library of Congress. In June 1939 he went to Columbia studios to make six sides, his first commercial solo recordings since 1930. (These were not issued until 1962, on an LP called *Father of the Stride Piano*.) The flurry of new interest in Johnson prompted Clarence Williams to publish Johnson's "Steeplechase Rag" in 1939. It was retitled "Over the Bars" and marked to be played in "Bright Jump" tempo.

In August 1940 Johnson's revival was interrupted by the first in the series of strokes that would plague his last years. He took it easy for a time, gardening and raising chickens at his home, at 171-38 108th Avenue in St. Albans, Queens. He came back strong in the spring of 1943, leading bands at Jimmy Ryan's and at the Onyx, two Fifty-second Street jazz clubs. He occasionally played at Small's Paradise, as well as at a neighborhood pub in Queens. In November and December 1943

Johnson recorded eight piano solos for Blue Note records. These included some experiments ("J. P. Boogie" and "Improvisation on 'Pinetop's Boogie Woogie'"), as well as two old-timers ("Back Water Blues" and "Arkansas Blues"). Best of all were four of his stride pieces: "Carolina Balmoral," "Gut Stomp," "Mule Walk Stomp," and "Caprice Rag." They are all taken at furious tempos, and they all swing hard. These records seem designed to say to the boogie boys, "James P. is still here, and he's still got it."

Johnson put on weight during his illness, and he had difficulty speaking. Photographs from the early 1940s show him—pudgy and pleasant-looking—sitting at various nightclub pianos. He is usually wearing a pinstripe business suit, with a cigar as his only "barroom" affectation.

Fats Waller's death in December 1943 severely depressed Johnson. He stayed away from the piano for a while, then he recorded eight Waller songs for Decca in the spring of 1944. He played at the Pied Piper, a Greenwich Village club, for most of that year but had to quit because of his health. He was the subject of two concert evenings in 1945: at Carnegie Hall on May 4 and at Town Hall on October 25. In 1946 Bregman, Vocco & Conn issued a folio of Johnson's recent pieces, including the tender "Blueberry Rhyme" and the boogie-based "A-flat Dream." The BVC folio also included "Fascination" and "Mule Walk Stomp," the last two of his eight rags to see print.

In 1947 Johnson was included in a group of jazz musicians assembled by Al Rose to play at Blair House at the request of President Truman. Johnson spent much of the evening happily propping up the bar while the leader of the free world spelled him at the piano.

In 1951 a massive stroke felled him. He became completely paralyzed, to be confined to beds at home or in a hospital for the remaining years of his life. Willie Smith helped to organize a benefit concert for Johnson at Town Hall on September 28, 1953. On May 5, 1954, *Down Beat*, having so little to report of Johnson for the previous few years, prematurely reported his death. He was hanging on though, and Willie Smith paid him a farewell visit. Willie wrote:

> The last time I saw my old friend, he was in a coma. For two weeks he hadn't spoken to anybody. . . . There was an old piano

in the room and I sat down. I played the "Carolina Shout." It was his tune. . . and I played it like he played it. It was stride piano, guys playing with two hands. Then Jimmy opened his eyes and smiled. He managed to write out a message. LION, it said, THEY WERE TOO GOOD TO THE PIANO PLAYERS WITH ALL THAT FREE BOOZE AND RICH FOOD. IT CATCHES UP WITH YOU.

James P. Johnson died at Queens General Hospital on November 17, 1955.

Johnson's work was so varied that the music business never quite got a handle on him. There was no manager or agent to push him, no publisher who was wholeheartedly committed to him. Since his proficiency as a player was always obvious, proficiency was what he became known for. He took the opportunities that came to him, and, famous or not, he changed popular music in ways that were both subtle and profound. Only his few peers appreciated the scope of his genius. There were about seventy-five people at the funeral of the man who had created so much great music for the guys with two hands.

Chapter 5

WILLIE THE LION SMITH

O NE WAY A MUSICAL STYLE stays alive is by inspiring experimentation. An enduring musical form, like good sculpture,
invites examination from all sides. It makes musicians want to
add to it, subtract from it, poke it, stretch it, see how far it will bend.
Classic ragtime did (and still does) this, as the cakewalks, intermezzos,
and idylls of the early century do not. Even offshoots of a form may be
large enough to warrant conceptual exploration, as were novelty rags and
stride piano. Sometimes the experiments produce good music, sometimes merely oddities and dead ends, such as George Antheil's novelty
rag–based multipiano works. There was not much experimenting done
with stride piano because to tinker with it, you had to be able to play it
well, and most pianists couldn't.

Willie the Lion Smith was almost alone in having hands and mind
nimble enough to play *with* stride, as well as to play it. In the '20s, Smith
was generally acknowledged to be the second-best player (after James P.

Johnson), but during stride's heyday he wrote very little, and he recorded no piano solos. When Smith finally came into his own, it was too late for the acclaim that should have come to him. Most pianists and piano fans of the time were into boogie-woogie. It looked harder than it was to play, and it was fast and hot.

Smith was middle-aged before his talents as player and composer were recognized beyond Harlem. But once his music was heard, there was no mistaking it for anyone else's. His unparalleled sense of harmony gave his work textures that were unique. In fact, his nearly forty works for piano constitute the most harmonically sophisticated body of popular piano music by an American composer. His pieces are hybrids, as evocative of Debussy as of 133rd Street. He made a sort of Harlem impressionism that influenced those looking forward (Duke Ellington, Billy Strayhorn, Joe Bushkin, and Mel Powell) as well as those looking back (the ragtime revivalists Ralph Sutton, Dick Wellstood, and Mike Lipskin). Smith never had a hit record, never wrote a hit song, and never composed for the theater. He earned his living as a piano player, and in his life as in his music, he went his own way. There was no personality, player, or composer quite like him.

William Henry Joseph Bonaparte Bertholoff was born November 25, 1897, in Goshen, New York. His mother, Ida, was a hardworking domestic, and when Willie was about two years old, she drove his idling father, Frank, out of their house. Ida got married again in 1901, to a mechanic named John Smith. The three Bertholoff children took their stepfather's surname, and, soon after the marriage, the Smith family moved to Newark, New Jersey. They took a house at 76 Academy Street, and John Smith took a new job, driving a meat wagon.

While the family was moving into the Newark house, Willie made a discovery in the basement: a pump organ had been left behind by its previous owners. Ida Smith, who was a church organist, was as happy as her son about the find. She hauled the instrument upstairs and began teaching Willie the hymns and old pop songs that she knew. Ida's mother, Ann, who had played banjo with the Primrose & West minstrel troupe, contributed more songs to Willie's repertoire. Ida's brother, Rob, a former vaudevillian, taught his nephew to dance. Soon after moving to Newark, Willie began to notice the raggy music that he heard when he walked past neighborhood dancehalls, and he practiced at playing it. His mother hated ragtime, but she tolerated Willie's ear version of "Maple Leaf Rag." When Willie was about twelve, he won a piano from Marshall & Wendell's music store by correctly guessing the number of dots in a circle in the store's newspaper ad.

In 1911 the Smiths moved to 28 Clayton Street in Newark. Willie was in high school by this time, more interested in basketball and track than in his studies. He began to frequent dancehalls and saloons, sometimes escorted by his Uncle Rob. He found that a few buck-and-wing steps could put coins in his hat in these places. If a piano player took a break, Willie was quickly in his place, pounding out his one presentable number, "The Grizzly Bear."

Newark's sporting district was called "the Coast," and Willie, in his midteens, became a prominent figure there. He went for the fun, but as his playing improved, he realized that he could earn money where he so enjoyed spending it. His first real job was at Bill Buss's saloon. Willie played afternoons, from 3 to 5 P.M., for a salary of $1 a day, plus tips and three free beers. His next job, at a large dancehall above Randolph's Cafe, brought him the acquaintance of other players. In the fall of 1914, a quiet, soft-looking young man about three years older than Willie came into Randolph's and sat down to try the piano. After hearing James P. Johnson play, Willie said, "Well, you may be able to play better than I can, but I'll bet I can beat you fightin'." Smith also met Luckey Roberts, at the dancehall, when Roberts stopped by, looking for suckers to shoot some lemon pool. He met Eubie Blake while scouting for work in Atlantic City in 1914, and he replaced Blake as pianist at Kelly's—a small "grotto" saloon there—in the summer of 1915.

Smith saw a lot of vaudeville shows in Newark, and he socialized with vaudeville performers, including an accompanist named Arthur Eck. Each had a skill that the other needed, so they traded lessons. Smith showed Eck some ragtime licks, and Eck taught Smith to read music. The newly literate hotshot began making trips across the Hudson to sit in at Manhattan clubs: Jim Allan's, the Jungles, and Barron Wilkins's.

In 1916 Willie Smith took a job playing for the floor shows at Johnson's Cafe in Newark. One of the singers he accompanied was a young white woman from Poughkeepsie named Blanche Merrill. (This was not the Blanche Merrill who wrote specialty material for Fanny Brice.) After a short, stormy courtship, they were married. Their union predictably hit the rocks, and they separated almost immediately. In November 1916, as much to escape battling with Blanche as to fight the kaiser, Willie Smith enlisted in the army.

Willie trained at Camp Dix, New Jersey, and was sent from there to the 92nd Division, 153rd Negro Brigade of the 350th Field Artillery at Camp Upton, on Long Island. The United States entered World War I on April 6, 1917, and the 350th was on its way to France by July. Smith became an expert gunner, the first in his company to become proficient with the huge 75mm French cannons that his division was assigned to use. The mission of the 350th was to stop the German advance on Paris, so about ten miles outside the city, the company dug in and braced itself for siege. Smith and his comrades held their ground for seven horrific weeks, hunkered down in muddy trenches that were crawling with rats. Oddly colored clouds of poison gas hung low over their heads, and the air stank with chemicals. Smith kept his cool in the hellish situation, and he scored heavily with his cannonry, making hundreds of accurate and devastating hits. His commander called him "a lion with a gun," and he proudly carried the nickname the rest of his life.

After the armistice of November 11, 1918, the 92nd Division converted to a labor battalion and remained in France to carry out the massive cleanup detail. In late 1919 Sergeant Smith was discharged with a commendation that "his conduct was excellent in battle, showing nerve, faith and intuition." Having whipped the Hun, the Lion would now enlist in the piano wars of Harlem.

Smith moved into Lottie Joplin's boardinghouse and went to work for Leroy Wilkins (Barron's brother). Leroy's was an upscale place on 135th Street—tuxedos were required for musicians and patrons on weekends—and it drew a smart clientele. Willie would keep his coveted position as Leroy's "house man" for two years. He organized a combo to accompany the star customers (including Ethel Waters, Florence Mills, and Bill Robinson), who were often moved to dance and sing. Smith was hired on a tips only/no salary basis, but he drew enough fans to ask his boss for (and get) $18 a week. His tips boosted his weekly take-home pay to $100 or so. He was still married to Blanche (in fact, they would never divorce), but he was long out of touch with her. Women who frequented Leroy's thought him to be both eligible and well-heeled, and he did his best not to disillusion them.

It was during his Leroy's period that Smith put the finishing touches on his personal style. He had studied the clothing and manner of piano sharks since his teens in Newark, and he took much from these early models. He wanted to make a striking impression before he sat down at the piano, so his first thoughts were of streetwear. His overcoat was a tasteful melton, with padded shoulders and plaid lining. His shoes were French, custom-made in the short-vamp style. The derby hat had been a Smith trademark since his days of passing it after dancing in Newark clubs, and he took to wearing one at the piano. His suits were conservative but expensive. He preferred a single-breasted cut, to show the gold watch chain that dangled across his chest. And he had spats made from the suit material. A silk shirt was best, especially if it was warm enough to remove the suit coat, which he folded over a chair, of course, to let the shiny lining show. A cigar and a cane completed the picture of elegance. He was six feet tall, handsome and muscular, with fierce black eyes and a withering glare. When the Lion entered a saloon, everyone knew a big shot had arrived.

Diamonds displayed on horseshoe stickpins and rings gave Smith the cachet of affluence, as did several gold teeth. (One Newark saloon player had a diamond set in the tooth of his bulldog, which he tied to a piano leg before he sat down to play. Smith must have considered this gauche, however, as he never added a bulldog to his ensemble.) Smith would change little in his appearance as he aged (affecting black horn-rims in the '40s and red vests in the '50s), because the Lion approved of what he saw in the mirror. For the next fifty years, he would look like a Harlem sport of 1920.

Willie's talk was even more intimidating than his clothing. He announced himself upon arriving at a club or party: "The Lion is here." From across the room, he would taunt whoever was playing: "When did you break your left hand?" He chatted noisily through other players' sets, oblivious to the music. After he had worked the room, he would dismiss the pianist: "Get up. I'll show you how it's supposed to go." The only compliment he could bring himself to give—and the one he gave when Johnson brought the terrified Fats Waller to play at Leroy's—was "He'll do." His temper was frightening. He was deeply offended by bad pianos and was known to explode at the sight of a stuck key. At rent parties—in private homes—he berated his hosts for untuned pianos and broken strings. He battled with club owners over the size and condition of his dressing rooms.

With few exceptions—Roberts, Blake, Johnson, and, later, Waller—Smith considered his contemporaries to be ham-handed. He said that Clarence Williams "played the piano as if he was wearing mittens." The only white pianist he respected was Arthur Schutt. He said of Vincent Lopez, "His left hand's like the bear, nowhere." His judgments were harsh, and he pronounced them loudly. Eubie Blake (who was nicknamed "Mouse") summed up sixty years of observing the Lion's cantankerous behavior:

> Of course the Lion never had *nothing* good to say about *anybody*, you know. Big mouth. But the Lion could play! He *could* play. But Willie always wanted to be the whole show. I guess he thought that if you always put the other guy down, it made *you* look good. But things don't work that way. Willie was good enough that he didn't need to act that way.

◆

Smith's musical style was not as well defined as his outward mien in 1920. His repertoire came mostly from Richard (Abba Labba) McLean, Jack the Bear Wilson, and One-Leg Willie Joseph, rough-hewn saloonists of a generation earlier. His sets were a mix of pop tunes and a few better-known rags, along with spicy club fare, such as "Don't You Hit That Lady Dressed in Green" and "Baby, Let Your Drawers Hang Down." Smith's best material was cribbed from the classics. He could rag Chopin's "Polonaise" as well as the "Miserere" from *Il Trovatore*, and in 1921 he devised his own version of "The Sheik of Araby," using a bit of "March Militaire" to replace the verse.

Willie clearly needed direction, and he got it when his friend and musical hero, James P. Johnson, became his mentor. The two were opposites temperamentally, but they had been close since their meeting in

Newark's "Coast." The Lion was watching closely during the evolution toward stride, and he assimilated Johnson's ideas quickly. He became proficient enough (and nervy enough) to play "Carolina Shout" in Johnson's presence. James P.'s generosity seems to have brought out Smith's better nature and inspired him to do some mentoring of his own. Along with Johnson, he also coached Fats Waller. The three became inseparable.

But Smith remained a neighborhood phenomenon, appreciated most by those in his profession and completely unknown below 131st Street. Why did Johnson, who had been making piano rolls since 1917, not pave his way at the QRS company? Why did Fats Waller, who began recording in 1922, not introduce him at OKeh or Victor? Whatever the reasons, it didn't happen. Smith never made a piano roll, and he didn't make instrumental recordings until 1925. (His next came in 1927, and his first piano solo recordings were not released until 1938.) The Lion's roar had narrow geographic limits.

Smith's career in the 1920s was a melange of clubs, shows, and, eventually, recordings. He could compete for and get good jobs, but there was no pattern to them. His first recording was as a barely audible sideman on the historic 1920 recording of "Crazy Blues," with Mamie Smith and Her Jazz Hounds. When "Crazy Blues" took off, he returned to OKeh to make two more sides with Mamie and her band. Smith left the Jazz Hounds when they began touring because he did not want to go South. He accompanied Clarence (Dancin') Dotson in vaudeville dates around the Northeast. He played in Will Mastin's *Holiday in Dixie*, which began as a club revue and later toured the Orpheum circuit. He left the Mastin show in Chicago and stayed for nearly a year playing at the Fiume Cafe there.

Back in Harlem, Smith performed at the Garden of Joy, the Capitol Palace, and the Rhythm Club. A few society parties came his way after the exposure he got when George Gershwin invited him—along with Johnson and Waller—to a celebration of the premiere of *Rhapsody in Blue* in February 1924. (The Lion was the only pianist ever to displace the ebullient Gershwin from the spotlight. At the *Rhapsody* party, when he thought his host had played long enough, Smith said, "Get up off that piano stool and let the real players take over, you tomato.")

It was in 1925 that Smith's patchwork recording career really began. In November he made two sides with the Gulf Coast Seven, in a

Columbia session produced by Clarence Williams. One of the tunes was Charley Straight's "Santa Claus Blues," and the other was Smith's first composition, "Keep Your Temper," both of which had been recently published by Williams. As written, "Keep Your Temper" is a driving stride number, but for some reason, in this recording Smith slowed it down and ironed out its syncopated kinks to make a run-of-the-mill dance record. Smith would not work in a studio again for two years, until a two-side 1927 Harmony session with Perry Bradford's Georgia Strutters. In 1929, Smith made two sides with Clarence Williams's Seven Gallon Jug Band for Columbia. These off-the-cuff recordings with ephemeral bands went nowhere and led to nothing better for the talent in the piano chair.

In 1927 Smith played the piano for a dance scene in a Broadway play, George Abbott's *Four Walls*, starring Paul Muni. Smith's time on stage at the Golden Theatre was about half an hour, and he would skip his curtain call to dash uptown to work in Harlem clubs. He kept up his two-jobs-a-night schedule during the show's entire 144-performance run. When the *Four Walls* tour was announced, Smith left the company, passing up his chance to be in the movie version that was made when the tour ended in Hollywood.

It was not until his late-'20s residency at Pod's and Jerry's that Smith began to attract fans from outside Harlem. This club was at 168 West 133rd Street, and, like the Cotton Club a few blocks away, it catered to the white show world. Its owners, Charles "Pod" Hollingsworth and Jeremiah Preston, called it the Catagonia Club, but everyone knew the place by their nicknames. Smith's workday began at midnight and ended at 7 A.M. His primary duties were to accompany the singing of Mary Stafford and Mattie Hite and the eccentric dancing of "Little Jazzbo" Hilliard, a hunchback. During his two years at Pod's and Jerry's, Willie acquired fans among jazz stars (Bix Beiderbecke and Jack Teagarden), bandleaders (Claude Thornhill and Benny Goodman), and songwriters (Hoagy Carmichael and Arthur Schwartz), as well as impressing Mae West and Mayor Jimmy Walker. After a year or so, Smith's salary went up to $350 a week, and he was given a 30 percent interest in the club. Tips still mattered to him, so he installed a mirror over the piano to keep an eye on where they went after the singers collected them. There was strict accounting to be done at dawn during the division of the "entertainer's fund."

Among the jazz players who came to Pod's and Jerry's to hear and to sit in with Willie Smith was Artie Shaw. Shaw was new in town, still waiting out the required six months to get his New York musicians' union card. But he was playing clarinet well enough to please the Lion, and he was an astute listener. Shaw heard something in Smith that went beyond the embellishments of other club players, even the gifted ones. Years later he would write in his autobiography, *The Trouble with Cinderella*, of the Lion's way of "introducing a melody, a thread of a tune, and then sliding into complicated little modulatory phrases of his own, which always, somehow or other, managed to get back into the tonality of wherever they started from." Smith's guide through these interesting musical byways was his idiosyncratic but unerring ear. He heard and played harmonies all his own, and Shaw encouraged him to use them in composition.

Smith had published only one piano work up to this time, his 1925 "Keep Your Temper," and he wanted more technical knowledge before he tried again. So, at age thirty-three, he began his first formal study of music, with a German professor named Hans Steinke, who taught him theory, harmony, and counterpoint. Steinke soaked him in classical piano literature, which Willie appreciated for its own sake as well for the technical benefits its practice offered. (Years later Smith would tell his biographer, George Hoefer, "The trouble with most piano players is that they don't play enough Bach. Bach develops the left hand.") He remained Steinke's pupil well into the 1940s, and he put his instruction to good use.

There were still clubs to play (Helbock's on Fifty-second Street, DeLuca's in the Village, and Club Napoleon—housed in the old Woolworth mansion on West Fifty-sixth Street) and singers to accompany (Nina Mae McKinney in vaudeville and Eva Taylor on radio), but Smith always made time to practice for his lessons with Steinke. And he began to shape his hodgepodge of pop/stride/classic playing into a compositional style. We can hear the new Smith emerging in his band records and in a few of his published piano pieces from the mid-'30s.

Clarence Williams had so far been Smith's sole publisher, and, despite the low sales of his sole instrumental number in 1925, Williams decided to commit to him in earnest in 1934. That year he published Smith's "Finger Buster," a hard-edged stride piece in the vein of "Keep Your Temper." (Smith made a recording—his first as a solo pianist—of

"Finger Buster" in May 1934 for ARC, but this record went unreleased until years later.) In April 1935, another of Smith's stride pieces, "Harlem Joys" (written with Walter Bishop) was recorded for Decca by Smith and His Cubs, a four-piece jazz band.

With "Finger Buster" and "Harlem Joys," Smith seemed to be continuing along the Johnsonesque path that he had been on since the early 1920s. But among the Williams publications of 1935 were two Smith pieces unlike anything he had written before, indeed unlike anything any ragtimer had written before. One of these was a four-themed work called "Love Remembers." Its arrangement is credited to "Hans Hanke" (surely a misspelling of Smith's teacher's name), and the piece is an outright reach into classicism. Its first and last strains are in 6/8 time, the second is in 6/16, and the third is in 4/4. The first section is marked to be played "Sweet and wayward (72 beats a minute)" and from there the number makes its impassioned way to the "Fast and shadowy (168 beats a minute)" fourth section in a swirl of notes. With "Love Remembers," the Lion was venturing from ragtime onto the terrain of "serious" music. He would not remain there, but he would keep his visa. For the rest of his life, his writing, including his rags, would sound as much like Ravel as like James P. Johnson.

Another unusual Smith work issued by Williams in 1935 was the one that is considered his masterpiece, "Echo of Spring." There is no arranger credit given on the published version, but there are two co-composers named: Clarence Williams (a great believer in the publisher cut-in) and Tausha Hammed (a Williams staffer who had been a cigar-box violinist in vaudeville). It is hard to imagine that Williams or Hammed contributed anything to "Echo of Spring," because it is far beyond anything written by either of them before or after its publication. It sounds like Smith and no one else, and it has the pastoral feeling that marks Smith's most personal work.

Smith said the tune came to him one morning around 6:30 while he was sitting on a park bench across from City College, near his St. Nicholas Avenue home. "Echo of Spring" is a raggy tone poem with a gently rocking bass line underneath a trilling, bird-note melody. It is full of harmonic surprises, but they are only surprises, not shocks. "Echo" takes its time; its unusual harmonies sneak up on, but never jump out at,

the listener. Smith uses chords as a painter uses splashes of color, and "Echo of Spring" suggests what we might see if Monet had depicted a peaceful scene of a corner in Harlem.

Smith began to record for Decca in the spring of 1935. His Cubs originally numbered four (including himself), and he would add three more players for his 1937 Cubs sessions. The scrappy band recorded mostly pop songs, lit by an occasional beam of stride in Smith's piano breaks. They chugged their way through a few intricate Smith compositions—"Harlem Joys" and "Echo of Spring" (both in 1935), "The Swampland Is Calling Me" and "I'm All Out of Breath" (both in 1937)—but the records were obviously made for dancing. The arrangements are so resolutely ordinary that they obscure the extraordinary material.

Late in 1937, after two years of freelancing for Decca, Smith was finally offered a one-year contract. There was a catch, however, and it was a big one: Smith was hired to beef up the records of Milt Herth, who had been making solo recordings on the electric organ for the company since June 1936 with no hits. By adding the piano of Willie Smith and the drumming of O'Neil Spencer to the perky stylings of Herth, Decca hoped literally to jazz him up. The Milt Herth Trio became a quartet in April 1938 with the addition of Teddy Bunn's guitar. The quartet records are somewhat better than the trio's, but they are all kept earthbound by their leaden star. Herth's taste in tunes ran from Dixieland clichés ("That's a Plenty" and "Jazz Me Blues") to pop clichés ("The Flat Foot Floogie" and "Home Cooking Mama with the Frying Pan"). It never occurred to Herth nor to anyone at Decca to record a Smith number. The era's most inventive composer of piano pop spent a year laying down the beat for a tin-eared organist.

Decca threw Smith a bone on January 10, 1938, by allowing him to record two piano solos (he chose "Passionette" and "Morning Air"), but it was not enough to mollify him. His happiest day at Decca was November 30, 1938, the date that he made his last session with Herth under his contractual obligation. As soon as he completed his servitude that day, he went directly to Milt Gabler's Commodore studio to record with Joe Bushkin and Jess Stacy. On their first number, "Three Keyboards," Smith chimed in on celeste, while Bushkin and Stacy played four-handed piano. The second side, "The Lion and the Lamb," was a stride duet by Smith and Bushkin. The session was a stunt, but the fun the pianists had is obvious in the loose and joyful playing.

Smith had been recording sporadically for ten years, but he had still not been heard at his best. Finally, on January 10, 1939, a year to the day after his two-tune date at Decca, he made a solo piano session for Commodore. He had been writing throughout the arid year he'd spent with Milt Herth, and he was ready. In a bravura feat, he recorded four-teen numbers, eight of them his own compositions. This Commodore session yielded a body of work unlike any in pop music.

Smith recorded six songs that day, including "Tea for Two," Vernon Duke's "What Is There to Say?," and Harold Arlen's "Stormy Weather" and "Between the Devil and the Deep Blue Sea." He begins them all with a clear statement of the melody, adding his harmonic colorations mostly as filler after the melodic lines. His phrasing is whimsical, and his bag of styles—from boogie to stride to Tatumesque runs—is ransacked for his improvisations on second and third choruses.

The only pure stride piece of the day was his "Finger Buster," and it stands in great contrast to his seven other originals, all of which show how far he had come since James P. Johnson was his only model. He rerecorded his two Decca solos, "Morning Air" and "Passionette," and both are improvements on the earlier versions. "Morning Air" is a stride piece with the striding removed. If it is supposed to suggest a matutinal stroll, it is a stroll taken at a very brisk pace. Smith's left hand is perpet-ual motion itself, keeping steady time but marking it in every way except the octave-chord way. "Passionette" bursts with energy, and "Concentratin'" has a call-and-response section that can only be described as rocking. "Sneakaway" is a rag, fluid and playful, unlike the bounding "Finger Buster." The first strain of "Rippling Waters" is a par-aphrase of the "dawn" theme from *Peer Gynt*, and Smith's performance of it shows what Bach did for his left hand: it is in constant and perfect con-trapuntal movement as it winds under the melody. "Fading Star" is a showpiece, full of broken tempos and rubato passages, ending in a burst of *scherzo*. If the eight Smith pieces had only their precision, their clar-ity, and their melodic invention to recommend them, they would be major contributions to the literature of popular piano music. But they have more: the Lion's singular sense of harmony.

◆

In his 1964 memoir, *Music on My Mind*, Smith does not mention the word "impressionism," nor does he cite Debussy or Ravel as influences on him. He said, "They talk about augmented chords, ninth chords, whole-tone progressions and all that. I've been using them for years but I didn't know what they were." He used such things, he claimed, only because "they sound good." If Willie were truly unaware that the impressionists got there first, his work is all the more miraculous, and his home-grown genius actually on a par with the French masters'. No three- and four-minute pop piano pieces were ever washed with such audacious chords, but his use of them is matter-of-fact. Like the impressionists, Smith disdained modulation; he just changed keys as he heard the need to do so. The chord isn't supposed to go there, but it goes there anyway, and it sounds fine. There is no self-consciousness in his work, and not a whiff of academic experimentation. However unlikely the voicing, there is no pomposity in it, no lingering to say, "Look what I did." Smith's tunes, even the pensive ones, are animated, moving along easily and letting the harmonies fall where they may.

Like Debussy, Smith saw chords not as steps along a mathematical progression, but as ends in themselves, like colors on a palette, sounds to be selected from to make something pretty. Even when he is improvising, he arranges his tonal colors in a pleasing way, and his pieces always have unity of mood. The frequent use of "passing chords" in the left hand gives his work a restless quality. "Echo of Spring," "Morning Air," and "Fading Star" are lively and dreamy at the same time. His right hand often seems to float free of his left, spinning gossamer embroidery over continually shifting colors in the bass.

Duke Ellington had been fascinated by Smith's sound since hearing him at the Capitol Palace around 1923. Smith took an interest in his young fan, and soon after their first meeting, he gave Ellington an impromptu harmony lesson. While riding around Central Park in a han-som, they created chords with their voices. In his autobiography, Ellington remembered Smith's "harmonic lavishness" and said, "I swam in it." The Ellington orchestra never recorded a Smith composition, but the Ellington mood pieces of the mid-'30s—especially "Bird of

Paradise," "Harlem Speaks," and "Echoes of Harlem"—show his influence. The Duke spelled it out in his 1939 "Portrait of the Lion," written as an homage to Smith and echoing his harmonic style. (Smith returned the compliment in a backhanded way with his 1957 "Portrait of the Duke." In its imitation of Ellington's playing, it is the sparest and plainest of all his piano works.)

Several recordings of Smith's work were made by others in the mid-'30s, notably Jack Teagarden's "Rippling Waters," Andy Kirk's "In the Groove," and Artie Shaw's "The Old Stamping Ground." But Smith's own 1939 Commodore recordings were the ones that defined him. Not long after these records were issued, Leo Feist published a folio containing seven Smith piano pieces, including the first printings of "No Local Stops," "Tango a la Caprice," and "Concentratin'." (Clarence Williams and others issued songs by Smith during this period, but, oddly, his songs sound nothing like his piano work. They are highly rhythmic but harmonically mundane. The only songwriter as harmonically adventurous as Smith was the Russian-born, conservatory-trained Vernon Duke.)

Smith's mother died in 1944, and he was deeply affected by her passing. Longing for spiritual support, he joined a black Jewish congregation in Harlem. (He had learned a bit of Hebrew as a child in Newark, and he had always had an affinity for Jewish beliefs.) A few years after Ida Smith's death, he became a cantor in a synagogue at Lenox Avenue and 122nd Street. Smith also began to teach music around this time, with Mel Powell, Joe Bushkin, and Dick Wellstood among his first pupils and Mike Lipskin among his last (in the 1960s). He moved to 300 West 151st Street, and around 1946 he cut back on drinking. His gilded teeth, an affectation from his rent party days, began to rot, so he had them removed.

Smith set out on his first international tour in December 1949. He played at jazz festivals and clubs in Europe for six weeks and received favorable reviews everywhere he went. Early in the tour, at the Vogue studios in Paris, he made the first of his several "memoirs" albums, in which he reminisces as well as plays. When he returned to New York, he became a regular at the weekend jazz sessions at Central Plaza, a Jewish catering hall at 111 Second Avenue.

In 1950, Willie returned to Commodore to remake the eight compositions from his historic 1939 session there. His playing was more relaxed and authoritative than it had been eleven years earlier, and this Commodore LP yielded the best studio work of his career. Other fine Smith albums from the 1950s are *The Lion Roars* (released by Dot in 1957) and *The Legend of Willie (the Lion) Smith* (made for Grand Award in 1958). In 1958 he was a featured performer at the Newport Jazz Festival.

Although the jazz world honored him, the Lion was not lionized by ragtime purists. Supervised by Mike Lipskin, he made a two-LP album of his *Memoirs* for Victor in 1968, on which he horrified revivalists by disassociating himself from their music. He said on the album, "Ragtime means a guy that don't know the keyboard. . . . This was the style of piano they played when they didn't have good left hands. . . . Some people think it's piano playing. . . . that's pure corn!" By the time he made these LPs, his own left hand was not the trusty machine that it had been, and Willie knew it. Once, while waiting backstage with Eubie Blake, Smith heard Don Lambert playing brilliantly and heard the audience's yells of approval. Blake jokingly asked, "How do we follow that?" Willie seriously replied, "I don't know about you, but I plan to do a lot of talking."

On April 29, 1969, Smith was a guest at the White House party given by President and Mrs. Nixon to celebrate Duke Ellington's seventieth birthday. After the Nixons went to bed, the Lion and the Duke played stride duets long into the night. Smith continued to headline jazz festivals in America and abroad—bullying concert promoters, upbraiding his audiences, and complaining about his dressing rooms—until his death in New York on April 18, 1973.

Willie the Lion, hard to like and easy to admire, brought something truly original to the composition of popular music. Like the semiclassicists of his era, he borrowed from European moderns, but he was the most creative of all the borrowers. In a time when "serious" composers spent careers trying to make a marriage between classical and pop, the two forms lived in common-law bliss in the work of Willie Smith. He alone made the match seem effortless. Others wrestled with long forms and with age-old structures that were literally foreign to them, but Smith never felt the need to write an extended composition. There are no Smith rhapsodies, symphonies, or sonatas. He borrowed only sounds.

Instead of making a poppish and ersatz classical music, he elevated pop by enriching its harmonic vocabulary. He took the busiest and most complicated kind of ragtime and, without being false to it, tinted it in pastels. The loudmouth who spent his life in smoky clubs left us music that is a breath of fresh air.

Chapter 6

FAT*S* WALLER

HARLEM'S BRAND OF RAGTIME was not made to accompany dancing or seduction; its only aim was aural delight. Its natural habitats were not the concert hall or the ballroom, but the small club and the parlor social. The music flourished where it could feed, and feed off of, high spirits. Players and listeners urged one another to exuberance, each relishing what the other had brought to the party. Through improvisation—his own or that of a rival—a player might find devices to be used in composition, but introspection came later. The first order of business was to lift the spirit and keep it high.

The pianist who personified stride's pleasure principle was Fats Waller. Although Waller was neither the best player nor the best composer of rags among his peers, nobody was more fun. He didn't merely brighten a party, he *was* a party. He was capable of powerhouse playing, but he seldom did it. Waller played not to overwhelm his rivals but to charm his listeners. He didn't assail the piano; he, alone among the so-called ticklers, actually tickled it. And he had more than musical tricks up his sleeve. Singing, mugging, and jokes complemented his teasing piano style and made it all the more delicious. Fats was good times rampant, everything a host could ask for.

Waller was the youngest of the stride masters, and by the time he began to record extensively, the style that he had devoted a decade of his life to was on its way out. In the late 1920s, players came to realize that stride alone could not sustain them, professionally or artistically. No one could center a compositional career on a form that had nothing but whoopee on its mind. Unlike classic ragtime, stride had one basic tempo (fast) and one basic mood (hilarity).

Some of those who began as stride fiends pared down their playing and became leaders of dance bands (Bill Basie, Duke Ellington, Claude Hopkins); others (James P. Johnson and Willie Smith) became all-purpose sidemen who occasionally led studio bands of their own. Some (Cliff Jackson, Don Ewell, Don Lambert) simply stayed in neighborhood clubs and leavened their stride repertoires with pop songs. James P. Johnson's invention took popular piano playing to giddy heights, but no professional could specialize in giddiness. (Even at today's ragtime festivals, which have spawned concerts built around every conceivable theme, an all-stride evening is rare.)

Fats Waller's ragtime-flavored piano was the underpinning of his popular recordings, but his impish vocals were why the records were made. His humor did more than save him from a sideman/neighborhood-bar career: it made him the most popular black entertainer of the 1930s. More than sixty of his five hundred or so recordings made it onto the *Billboard* charts. Fats composed music for three hit shows (and performed in two of them); he sang and played in three major films; he was ubiquitous on radio, as host and guest. There are about a dozen standards among the two hundred or so published songs and piano pieces that bear his name. Spontaneity was part of his genius. The effort of writing never showed because there was no effort to it. Most of his songs were composed in the time it took to jot them down, and most of his recordings were made in the time it took to sing and play them.

Despite the solid musicality of his work, he was taken for granted by the public and by the record industry—as Fatsy-Watsy, the merry prankster who happened to play piano—and he was a sculptor of his own frivolous image. His personal life was a mess, as was his professional one, and to satisfy his appetites, he could be an eager collaborator with anyone who wanted to exploit him. He was a legendary eater, a nonstop drinker, a tireless reveler who could be seen reeling through Harlem at midmorning, looking for another party or a club that was still jumping from the night before. To pay for his eating, drinking, and reveling, he sometimes sold himself too cheaply, and he often worked himself too hard.

Despite his childish nature, Waller was the most successful of all the Harlem pianists. In the late '30s, his name was as well known as Louis Armstrong's; by the early '40s, he was earning more than the president of the United States. He was the royal nonesuch of jazz, the clown who sang in funny voices and ad-libbed his way through soppy song lyrics. But he was also the one who did the most to keep improvisational small-band jazz alive in the tightly charted big-band era. His piano was the bridge between the precision of stride and the looseness of swing. He swung hard enough to influence the forthright Bill Basie, and his treble filigree inspired the lighter-than-air stylings of Art Tatum.

Thomas Wright Waller was born on May 21, 1904, in an apartment rented by his parents, Edward Martin Waller and Adeline Lockett Waller, on Waverly Place, in Manhattan's Greenwich Village. He was fourth among the five Waller children who survived past infancy. Edward Waller had a small trucking company, and Adeline was a housewife, but their consuming interest was their church, Abyssinian Baptist, in Harlem. Soon after Tom's birth, the Wallers moved uptown to be nearer their spiritual home. Edward served as Abyssinian's superintendent of Sunday school, and he was also chairman of the board of deacons; Adeline sang and played the organ for services. There was daily prayer and Bible reading at home, and Adeline kept an eye on her children's playmates, weeding out those who might be bad influences on them. Young Tom and his sister Naomi were close partners in naughtiness, and they learned to use their parents' piety to avoid punishment. If threatened with a spanking for one of his capers, Tom would suggest prayer, rather than the hairbrush, as a solution. And he could sometimes change the subject merely by beaming angelically and claiming that he had recently had sweet dreams of Jesus.

When Tom was about six, his mother began to show him some hymn tunes on the family's wheezy little harmonium, and his musical interest was piqued further by his discovery of a piano in a neighbor's apartment. After much calculation, the Wallers decided that they could afford a piano, too, and that Tom and Naomi should begin lessons with Miss Perry, an elderly woman who lived near their West 134th Street apartment. Naomi hated her lessons, but Tom loved his. Using his considerable wiles on Miss Perry, he could sometimes deflect his study from scales and exercises to the playing of popular song sheets that she owned. His ear was so good that he saw no need to practice. Realizing that he would always choose the fun of playing over the chore of practicing, Miss Perry dropped him as a pupil.

Despite his flirtation with the piano, Tom remained loyal to his first love, the harmonium. When his father left Abyssinian Baptist Church to join a Pentecostal congregation, Tom was, at age ten, able to accompany him on the family's portable organ while he evangelized on street corners in Harlem.

Tom Waller was enrolled at P.S. 89, where he acquired the nickname given to roly-poly boys, and where a music teacher, Miss Corlias, taught him violin and piano (and note reading on both). He played the violin in the school orchestra and clowned as he played piano for assemblies. His father disapproved of worldly music, and, to point Fats in the right direction, he took his eleven-year-old son to hear Ignace Paderewski at Carnegie Hall. The boy raved for days about the concert, but his practice was still taken up by rags and songs. His father whipped him for ragging hymns, and their ongoing conflict became a strain on Adeline, who had developed diabetes. She was forever in the middle of their rows, and to give his wife some peace, Edward Waller allowed his son to drop out after one year at De Witt Clinton High, to try to become a musician.

Fats and Naomi took jobs at a jewel-box factory in the Battery, near enough to Trinity Church for Fats to spend his lunch hours ingratiating himself with the organist so that he might be allowed to play. He quit the factory job to become an errand boy for two brothers, Connie and George Immerman, delivering cold cuts from their Harlem delicatessen (and the bootleg liquor that was their sideline). Still in his midteens, Fats was his own man now, free to roam the streets and to explore clubs and cabarets, the occasional clash with his father being the price of living at home.

Waller's favorite stop in his meanderings was the Lincoln Theatre, a huge silent movie house on West 135th Street. He was not interested in the films, but in the giant Wurlitzer organ used to accompany them. He befriended Maizie Mullins, the organist, and she often invited him into the pit to watch her play. Before long, he was surreptitiously subbing for her when she took her breaks. When she left in 1919, she recommended Fats to the theater owner, and, at $23 a week, the $10,000 Wurlitzer became his charge. This job would be the mainstay of his income for the next several years, and he drew customers to the Lincoln just to hear him. Jazz pianist and arranger Mary Lou Williams recalled that "people just screamed, he was so good." At fifteen, Waller was at nearly his full height of six feet, and already at his full weight of about 300 pounds. And he was all devilry, with eyes rolling and lips pursed as he played inappropriate music underneath newsreel pictures of statesmen's funerals on the screen.

Fats was asked to play with a band at a block party, and it was there that he met a pretty teenager and became smitten with her. Her name was Edith Hatchett, and when he took her home to meet his family, they approved of her sweetness and demure manner. Fats began seriously courting her. But during the heady days of his first crush, there was still browbeating by his father, and there was increasing worry about his mother. Adeline was losing ground to diabetes, becoming grossly overweight and bedridden. Nonetheless, as he always would, Fats looked on the sunny side. Life was generally good: he had a girlfriend and a job, and he was making music and listening to it everywhere he went.

The relative tranquillity of Waller's life ended on November 10, 1920, when his mother died of a stroke. Her death was the breaking point for a fragile family. Fats was inconsolable, as was his father, and their tempers were raw. After a last violent row, Fats left home in despair. He was taken in by the family of a school friend, Wilson Brooks.

The Brookses owned a player piano, and Wilson's older brother, Russell, was the family pianist. Russell especially liked the music of Luckey Roberts and James P. Johnson, and he proudly showed Fats his collection of their rolls and sheet music. Fats learned to play Roberts's "Pork and Beans" from its published version, and he immersed himself in the Johnson rags on rolls. When Russell boasted that he knew Johnson,

Fats begged for an introduction. Waller was thrilled when Russell invited their hero to the apartment.

Johnson accepted the invitation because he had heard Waller at the Lincoln Theatre and had seen promise in him. He sent Russell away as the nervous novitiate made his way to the piano. They spent the afternoon together, Johnson suggesting fingerings and modulations and Waller trying them. Fats was disheartened to hear Johnson recommend the same scales and exercises that Miss Perry had urged on him years earlier, but he promised to work at them. At the end of their session, Waller was grateful to have had a few hours with his idol, but Johnson saw a chance to do more. He went home and told his wife Lillie, "I know I can teach that boy." Johnson's decision to coach him began a deep personal and musical relationship that was the bulwark of Waller's life.

James P. and Lillie Johnson took him over. Johnson let Fats tag along to clubs for informal coaching while he worked. He brought him to rent parties, saw that he met Blake and Roberts, and made sure that he heard everyone worth hearing. Lillie saw to it that he got sleep and food, and she bought him clothing. Fats had two havens now, and he began dividing his time between the Johnsons' and the Brookses' homes. He would have slept on the street to avoid going back to his father.

The most frightening rite of Waller's initiation into the Harlem piano world was Johnson's presentation of him to Willie the Lion Smith, who was playing at Leroy's. Waller was wearing a wrinkled suit, the best he had, for the occasion. Johnson introduced the timid boy to the Lion and asked that he be allowed to play a few numbers. The Lion's scorn was shattering: "I can't be bothered listening to some punk kid. Get that guy down because he looks filthy. Get them pants pressed. There's no excuse for it." Johnson persisted, and Smith reluctantly ceded the piano to the nervous fat boy. As he always did when anyone else was playing, the Lion wandered about the club, grumbling and talking with customers, conspicuously inattentive. Then Waller lit into "Carolina Shout," and the Lion stopped his milling until it was over. He could not bring himself to utter praise, of course, but he whispered to Johnson, "Watch out, Jimmy, he's got it." The third musketeer had arrived. The masters and their prize pupil prowled Harlem every night in search of pianos on which to mow down any upstarts and to show off for each other.

Early in 1921, Fats Waller traded a bad domestic situation for a worse one when he married Edith Hatchett. The teenage newlyweds moved in with her parents in the Bronx, and the Hatchetts began a campaign to force Waller to give up music. He was still playing at the Lincoln Theatre, but his salary wasn't enough to support a wife. The situation became grim when Edith announced to her family that she was pregnant. Her father demanded that Waller learn a trade—he suggested carpentry—take responsibility, be a man. Waller's response was to grab every piano job that came his way, to earn as much as he could, doing what he knew how to do.

When the Lincoln Theatre changed its management later that year, Waller changed jobs, taking over the organ at the Lafayette Theatre, on Seventh Avenue between 131st and 132nd streets, for $50 a week. Needing the food as well as the tips, he pressed the self-anointed flack Lippy Boyette for rent party dates. He subbed for Willie Smith at Leroy's. He went on a six-week tour of the Northeast as accompanist for a minor vaudeville act, Liza and Her Shufflin' Six. Nothing would satisfy the Hatchetts. Their disapproval of him was boundless, and he began to stay away from their home, and away from his wife, to avoid it.

His friends tried to help. Clarence Williams recommended him to producer Fred Hager at OKeh records as accompanist for the blues singer Sara Martin. Waller was scheduled for two Martin sessions, but he failed to appear at either one. Williams gave him a talking-to about his irresponsibility, and the chastened Waller asked for another chance. Williams prevailed on Hager again, and in late October 1922 Fats Waller entered the OKeh studios to make the two piano solos that were his first recordings. One number was "Muscle Shoals Blues," a tune that Hager thought would sell in the "race" market; the other was a song that Waller chose, "Birmingham Blues," by McCord and Matthews. The playing is good on these two middle-tempo pieces, but there is a stiffness in them that makes them sound like piano rolls. However, Hager was pleased enough to keep hiring Waller. Before 1922 was out, he had made another four sides at OKeh, all as accompanist for Sara Martin.

James P. took Waller to the Bronx to meet the owners of the QRS Company, where Johnson was in great favor as a piano-roll artist. (QRS used the slogan "Quality Reigns Supreme," but its slogan did not inspire its name: the three initials came from the marking over a mail slot in their building.) The company was a subsidiary of the Melville Clark Piano Company, a manufacturer of player pianos. It was run by Max Kortlander, a white player and composer of novelty rags, and J. Lawrence Cook, a black arranger who was the most gifted creator of piano rolls. Cook—who plied his artistry well into the 1960s—skipped the piano-playing part of the process. He worked directly on the heavy paper "master," cutting so precisely as to produce "piano reproductions" that sounded hand-played, but which had, in fact, never been played at all. He was a musical chameleon, punching out tunes in the styles of many well-known pianists, and even able to add extra "hands" in anyone's idiom. Many QRS rolls attributed to major performers were really the ghostly work of J. Lawrence Cook. (The QRS rolls labeled "Played by Thomas Waller" are Waller's own; those attributed to "Fats Waller" were created by Cook.)

Kortlander and Cook decided to give Waller a try, and in March 1923, Fats cut his first roll, a Spencer Williams tune called "Got to Cool My Doggies Now." Waller would make nine more pop song rolls for QRS—at $50 each—in 1923 alone, with "Your Time Now" a standout among them. (Waller made no piano roll versions of his rags. He did not start writing his stride pieces until the late '20s, by which time the piano-roll market had dwindled.)

Clarence Williams began to buy Waller's compositions in the summer of 1923. The first two purchases were songs, "It Seems to Me" and "All Alone" (with words and music by Waller), neither of which was published. But in September 1923, Williams bought a Waller song called "Wild Cat Blues," which he overhauled and turned into a piano rag to issue in October (with his own name appended as co-composer, of course). The blues boom was then at its height—and Clarence Williams was the blues' leading entrepreneur—but the title of Waller's first publication is more than a publisher's marketing ploy. "Wild Cat Blues" is a rag, but it obviously began its life as a blues. Its four melodies are conceived in two-bar phrases, and its first and fourth strains are twelve-bar melodies with four-bar codas attached. Like Johnson and Smith, Waller never took the blues seriously, but his writing was informed a bit more by the style than theirs was.

Waller was encouraged by his first publication, and he plunged into a frenzy of songwriting in collaboration with lyricist Jo Trent. Clarence Williams bought more than a dozen Waller-Trent songs before he finally issued one (Waller's second publication), "In Harlem's Araby," in the summer of 1924. Williams took another dozen or so Waller pieces before his faith in Fats paid off with "Squeeze Me," a minor hit of 1925. He also issued Waller's instrumental "Oriental Tones" that same year.

Waller's career was on the upswing in 1923, but his personal life went further askew when Edith filed for divorce. In her settlement, she was awarded $35 a week to support herself and their son, Thomas Jr. The amount was reasonable, but it was a commitment that Waller seemed unable to keep. His payments came late, came up short, or came not at all. For the rest of his life, including the years when he was making big money, he played hide-and-seek with process servers sent by Edith to extract alimony from him. Fats got ultimatums from judges and lectures from his mentors, all to no avail. He would do two stints in jail for non-payment, and his scapegrace ways were a standing joke among his friends.

The dark side of the joke, which everyone around him seemed to ignore, was that by the time he was twenty, Waller was on his way to chronic alcoholism. From the time he began to stir in the piano world, when he was about fifteen, he had had a bottomless thirst for the boot-leg gin that flowed at clubs and rent parties. The bottle and glass that he kept on his piano during his performances were not props. He could polish off a fifth in the length of a set, and when he called for another, it always appeared. When he played in theaters, where the bottle on his piano would have been unseemly, it was kept just offstage. Waller would excuse himself between numbers, take a swig behind the curtain, and return to his playing. When Prohibition ended, he switched from gin to bourbon, carrying cases of Old Grand-Dad with him when he toured. Waller was given a dire warning from his doctor in the late '30s, and he went on the wagon for a short time. Then, after a brief experiment with sauterne, he and his Old Grand-Dad were reunited. His drinking rarely affected his playing, but his bouts with the bottle weakened him and probably shortened his life.

Waller could not control his passion for food any more than his craving for alcohol. By himself, he could put a dent in the spread at any rent party. His friends remembered his eating a dozen hamburgers at a sitting, ordering four whole chickens—three fried, one roasted—in diners at 6 A.M., finishing a dishpan full of spaghetti at Clarence Williams's housewarming, then inhaling a pie for dessert. Fats liked everything, and lots of it.

To stay on the boozy merry-go-round that was his life in the '20s, Fats needed cash, and he often needed it in a hurry. When he was broke, he had a commodity that was almost as good as cash: his songs. He stuffed his pockets with manuscripts and made rounds of downtown publishers' offices, offering to sell any melody outright for $5 or $10. He suggested that Fletcher Henderson take nine tunes in payment for nine hamburgers when Henderson bought him dinner. Once when he was particularly desperate, he offered J. Lawrence Cook a stack of manuscripts for $10. Cook refused to take advantage of him that way, so Waller proposed another way: a bargain rate of $5 each for making some piano rolls. (Cook did not accept, and he chastised Waller for making the offer.) Fats burst in on one publisher with the announcement: "I'll write you a song for $2.50." Melodies came easily to him, and even after admonitions from friends like Cook and publishers like Harry Link and Clarence Williams, Fats continued to use them for barter.

In 1924 Connie Immerman, the deli owner for whom Waller had worked as a child, took over a failing club called the Shuffle Inn, next door to the Lafayette Theatre. He renamed the place Connie's Inn, and he was happy to have Waller sit in on piano when he took his breaks from the Lafayette. One of the regular customers at Connie's was a press agent, "Captain" George H. Maines, and he was impressed by Waller's ability to entertain. He offered his services as a manager, and Waller, enjoying his ride but knowing he was getting nowhere, accepted.

Maines knew that Waller needed exposure outside of Harlem. He got him an audition at the Kentucky Club, a showcase for black talent at Forty-ninth Street and Seventh Avenue. The management hired Waller with the idea of using him as pianist in the house band, led by Duke Ellington. Ellington demurred at turning over his piano chair, so Waller went on as a single, performing during intermissions. He clowned outrageously, yelling offstage to announce himself as "Ali Baba, the Egyptian Wonder," then appearing with a turban on his head as he danced a hula holding a corner of the stage curtain in front of him. It was white New York's first look at Fats Waller.

In 1925 Louis Armstrong invited Fats to come to Chicago, where he got a job playing at the Hotel Sherman. Waller became such a pet of Chicago mobsters who hung out at the Sherman that he was kidnapped from the hotel and taken to Al Capone's headquarters. He was showered with champagne and hundred-dollar bills as he played for a surprise birthday party for Capone that lasted three days.

When he returned to New York, Fats resumed his tentative courtship of Anita Rutherford, whom he had met at a Harlem luncheonette. Captain Maines thought that the levelheaded girl might bring some stability to Waller's life, so he encouraged him to propose. They were married in 1926. Waller would not be a model husband to Anita, but he buckled down to his responsibilities as provider as he never had before.

In 1926, at George Gershwin's suggestion, Fats enlisted Leopold Godowsky to teach him harmony and counterpoint. Waller had had some success with a revue score written earlier that year (*Tan Town Topics*, presented at Harlem's Lafayette Theatre), and, if other chances for theater composition came, he resolved to be ready for them. His work with Godowsky was brief but intensive. Fats took in what he could for as long as he could, then, with no more reluctance than he had had at leaving De Witt Clinton High, he left Godowsky.

◆

The two piano solos that Fats Waller recorded for OKeh in 1922 did not sell well, so his studio work in the mid-'20s was as an accompanist for singers—Sara Martin, Anna Jones, Alberta Hunter, and Caroline Johnson—on blues-tinged pop songs for various "race" labels. Waller was on the first recording of "Henderson Stomp," as temporary pianist for the Fletcher Henderson Orchestra in the Columbia studios on November 3, 1926. But as yet there were no definitive, or even distinctive, Fats Waller piano recordings.

For two years Waller's manager, Captain Maines, pushed Victor to sign him. The company wasn't ready to go that far, but Victor's A&R

man, Ralph Peer, did agree to record him. Peer was particularly interested in Waller as a jazz organist. The idea of playing jazz on the organ was a novelty then—no one was doing it except Waller—and Peer wanted something new for the race market. On November 17, 1926, Fats was sent to the Victor studios, a converted church building—with a leftover organ—in Camden, New Jersey, and the experiment was begun.

Waller recorded two sides that day, a stately and seductive "St. Louis Blues" and his own "Lenox Avenue Blues." The record was not a commercial success, but Peer liked it. He got Waller back in January 1927 to try again. Fats turned out "Soothin' Syrup Stomp," "Sloppy Water Blues," and "Rusty Pail" on the organ and did a couple of songs as piano solos. In February he made "Stompin' the Bug" and "Hog Maw Stomp"; in May, "Sugar" and "Beale Street Blues." Although "Beale Street Blues" sold better than the rest, the record-buying public was not as interested in jazz on the organ as Ralph Peer was, and Victor finally shut down Peer's experiment. The organ would remain Waller's favorite instrument, and he would make occasional organ recordings in the 1930s. But with Waller's recordings of the late '20s, the organ had its best shot at acceptance by the jazz world, and it didn't catch on. Waller's remaining 1927 recordings found him back in a sideman's chair, as pianist for Tom Morris's Hot Babies in two Victor sessions. (One of these Hot Babies sessions yielded "Red Hot Dan," on which he sang, but his vocal made no more stir than had his organ solos.) Peer didn't know what to do with Fats, so he did little with him for more than a year.

Waller was only gigging in the late '20s, but the gigs were getting better. In 1927 he toured to several Ivy League schools during prom season as pianist with the Fletcher Henderson Orchestra. Next, he spent a few happy months back in Chicago living with Louis Armstrong, while they played in Erskine Tate's Vendome Theatre Orchestra. His Chicago stay was cut short when Edith had him arrested and brought back to New York to face new charges in alimony court. Promising to be more timely in his payments, he was released after a sermon from the judge. In September Fats's financial responsibilities increased when Anita gave birth to their son, Maurice Thomas Waller.

Clarence Williams issued two Waller piano pieces in 1926 ("Old Folks Shuffle" and "Midnight Stomp"), but, as was often the case with

Williams publications, they didn't get much distribution. In 1927 Fats began seriously shopping his work to other publishers. Robbins-Engel issued one Waller instrumental that year, and Gotham Music Service issued four. The most important publishing contact Fats made that year was with Joe Davis, the white owner of Triangle Music Company, which specialized in the publication of black writers. Davis issued Waller's "Meditation," as well as his "Alligator Crawl" (which would stay in print for a decade, with reissues in 1934 and 1937). It was a leap of faith for a publisher to buy any of Waller's instrumentals, as only one of his published piano works had yet received a recording (Clarence Williams's Blue Five's "Wild Cat Blues," in 1923) and none had been issued on Waller's own piano rolls. Fats himself apparently did not see any connection between recordings and sheet music sales. He invariably chose his unpublished tunes for the organ records (as well as for his two Victor piano solos).

Waller (writing with lyricist Andy Razaf) contributed half of the score to *Keep Shufflin'*, a musical that began a successful run at Daly's Sixty-third Street Theatre in February 1928. The show's other main composer was James P. Johnson, and the two played twin pianos in the orchestra pit during intermissions, bringing the gusto of stride to the Broadway stage for the first time.

From June to October, Waller played the organ at Philadelphia's Grand Theatre, the last time he would accompany silent films. As soon as he came back to New York, Edith had him arrested again. There was no judge's sermon this time: Fats was sentenced to six months in jail on Welfare Island. His father died during his incarceration, and Waller refused to go to the funeral because he was embarrassed by the leg irons that he would have to wear to attend. In November, while he was still in jail, his third son, Ronald, was born.

Waller's reputation for good-time jazz kept growing, so Ralph Peer decided to build some band sessions around him early in 1929. His reputation as a no-show was also firmly in place by then, so Peer sent banjoist Eddie Condon to make sure that Fats got to the studio on time and in shape to play. Condon took his duty seriously, trailing Fats around Harlem for three days before the scheduled session. Waller was pleased to have the young man's company, and he soon converted Condon from shepherd to fellow roisterer. Between binges, Condon tried to steer him to make some decisions about personnel for the recordings and about material. When the exasperated Condon asked, "What'll we play?" the answer came: "Why, we'll play music."

March 1, 1929, dawned to find Condon and his charge sleeping it off underneath tables at Connie's Inn. Condon awoke at half past 10, in a panic. They were due at the Victor studios at noon, and there had been no preparation for the session. Condon roused Fats and alerted him to the crisis. Waller said, "That's fine! That's wonderful! That's perfect! Now we've got to see about that band. Look around for some nickels so I can make that telephone go." Fats assembled a small band—trumpet, trombone, and clarinet—over the telephone. During the cab ride to the midtown studios, he hummed a few snatches of tunes to his four side-men (including Condon) and improvised some ideas for recording. At 11:50 A.M. the band that would be called Fats Waller and His Buddies walked in. Ralph Peer thanked Eddie Condon for a job well done, and they went to work. The four sides they made that day rank high among the jazz records made in the vintage year of 1929.

There were two sides by Waller and the band: "The Minor Drag" and the hot and nervous "Harlem Fuss." The "Fuss" begins with a round-robin of solos—clarinet, muted trumpet, trombone, piano—then esca-lates to a scuffling jam, driven by Waller. Each of Fats's "Buddies" played better than he ever had in a studio that day (as "His Rhythm" men would often do in the '30s), and they had the tight sound of a group that had been together for years. There would be two more Buddies dates in 1929, made with different personnel and instrumentation, but the piston in all the Buddies sessions was Waller. He doesn't hog the proceedings, but he is underneath everything, shining during his own solos and prodding His Buddies to shine in theirs. The swinging is diamond-hard.

Waller also made two piano solos on March 1, and they were reve-lations, showing him off as performer and composer as nothing he had recorded before. "Numb Fumblin'" is a twelve-bar blues hung with the ornaments of stride: tinkling triplets, swirls of sixteenth notes, voicings that leap octaves. There is a rocking bass line under one chorus and a dash of bitters in its exotic minor harmonies. The other solo was "Handful of Keys," which became Waller's signature stride-ragtime piece. Like Johnson's "Carolina Shout" and Smith's "Finger Buster," "Handful of Keys" became a must-learn for Harlem pianists. It pounces out of the piano, coming at the listener like an overgrown puppy. Waller's playing of it is loose and light, with his right hand dancing by itself in a one-handed call-and-response section.

And there were still more stride masterpieces to come from Waller in 1929. On August 2, at another Buddies session, he recorded piano solos of "Gladyse" and "Valentine Stomp" (named for Hazel Valentine, proprietor of a Harlem bordello called the Daisy Chain). "Gladyse" is tinkling and jovial, its first strain suggesting a tipsy music box. "Valentine Stomp" is a rag made of characteristic Waller devices: chimelike triplets scampering down from the upper octaves; tenths in the left hand to make a bass line described by Eudora Welty as "deep and coarse as a sea net"; and pristine voicings of chords—all set to an easy swing. In the same August session, Waller made piano solos of "Ain't Misbehavin'" and "Sweet Savannah Sue," two hit songs from his revue *Hot Chocolates*, which had opened in June at the Hudson Theatre. In September, there was more brilliance: his solos of "Smashing Thirds" and "Goin' About."

Waller's newly thriving career was derailed by a disastrous business deal that he entered into in midsummer 1929. For some unfathomable reason, he and Andy Razaf sold their *Hot Chocolates* copyrights to Mills Music—including the hit "Ain't Misbehavin'"—for a flat fee of $500. The two songwriters, who should have been set for life on the income from these songs, were suddenly broke. Waller's scramble for money would send him to a day job (on the staff at Joe Davis's publishing company), to Chicago (to play the organ at the Regal Theatre), to Paris (on a vacation with Spencer Williams, to escape his worries about money), to Cincinnati (to host a radio show)—to everywhere except the place he should have been, the Victor studio.

When Fats returned to New York from Cincinnati early in 1934, his new manager, Phil Ponce (who had inherited Waller from Captain Maines in 1932), took him back to Victor. With eighteen months of wide exposure—and wide popularity—on radio, Waller was on the brink of stardom now, and the company's executives knew it. He was at last offered a Victor contract, and on May 16, 1934, he took a five-piece band into the studio to make the first of several hundred recordings by "Fats

Waller and His Rhythm." The Cincinnati radio programs (along with the touring shows and the remote broadcasts they spawned) had polished Waller's performing to a high gloss. He had always been an entertaining pianist, and now his singing and comedy were as good as his playing. No one else had Waller's rag/swing/jazz/pop style, and this unique package would bring Victor literally dozens of big-selling records, including six that hit Number 1 on the *Billboard* charts. In 1935, Fats received the ultimate show business accolade, an outright imitator: Bob Howard, who would provide Victor's rival, Decca Records, with "Fats Waller vocals" for four years.

Waller's singing was such a safe commercial bet that a Waller piano session became something of a rarity. His last important piano work came early in his tenure at Victor, on November 16, 1934, when he recorded four solos: "African Ripples," "Clothes Line Ballet," "Alligator Crawl," and "Viper's Drag." Music publisher Joe Davis took the occasion to issue three of these numbers (all except "African Ripples"), along with a piece called "Effervescent," a reworking of Waller's 1927 "Meditation," in a folio in December of that year. There were no more piano solos until 1937, when Fats recorded five pop songs.

Waller's life became even more cluttered as his fame grew. He was one of the busiest performers of his time, and his touring schedule was erratic and relentless. He took His Rhythm everywhere, on buses, on trains, in cars. He would go anywhere, and he would take any request except one: to play the only music he detested, boogie-woogie. He had a clause in his personal appearance contracts that recused him from playing boogie, even if his audiences or sponsors asked for it.

◆

In the summer of 1938, Ed Kirkeby, Waller's current manager, booked him on a ten-week tour of the British Isles. He went as a solo performer, playing and singing in the largest variety houses in England and Scotland. Mills Music, in celebration of his triumphs there, issued its third Waller folio, *Fats Waller's Swingtime in Scotland,* which contained Walleresque arrangements of Scottish folk songs. Sam Fox, a Cleveland publisher, brought out six of his instrumentals (including "Fractious

Fingering," "Black Raspberry Jam," and "Lounging at the Waldorf") that same year.

In March 1939, Kirkeby sent Waller back to England, and it was during this tour that he made his sole attempt at an extended composition, "London Suite." The Suite is a set of pieces written to capture the moods of various areas that he saw in the city ("Chelsea," "Bond Street," "Piccadilly," etc.). The themes are pretty, but none of them are thoroughly explored. The six "movements" of the Suite have a truncated feel, making them pleasant program music and no more. Waller recorded them in London, in June 1939, for HMV, but these recordings were not released until 1950. (His woozy "Jitterbug Waltz" of 1942 is a more imaginative mood piece than anything in "London Suite." It is sly and tired-sounding and very tender, evoking a jitterbug taking a serious look at his date after a long evening of dancing.)

With America's entry into World War II, Fats added dozens of unpaid appearances at military bases to an already impossible list of commitments. In November 1943, after playing a string of service shows, he headed for Los Angeles, where he was booked in the Zanzibar Room. He caught the flu from sitting under the Zanzibar's powerful air-conditioning vents for hours every night while he was soaking with perspiration, and his work at the club was interrupted by a ten-day stay in the hospital. Fats returned to finish out his contract, playing to enthusiastic audiences. Then, after a flurry of guest spots on Hollywood radio shows, he and his manager, Ed Kirkeby, boarded the Santa Fe Chief for New York.

Waller was sick and exhausted. He told Kirkeby, "Oh, man, I can't take this much longer!" He rallied when passengers in the club car recognized him, however, and he spent hours drinking with them. Kirkeby got him to bed and went to his own compartment. When he checked on Waller the next morning, Fats said he planned to sleep all day. He slept through the day and into the night. Kirkeby looked in on him again about 2 A.M. Fats complained of being cold and went back to sleep. About three hours later, Kirkeby heard him choking. He sprang to Waller's berth and found him shaking uncontrollably. He called for a porter, who fetched a doctor while the train was stopped in Kansas City's Union Station. The doctor quickly checked Waller's pulse and breathing

and, after a long silent moment, pronounced him dead. He had suc-
cumbed to influenzal bronchial pneumonia on December 15, 1943, at
thirty-nine years of age.

Waller was bitterly mourned, by his fans and his fellow musicians
alike. Besides the loss of unheard music in him, there was the loss of the
man himself. Louis Armstrong spoke for all who knew him:

> Fats is gone now . . . but to me he's still here with us. His
> very good spirit will keep him with us for ages. Right now,
> every time someone mentions Fats Waller's name, why,
> you can see the grins on all the faces as if to say, "Yea,
> yea, yea, yea, Fats is a solid sender, ain't he?"

Chapter 7

JELLY ROLL MORTON

BEGINNING IN THE 1960S, various chambers of commerce awoke to the fact that they could attract tourists by staking claim to whichever pieces of jazz history were theirs. Cities that had been oblivious to the early jazz made within their boundaries began to advertise that so-and-so was born there, that so-and-so played there, that they had lively saloon districts around the turn of the century. Weekend festivals were organized to honor native sons (and a few daughters), and neighborhoods with cobblestone streets were tricked out to look "old-timey." Travel agents were notified of the dates. St. Louis celebrated the ragtimers who had rocked the rafters at Tom Turpin's bar; Kansas City recalled its days as a hub on the wheel of territory bands; Chicago touted itself as the crucible in which hot playing was forged; Memphis proclaimed itself the home of the blues. For the newspapers, old-timers racked their brains to recall the first syncopated playing they ever heard, and, whatever they remembered, they called "jazz."

America first became aware of jazz early in 1917, when recordings by the Original Dixieland Jazz Band began to blare from parlor phonographs. The ODJB, a five-piece white band from New Orleans, had set Chicago on its ear a few months earlier with its whipped-up tempos and loose-jointed fun; now they were based in New York, packing them in at Reisenweber's cabaret and making their hyperactive music for Victor. For the next five years, ODJB hits poured out: "Livery Stable Blues," "Original Dixieland One-Step," "St. Louis Blues," "Tiger Rag," "Bluin' the Blues," and "Fidgety Feet." They were simply the damnedest thing ever on records, and people wondered, for the first time, "Where did jazz come from?" Because of the ODJB's raging success, the answer had commercial, rather than historical, import.

Wherever jazz came from, record companies wanted to go there and get more of it. In mid-1918, when the ODJB was securely tied to Victor, the Columbia Record Company sent its A&R man, Ralph Peer, to search for jazz in the hitmakers' hometown. The city was alive with music, of course, as it had been since French rule, but none of it sounded like the ODJB. Peer heard some raggy playing, and he heard some soloists improvising. But he did not hear the communal clash and drive he was looking for in the laid-back bands there. He wired his bosses: "NO JAZZ BANDS IN NEW ORLEANS."

For half a decade—an eternity in the music business—the ODJB had the field to itself, doing what no one else was doing and selling records like crazy. Dance bands imitated its effects—smears, growls, and frantic tempos—but none had the ODJB's exuberance or musicality. In February 1921, Perry Bradford talked OKeh executives into recording a black jazz band, Mamie Smith's Jazz Hounds. The following year, two young white bands, the Original Memphis Five and the New Orleans Rhythm Kings, began to add their imitations of the ODJB to the body of recorded jazz. And in 1923—the year that saw the studio debuts of New Orleanians King Oliver, Sidney Bechet, and Jelly Roll Morton— the Big Bang theory of jazz was born. It postulated that New Orleans was indeed the foundry of jazz but that no one had noticed this until, for some reason, jazz burst northward out of the city in the late teens, as though shot out of a cosmic cannon aimed at Chicago.

Every city had its own pop sound in the early century: the stately and lyrical classic ragtime of St. Louis; the eccentric pianism of Eubie Blake and Hughie Woolford in Baltimore; brass-heavy concert orchestras like that of Detroit's Old Man Finney; the two-fisted piano of Luckey Roberts and Abba Labba in Harlem. The distinctive music of New Orleans was the good-natured, anything-goes ragtime played by the city's (mostly black) marching bands. Other cities had brass bands, too, usually quasi-military ensembles that prided themselves on their reading ability and on the precision of their marching and playing. New Orleans bands, even on formal occasions, played for fun, and precision was not their object. The Crescent City had scores of lodges, social clubs, and benevolent societies, and they all loved a parade. They jammed the streets on religious holidays, during Mardi Gras, at funerals, to and from weekend excursions to Spanish Fort and Milneburg, and sometimes for no reason except the sheer love of a movable party. In the spring, summer, and fall, it was the rare Sunday in New Orleans that did not see eight or ten parades winding about the city.

New Orleans parade bands had permanent leaders, but few had permanent personnel. The leader of a brass band—the Excelsior, the Onward, the Tuxedo, or the Eagle—was hired by an organization to recruit players for a parade. He would receive $5 for his trouble, and he was authorized to pay so many musicians at a dollar or two a head. Because the jobs included free food and drinks, there was no shortage of players. Demand was constant, and the supply was high.

But not all players were equally skilled at following the printed scores of the marches, dirges, and rags used in parades. In these pickup bands, highly trained reading musicians were thrown into ensembles with "catchers" (those who learned their parts by imitation and memorization) and "fakers" (those who played whatever came into their heads). Even the most familiar pieces, like "High Society" and "Panama," never came out quite the same way twice. High demand for players necessitated a tolerance for embellishment, decoration, and improvisation. This acceptance of individuality was liberating for musicians and instructive for listeners. New Orleans parade goers knew that the best music was not necessarily made by note readers.

Besides offering musicians hundreds of places to play—in the streets, hotel ballrooms, amusement parks, lodge halls, saloons—New

Orleans also offered them a vast menu of music to hear and think about. The city had spent the eighteenth century under the rules of France and Spain, and music from both countries took firm root there. Waves of immigrants over the years—from Italy, Canada, Cuba, the Caribbean isles—added their music to the city's mix. The sound of African drumming in Congo Square was as familiar to New Orleans ears as the formless, improvised tunes of Italian street vendors advertising oysters and strawberries with song. New Orleans had the right music for the patterned dancing of French aristocrats and for the shindigs of keelboatmen in muddy boots.

The French Opera House, which opened at the corner of Bourbon and Toulouse streets in 1859, was the high-culture end of the city's music. And on every street corner three or four urchins held forth. These groups were called "spasm bands," and they played pots and pans, combs, and homemade fiddles. They didn't have the skill to hold a crowd for long, but they kept caps at their feet to catch any pennies that passersby might throw to them. City churches rang with sacred music, from Bach to spirituals. A new saloon often marked its opening by removing the front door from its hinges, because it was expected never to close; day and night, piano music rang from these doorless dives. There were bands everywhere outdoors—at picnics, at political rallies, on excursion boats—and pianists everywhere indoors. And it seemed that no music that came to New Orleans ever left. The city took every style that was brought there and found a use for it: dancing, entertaining, mourning, parading, partying, worshiping. New Orleans was a city with a soundtrack, a place where the exotic and the ordinary, the high and the low, were on easy terms with each other because they mingled in the streets all the time.

In a testy letter to *Down Beat* in 1938, Jelly Roll Morton wrote, "It is evidently known, beyond contradiction, that New Orleans is the cradle of jazz, and I, myself, happened to be the creator in the year 1902." Morton was twelve years old in 1902, and, on the face of it, his claim seemed absurd. He had always been arrogant, and by 1938, at the bottom of a ten-year slide in his career, he had become downright cranky. Morton knew that he was far out of fashion and that a letter to *Down Beat* would not turn the tide of opinion running against him. But he had never given a damn how outrageous he seemed, so he wrote it. Sometime in the early century he *had* done something important, and he wanted credit for it. What he had done was to create *his own sound*, and, given the nature of that sound and the time in which he developed it, his creation looks very much like the invention of jazz.

Morton had been playing the piano since he was about seven years old, and by the time he was twelve, he was a keen student of the whorehouse professors of Storyville. He could walk along North Basin Street and identify the players in the houses and bars that he passed without looking inside, recognizing each pianist by his harmonies and embellishments. He could replicate many of the tricks he heard, but he wanted more than a bag of tricks, more than a set of "New Orleans" devices to flavor his playing. He wanted to write his own tunes, to develop harmonies that were his alone, to put it all to his own rhythms, even to stake out a tempo that was no one else's. In short, he had the audacious idea to remake New Orleans music in his own image. And by age twelve, around the time that he began playing professionally, he had much of it figured out. The sound that he fashioned was as different from his idols' as from his rivals'. ("Mortonesque" playing is especially evident on his piano rolls. He was the only pianist to surmount the "roll sound" of the 1920s. Other who cut rolls—including fine players like Pete Wendling, J. Russel Robinson, and Max Kortlander—all sound like they have the same arranger. Fats Waller often sounds like James P. Johnson, and Clarence Williams sounds sometimes like Richard M. Jones, sometimes like Lem Fowler. Nobody else in the medium sounds like Morton. His attack, his harmonies, and his tempos are immediately identifiable.) His overhaul of the local piano sound was so meticulously done that his music didn't even sound like New Orleans anymore; it just sounded like Morton.

The creation of a unique piano style would be reason enough to celebrate Morton, but the principle he arrived at in creating his style is the bedrock of jazz theory. His tenet was that the musicians—and their musical ideas—are the most important element in jazz music. The performance is supreme over *what* is being played and *where* it is being played. This is the declaration of independence for jazz.

Freedom implied responsibility to Morton, of course. If the player is more important than the composer or the occasion, then every player had better be there with the goods, able to invent, to transpose, and to complement a solo as well as to create one. Morton heard the bands of New Orleans's legendary leaders, such as Buddy Bolden, but he didn't think much of them. He was impressed by Bolden, but he never mentioned liking his band. The leader was all, and that was not enough. He thought that jazz should have more to offer than a star soloist, no matter how good the soloist was.

At age twelve, Morton didn't have a band, of course, so he tried to make his piano sound like a band. He began to think of his playing in orchestral terms, and he layered his improvisations with bandlike devices. He used single-note tympani lines in left-hand patterns, and he could slip from a tympani sound into the downward walk of a tailgate trombone. His right hand could thrum like a guitar in the middle register, then spin high, whirling figures like a clarinet.

In the teens, as he organized bands in various cities, Morton began to morph his piano-as-orchestra idea into orchestra-as-piano. His experiments with this notion would make him the first important jazz arranger. Morton's earliest band records are nothing special—his own piano is not even prominent in them—but by the time he introduced his Red Hot Peppers to the world, his orchestral passion was in full flower. The Peppers recordings have a design—shapes, forms, harmonic colors, a guiding sensibility—that no other 1920s jazz band records have.

Morton saw the contradiction implicit in the phrase "jazz arranging," and he never let his "arranging" supercede his "jazz." He planned variations in structures and textures that left room for his players to improvise their solos. The Peppers records never sound constricted by their three-minute time limit, nor do they sound as though they are indulging soloists (including Morton). They are Morton's theories put into perfect practice, so they sound like him.

There were wheels within wheels in Morton's arrangements, and, as he knew they would, his Peppers began to sound like his piano. Morton gave sidemen more freedom than any other leader of his time, and they responded by echoing his ideas in their solos. And in a *lingua franca* of jazz, his piano often paraphrases (and imitates) the other instruments in its conversations with them. On the Peppers sides, Jelly Roll Morton was in complete control of his medium and his materials. In other words, he was an artist, one of the most important and original in American music.

Earlier in the year that he vented his spleen to *Down Beat*, Morton was invited by Alan Lomax to tell his story for the Archive of American Folksong at the Library of Congress. Lomax was looking for the link between folk music and early jazz, and Morton gave him an earful. Sitting at a Steinway grand, with a Presto recorder and a large bottle of whiskey nearby, the guest of honor spun his tale. He was a Storyville Scheherazade, with a photographic memory of everything he had seen there as a young man and a phonographic memory of everything he had heard. He demonstrated Creole songs that he had not thought about for forty years; he imitated a dozen New Orleans piano players—bad ones as well as good ones. He played a funeral march, a quadrille, hymns, pop songs, opera themes; and he sang some wildly pornographic blues. His stories are full of gore, and they paint Storyville as a dangerous, as well as an exciting, place.

The interviews are self-congratulatory, but they are not egomaniacal. Morton demonstrates various styles, some of which he admired, and shows how he "changed every style to mine." On these records, his rags don't sound like other players' rags, nor do his blues sound like others' blues. Like him or not, believe him or not, Morton made his case at the Library of Congress. His oral memoir is one of the great American cultural documents—and it takes us as close as we will ever get to answering the old question, "Where did jazz come from?"

◆

He was born in New Orleans on October 20, 1890. His name at birth was Ferdinand Joseph LaMothe (misspelled "LeMott"—as it was pronounced—on his baptismal certificate), and he was the only child of Edward J. LaMothe and Louise Monette. The dominant figure in his family was Louise's grandmother, Mimi Peché, a haughty old terror whose mission in life was to remind her descendants that they came from French aristocracy.

The Pechés, LaMothes, and Monettes indeed carried old French names, but Morton's ancestors were not "directly from the shores of France," as he said they were. They came to Louisiana from Haiti in the early nineteenth century, and they were "Creoles of color," a term used to designate the descendants of French and Spanish aristocrats and their slave mistresses. The "Creole" part of the term precluded their being sold into slavery, but "of color" was a disclaimer that they were not really white, however light-skinned they might be. At the death of a white ancestor, his "colored" descendants might inherit a bit of his money and property, and most of them would keep his name, but they were cut off by the legitimate (white) side of the family. Many white families in Louisiana carried the pretense through generations that, merely by coincidence, there happened to be "Creoles of color" living nearby who bore the same last name.

"Creoles of color" worked mostly as craftsmen and tradesmen. Morton described his ancestors as being "somewhat rich," and, compared to the African Americans around them, they were. His maternal grandfather, Julian Monette, was a liquor wholesaler, and he had served briefly as a state senator in Louisiana's Reconstruction government. *Arriere grandmere* Mimi's husband, Pierre, was a cigar maker, and she worked as a ladies' maid for the wealthy Solaris family. The Solaris women took her with them on their annual trips to Europe, and she spoke only French all her life.

Whatever pretensions to gentility the Pechés and LaMothes may have had were crushed by an act of the Louisiana legislature. The state had, since the Reconstruction era, tried to identify the ingredients in the racial gumbo that made up its population, to define whiteness by codifying various degrees of blackness. Official documents—wills, deeds, birth certificates—classified Louisiana's citizens by their color. Louisianans came in many colors, of course, and the colors were given official and specific names, some of them—mulatto, quadroon, octoroon, mustifee, mustifino, casco, sambo, mango—taken from the demeaning glossary of seventeenth-century slave traders.

After decades of disputation and confusion, Louisiana decided to settle its racial hash once and for all by enacting State Code 111 in 1894. According to this statute, "one drop of black blood" meant that its bearer was black. The racial dynamic in New Orleans was suddenly transformed; Creoles who had for years considered themselves superior to their darker neighbors were suddenly lumped together with all other blacks, and treated with the same level of disdain. For light-skinned "Creoles of color," the question became whether or not to try to pass for white. Whatever Mimi Peché may have felt about the code, her great-grandson grew up accepting its implications. There is no evidence that Jelly Roll Morton ever tried to pass, even though his complexion could have allowed him to. He clung to the notion of Creole superiority that was pounded into his head in childhood, but throughout his life, he lived in black neighborhoods and worked at black clubs. His bands were made up almost exclusively of African-American players. He treated them as equals, and, to a man, all who spoke or wrote of their time with him remembered him as a fair and friendly leader.

Ed LaMothe, a likable, easygoing fellow, worked as a contractor, but he was as interested in playing the trombone and in attending the opera as he was in the construction and demolition of buildings. Ed kept musical instruments around his house at 141-1/2 Perdido Street, and he encouraged his young son to try them all. Ferd tooted the harmonica and twanged the Jew's harp, made drums out of kitchenware, and flailed away at a guitar. There was a piano in the parlor, too, but he saw only women play it, so he eschewed it as a "sissy" instrument.

The guitar intrigued him first, and Ferd joined a string trio of neighborhood boys who played on street corners. His friend Bud Scott so far surpassed him on the instrument that he gave it up in disgust. He next joined a boys' vocal quartet whose specialty was comforting the bereaved. If any of the four heard of a death in the vicinity, he would assemble the others and they would head for the home of the deceased. They sang spirituals in the parlor where the corpse was laid out, then the comforters would be comforted with generous helpings of the food that neighbors had brought to the family in mourning.

The idea of making music and getting something in return for it was implanted in Ferd, but he was still undecided about what kind of music to make. Finally, he saw a short-haired, masculine-looking man play a concert of classical piano music at the French Opera House. This settled the matter. If the piano was not exclusively the domain of women and sissies, he would get serious about the piano.

Ferd's mother, Louise, having had enough of the lackadaisical Ed LaMothe (to whom she may not have been married), sent him packing. She soon found another man more to her liking, an African-American hotel porter named Willie Mouton. They were married in 1894, and

Louise and Ferd moved into his modest house at 1443 Frenchmen Street. When Mouton anglicized his name to "Morton," Ferd began using the name as well. Louise and Willie Morton began a family of their own with the birth of a daughter, Amide, in (Amide thought) 1897.

With his parents' separation and his mother's remarriage, Ferd's life lost all coherence and routine. Ed LaMothe tried to maintain their relationship by offering the child a job as a bricklayer, but Ferd declined. His great-grandmother swooped in from her trips to Europe, prattling grandly in French, and laden with gifts and clothing for everyone except him. Mimi kept up her monologue about the Pechés' aristocratic past, but Ferd saw that, despite its noble heritage, his family was always broke. He took a job washing dishes at a restaurant for seventy-five cents a week, but he was stiffed for his first month's salary.

Ferd worked to teach himself piano and guitar, but no one noticed, much less encouraged, his effort. He dropped out of St. Joseph's Academy, the nearby Catholic school he attended for a time. (His relatives disagreed years later as to whether he had made it to the fourth or to the eighth grade.) He couldn't discuss his ambitions with anyone, because he knew his family would never tolerate a "tramp musician" in its midst. His home seemed to him to be "full of spirits." He heard noises late at night when the house was dark—dishes clattering, the sewing machine running—and he kept cups of holy water around his bed as he slept. He began spending time with the most stable—and most prosperous—adult he knew, his godmother, Eulalie Echo.

Eulalie Echo (a professional name, spelled the way her husband, Paul Hecaud, pronounced his surname) doted on her godson. When Ferd was a baby, she had often spent afternoons with him, taking him on her rounds through the French Quarter, sometimes telling strangers that he was her own child. She made sure he was dressed well and bought him natty suits with short pants. She sometimes adorned him with a diamond or two from her jewelry collection. She lived in the Garden District of New Orleans, and she also had a country house in Biloxi, Mississippi. In the summer she took Ferd to the Biloxi house and let him pick all the strawberries he wanted.

The source of Eulalie Echo's fine living was her reputation as one of the most effective voodoo practitioners in New Orleans. Prominent people from all over the city sought her out and paid her well to summon their dead loved ones in séances at her home. She mixed charms and cast spells for them.

The specter of voodoo had worried Spanish governors as far back as the 1780s, and nineteenth-century New Orleans had shivered in fear of two successive voodoo queens, each calling herself Marie LaVeau. After the deaths of the two Maries, voodoo continued to thrive, as Zozo la Brique, Julia Jackson, Doctor Yah Yah, and Doctor Beauregard dispensed their magic in the Vieux Carré. New Orleans pharmacies stocked such over-the-counter necessities as Controlling Powder, Love Oil, Mind Oil, and Get-Together Drops. But if the job was to be done right, a professional had to be consulted, and Eulalie Echo was near the top of her profession. Ferd watched her preparing *gris-gris*, and he heard voices that seemed to come from the glasses of water she placed around her house.

Eulalie Echo was generous to Ferd, and she was perceptive enough to provide him with just what he needed during this troubled time: she paid for his piano lessons. His first teacher was a neighbor lady, Mrs. Rachel Moment, but when he caught her faking at reading the pop tunes printed in the Sunday newspaper supplements, he quit going to her. He studied privately with a music teacher at St. Joseph's with better results. His best early teacher was his third, the black pedagogue William J. Nickerson, one of the most respected musicians in the city.

Around the time that Professor Nickerson introduced him to the classics, Eulalie Echo's next-door neighbor showed him the power of the blues. The neighbor was Mamie Desdoumes, and, although she was missing two fingers, she was one of the few women pianists in the Tenderloin. She had a haunting tune that she played and sang over and over, and her music in the early-morning stillness of the Garden District moved Ferd enormously. (He published his recollection of her words and music in 1939 under the title "Mamie's Blues.")

Ferd ran with a fast crowd in his early teens. He remembered them as "tough babies" and "tremendous sports," which they were. They wore trousers as tight as sausage skins, Stetson hats, and cork-soled shoes. They left the top buttons of their shirts open to show the red undershirt beneath. They affected a slow and cool way of walking that they called "shooting the agate." They flirted with housemaids, called them "sweet mamas," and were rewarded with pans of food from their employers' kitchens. They liked to go to Storyville to take in the sights. Morton's family would have been horrified to think that he had been anywhere near the sporting district, but they paid so little attention to him that he went there almost every night.

On one of these surreptitious jaunts, his friends led Ferd into a whorehouse and sat him at the piano. They begged him to play, and the smiles of the girls convinced him that he should. He played for nearly an hour, and when he got up, he was showered with coins. Even the madam was impressed with his $20 windfall, and she offered him a job. At this time, he was working at a cooperage, tacking metal strips around sugar barrels for $3 a week. There was no question of where he'd be the next evening at 9 o'clock. His Storyville life had already begun.

◆

New Orleans was always more proud of than embarrassed by its reputation as a red-hot town. It had been a whoring center since the early nineteenth century, when traders and trappers jumped over the sides of flatboats to visit the floating brothels moored in the Mississippi along Tchoupitoulas Street. Beginning in the 1820s, the action moved to a six-block, crime-ridden strip of Girod Street known as "the Swamp," about a half-mile west of the river. The Swamp was sodden with violence—knife fights, bludgeonings, shoot-outs, arson—and it was said to be so awful that, despite an average of six murders a week in the area, no New Orleans policeman set foot there for twenty years. For a picayune (a six-cent coin) a traveler could get a drink, a woman, and a bed for the night at places like the Sure Enuf Hotel and the House of Rest for Weary Boatmen. Hoping that if vice could not be stopped it could at least swell the public coffers, the city tried issuing brothel licenses for two years in the late 1850s. The licenses cost $100 per whore and $250 per madam, and nearly $100,000 was collected in each year of the statute's existence.

By the 1880s the burghers of New Orleans could hardly avert their eyes from the city's wickedness, because two new muckraking newspapers, The *Mascot* and The *Sunday Sun*, wouldn't let them. Throughout the decade, first in the *Mascot* and later in the *Sun*, horrific stories blared out.

Underneath banner headlines—SINNING FOR SILK; DISGUST-
ING DEPRAVITY; HOW CHILDREN ARE RUINED—the papers
described the wiles of procuresses, charted the rates for virgins on the
open market, chronicled gruesome murders among the *demimonde*,
pointed fingers, gave addresses, named names. The *Daily Picayune* took
up the cry for reform in the mid-1890s, hounding government officials
relentlessly. The city fathers had a clear mandate: to do something about
prostitution and its attendant ills, corruption and crime.

Local lawmakers studied the problem. Alderman Sidney Story, a real
estate broker, looked to the sophisticated cities of Europe for guidance.
He reported to the city council that his research showed that New
Orleans would more likely be successful at regulating prostitution than
at abolishing it. On January 26, 1897, Alderman Story introduced, and
the council passed, an ordinance creating an area where vice would be
permitted but not legalized. There followed months of argument over
the boundaries of such a district. There was also discussion of the possible need for two districts, one for whites and one for blacks. (The creation of a black district was tabled for twenty years. In the meantime, an
informal black district thrived uptown, not far from the white one.)

Finally, on September 1, the council passed an amended ordinance
that spelled out where this experiment in tolerance would take place:
"from the South side of Customhouse Street [later renamed Iberville
Street] to the North side of St. Louis Street, and from the lower or wood
side of North Basin Street to the lower or wood side of Robertson
Street." In addition to the main area, another (smaller) outpost of prostitution was created about three blocks north and east of it. Moralists
were appalled at such pusillanimous action in the face of galloping vice,
but their pleas to ban prostitution altogether could not sway the council.
As of January 1, 1898, prostitution would not be legalized in New
Orleans, but it would be tolerated. Well before his ordinance took effect,
Alderman Story was embarrassed to see that newspapers were already
calling the district "Storyville."

What the city council wrought was thirty-eight square blocks of solid
sin abutting the French Quarter. A study conducted at the request of
Mayor Walter C. Flowers in 1899 showed that there were more than two
thousand prostitutes in Storyville, employed in about 230 houses and

cribs. (A crib was a single room rented by the day to a prostitute. The furnishings of a crib were usually the minimum needed to conduct business: a cot and a wash basin. Crib girls charged as little as a quarter for a few minutes of sex, while the price for an evening at a fancy house might be as high as a $100 plus tips.) Besides sporting houses, the district offered visitors gambling dens, saloons, and cockfights. It was a theme park for the fourteen-year-old male libido, and Ferd Morton reveled in it.

Most of the houses could not afford music, but those madams who went in for opulence—Josie Arlington, Countess Willie Piazza, Gypsy Shafer, and Lulu White—saw it as a necessity for entertaining big spenders. Within a year or so of his Storyville debut, Ferd Morton had played for them all. The bassist Pops Foster was not a wholehearted admirer of Morton, but he admitted, "Jelly was the best entertaining player by himself in the sporting houses. He knew all the dirty songs and that's where he was great. When a customer would come in the door, Jelly would make up a dirty rhyme on your name and play it to his piano playing." Morton was also making a reputation as a ladies' man (and as a part-time pimp), and he acquired the nickname "Wining Boy"—a corruption of "Winding Boy," which implied that he had great movements in bed. He was so proud of his renowned hips that he made up a dirty blues about himself, using his nickname as its title.

Sporting-house piano jobs were the best that a musician could get (a $2 or $3 minimum guaranteed by the madam, plus the chance to make $100 or so in tips on a good night). Competition was keen, and Morton took the measure of all his rivals. He was impressed by Sammy Davis, a ragtime player whom he called a "great manipulator." He heard Alfred Wilson, the Game Kid, Albert Carroll, and the only white pianist in Storyville, Kid Ross.

Morton's favorite was Storyville's favorite: Tony Jackson, whom he called "the greatest single-handed entertainer in the world," known for the breadth of his repertoire and for his ability to play and sing in every style. He had a wide vocal range that allowed him to deliver operatic selections with as much conviction as his pop songs and blues. Morton credits him with writing the classic "Michigan Water Blues," and one of Jackson's early pop songs, "Pretty Baby," written in honor of a current boyfriend, finally saw print—with an added verse and a revised chorus lyric—in 1916. Two more of his numbers, "I'm Cert'n'y Gonna See about That" and the poignant "Some Sweet Day," have remained in the traditional jazz repertoire.

Jackson didn't get publications until late in his life, so most of his early work is lost. One of Jackson's originals, "I've Got Elgin Movements in My Hips," is among the missing pieces, but another of his numbers was salvaged in a re-creation by Morton. Jackson's home base in the early century was Gypsy Shafer's, where the house specialty was the "naked dance." If a customer wanted to see—and could pay for—this spectacle, Madam Shafer would arrange it. It began when a nude woman entered the parlor with a raw oyster balanced on her head. To the accompaniment of Jackson's piano, and without using her hands, the woman demonstrated her muscular control by slowly steering the slithering oyster down the length of her body to the tip of her toe. When the oyster reached its destination, she flipped it high into the air with her foot, then caught it in her mouth. It was a thrilling sight, and it required thrilling music. The melodies of Morton's jangling "Naked Dance," which he recorded in 1939, are his own, but the heat in them comes from his memory of Tony Jackson's playing.

The most important early influence on Morton was a pianist we know almost nothing about, a teenage journeyman named Frank Richards. Although Morton chose not to emulate his style, he thanks Richards on the Library of Congress recordings—three times, for emphasis—for teaching him and for helping him "in a perfection way." The first tune that Morton claimed to have written, in 1902, was the sexy, tango-tinged "New Orleans Blues," and he says that Richards "corrected" his writing of the number to make it the "first blues written as a playable composition" (that is, a blues with several melodic themes and a set structure to them). Morton would far surpass his young Storyville professor, but Frank Richards's technical guidance meant a lot to him as a beginning composer.

Storyville pianists fell into two camps, ragtime players and blues players, and Morton didn't like the tempo of either style. He thought that the 2/4 march tempo of ragtime gave it a jerky feel when piano players sped up, as they invariably did. Trying to show off, they lost control of time and played erratically. Morton liked the precision of ragtime writing and the accuracy that it demanded, but he knew that it was impossible to dance to a rag that was literally running away with its player. He was never in a band in Storyville, but he believed in the dictum of Buddy Bolden: "Play it low so I can hear those whores drag their feet on the floor." Bolden was a cornetist of legendary power, but he knew that it was neither speed nor noise that brought people into each other's arms on the dance floor, it was insinuation.

Morton liked the lyricism of the blues, but he referred to the Storyville blues specialists as "one-tune players." The main duty of a sporting house player was to keep playing, and Morton knew from experience that one could wander around in the blues for a long time. The standard blues tempo was good for dancing, but Morton felt that monotony set in without extra rhythmic devices—such as his backwards-walking bass, breaks, and "Spanish" figures—to break up the predictability of blues structure.

Morton borrowed from both ragtime and blues to make something uniquely his own. He took the three-strain structure of ragtime—especially favoring the songlike third strain—and he set his syncopated melodies to a bright, medium 4, slower than ragtime but faster than the blues. In shifting the feel of ragtime from the brisk 2/4 to the looser 4/4, he removed the stiffness from his ragtime playing. He took the traditional three-chord harmonies of the blues and gave them an array of colors. Any good jazz player varies his effects, but Morton built variations into his composition as well as his performances. Ragtime was the basis of his writing but not his playing. If *you* play "Grandpa's Spells" as written, it's a rag; when *Morton* played it, it was jazz.

In 1906, when Morton was fifteen and, by his own estimate, "one of the best junior pianists in the whole city," his mother died. Willie Morton had long since fled the household, so the care of Ferd's two half-sisters, Amide and Frances Morton, fell to great-grandmother Mimi Peché. Ferd was sent to live with an uncle, who was a barber. He tried to teach the boy his trade, and he let him run errands and shine shoes in his shop. Morton must have laughed at his uncle's notion of a salary (twenty-five cents a week), as he had made a hundred times that on his worst night in Storyville. He drifted away from his uncle and became a citizen of the district. He was walking the walk and talking the talk now, living by his wits as well as his piano playing. He gambled at pool and cards. He looked like a pimp—strutting around Storyville with gold in his teeth and girls on his arms—and sometimes he was one.

A year or so after his mother's death, Morton was walking home from work one Sunday morning when he ran into his great-grand-mother, who was coming back from Mass. Mimi Peché saw the wages of sin hanging all over him—fancy suit, Stetson hat, and turned-up St. Louis flats on his feet—and she plunged into the confrontation that had been inevitable. She opened with accusatory questions (in French): "Have a good job now, Ferd? Making plenty money?" Morton took the bait. He made a flip reply to the effect that he was doing very well. She trained him in her sights and let him have it. She told him that he was a disgrace to his family, called him "a bum and a scalawag," reminded him of the orphaned Amide and Frances, and said that he was a horrible influence on them. In the name of generations of his ancestors, she dis-owned him. Morton was so shaken by this outburst that he did what was for him seemingly unthinkable. He reckoned that Mimi Peché was right, and he left town.

Eulalie Echo came to his rescue again. She offered her Biloxi house to Morton for his base of operations, and for about a year he used it. He did not change his ways, he merely changed his scenery. He bummed around Biloxi, hustling pool and pimping. He thrilled the Mississippi girls with his endless supply of sharp clothes. When one of them com-plimented his attire, he made his standard quip, "I'm the suit man from suit land." He helped manage a whorehouse in Gulfport, run by a white madam named Mattie Bailey, until the locals expressed their disapproval of the obvious intimacy between them by threatening to lynch him. He caught typhoid fever in Meridian, and Eulalie Echo nursed him back to health, with a three-week diet of whiskey and milk. He tried to stay away from New Orleans, but Mississippi held so few opportunities for a young sport that he was going broke. He decided to risk the wrath of Mimi Peché and go back to Storyville.

But soon after Morton returned to New Orleans, a malaise gripped him. He felt ill, and he couldn't play because his fingers didn't obey his brain. He was losing jobs and worried about it. One day as he was sitting in a saloon, an elderly stranger came in and looked him over. He asked

Morton if he were sick, and Morton admitted that he was. The old man said, "Don't you worry, son. Papa Sona gonna cure you."

Papa Sona's treatment was a series of three baths, on three successive Fridays, "in a tub with some kind of grass in it," Morton recalled. The old man stripped the boy and sat him in the tub. He rubbed the grass over his body and "mumbled and shook" as he made an incantation. After the third bath, Papa Sona said it was time to get a job, "so you can pay me." Ferd walked him by Hilma Burt's house, one of the grandest in the district, and he touched Papa Sona's arm as they passed, using the pre-arranged signal to be given when he spotted the place he wanted to work. Three days later Morton got a call to come to Hilma Burt's immediately to replace an ailing piano player. He played like mad, and Burt offered him steady work. Within a week he was back on his feet, restored to health and rolling in money again. He never paid Papa Sona, and thirty years later he said, "I have lived to regret this ungrateful action."

Morton's nerve was up, and he was ready to explore the wider world again. He went around to say goodbye to Amide and Frances. Amide, who was then about ten, asked him to play for her. They walked across the street to a neighbor's piano, and the little girl heard him play for the first and last time. She didn't remember much about the music, but she remembered his "loud silk candy-striped shirt and loud suspenders." For years afterward, Morton would send money to the half-sister he hardly knew.

In 1908 Ferd moved away from Storyville as casually as he had moved into it. He signed on as pianist for William M. Benbow, a veteran black producer of minstrel shows that starred himself and various members of his family. For a while, Morton's wandering had a pattern, the schedule of the Benbow troupe; after that, chance, whim, and necessity moved him. For years, he would shuttle between the old black show business (minstrelsy) and the new (vaudeville), playing piano, trombone, drums, telling jokes, hustling pool, improvising a living.

Morton left New Orleans, but the city never left him. For the rest of his life he held with New Orleans music and Storyville ways. A whorehouse would always be his idea of class, he would always dress like a tremendous sport, and there would always be a streak of voodoo in his Catholic beliefs. The earliest known photograph of Morton was taken around the time he went with Benbow. In it he stands in front of a painted backdrop in a portrait studio. He is about seventeen, sharply dressed in jacket and matching cap, with a jeweled stickpin and a gold watch chain slung across his chest. He is not smiling, and his eyes look very old.

◆

Morton stayed with the Benbow company for about a year before he dropped out. He fell in with a fellow vagrant, a Mississippian who called himself Jack the Bear, and together they went scrounging around Jack's home state. Morton was the breadwinner, hustling low-stakes pool in Yazoo and Clarksdale and flirting with landladies to get them free lodging. They mixed Coca-Cola with salt and sold it door-to-door as a consumption cure. Jack the Bear posed as the doctor who had invented the miracle tonic, and Morton did the talking. (His opening gambit: "Have you anyone in your family with the TB's?")

Wherever they went, Morton sought and challenged the hometown piano stars. He easily cut them in contests, and he found that all the local girls loved a winner. The only pianist who impressed him during this period was a ragtimer from Mobile named Porter King. Morton wrote a ragtime piece in his honor, "King Porter Stomp," not to copyright or publish but to use against his rivals in piano showdowns. (Lottie Joplin claimed that Morton sent the manuscript of "King Porter" to Scott Joplin in New York and asked him to edit it. Joplin supposedly fixed up a few of Morton's passages and sent the tune back.) Morton said that he wrote "I'm Alabama Bound" around this time, too, but that it was stolen by a white composer, Robert Hoffman, who copyrighted it and published it in New Orleans in 1909. Morton would reclaim the piece in 1939 by writing a lyric for it and renaming it "Don't You Leave Me Here."

In late 1909 or early 1910, the two adventurers decided to try Memphis. Jack the Bear assured Morton that he knew all about Memphis and that he had big-time connections there. After they arrived, it became obvious that his partner had never been to Memphis before, so Morton went nosing about Beale Street to see what he could turn up. He trounced a local favorite, Benny Frenchy, in a piano battle at the Monarch Cafe. He met the city's most prominent bandmaster, W. C.

Handy, and disliked him on sight. (Morton always believed that Handy stole the "St. Louis Blues" melodies from a Memphis guitarist named Guy Williams, and years later, to discomfit the grand old man of the blues, he would yell out Williams's name if he saw Handy on a New York street.)

Morton landed a short stint as a replacement pianist for vaudeville acts at the Savoy Theater in Memphis, and when it was over, he rejoined the Benbow show. Because the popular comedy duo Stringbeans and Sweetie May were now in the company, the troupe did good business in the Southeast and the Midwest. Stella Taylor was Morton's girlfriend, and when she quit the show in Jacksonville, Morton quit, too. She repaid Morton's show of solidarity by leaving him for another man. Morton "looked this gentleman up in a pool hall and just naturally beat him to death playing pool and took every nickel he had in the world." He consoled himself after the breakup by learning to play the trombone. When he heard that the old-time minstrel impresario Billy Kersands was auditioning bandsmen, he left Florida to go to back to Memphis for the tryout. He played enough trombone to get the job.

Besides his duties as musician in the Kersands company, Morton was chosen to be straight man to Sammy Russell in a blackface comedy act. The team often strayed from their written material, and it was an improvised retort to Russell that gave Morton his famous nickname. In a sketch, Morton asked Russell his name, and he got the scripted reply, "I'm Sweet Papa Cream Puff, right out of the bakery shop." While waiting for Russell's laugh to subside, Morton thought up a comeback. He announced that he was "Sweet Papa Jelly Roll, with stove pipes in my hips and all the women in town just dying to turn my damper down!" Morton's line topped Russell's. The sexual connotation was even more explicit than that in "Wining Boy," so "Jelly Roll" he became. He liked it, even when it was shortened to "Jelly."

Morton was still on the periphery of show business, but at least he was working. He re-upped with Benbow late in 1910, and the show's route took him to the Northeast for the first time. Every place he went, he heard piano players and made sure that they heard him. James P. Johnson caught him at Barron Wilkins's Little Savoy in New York's Tenderloin in 1911. He said Jelly Roll had "just arrived from the West and he was red hot. The place was on fire!" Morton had a couple of girls with him, and Johnson suspected that he was doing some pimping as well as piano playing. While admitting that Morton could stir up a crowd, James P. still belittled him: "Of course, Jelly Roll wasn't a piano player like some of us down here. We bordered more on the classical theory of music." Morton's slight classical training was at least the equal of Johnson's, but his playing was so different from what was being heard in New York—and so much less flamboyant—that Johnson did not appreciate it.

Morton left Benbow in 1912 to visit Tony Jackson in Chicago. He was glad to see his Storyville idol again, but Morton did not like the Levee district. There were plenty of piano jobs in the city's red-light area, but they did not pay well. Even worse, there were no local players good enough to inspire and challenge him. So he went to Houston to ply his fallback trade, pool hustling.

Morton's M.O. at pool was to shoot left-handed for a while, to intrigue a chump with the possibility of winning and to get the bets high. Then, after the stakes escalated, Morton would switch to shooting with his right hand and wipe out his opponent. In Houston his sportsmanship was questioned by a bettor with a drawn pistol. As bullets flew around him, Morton dove under a pool table and made a narrow escape out the back door. He retired from Houston's pool emporia and spent the rest of his time in Texas showing girls his suits. He bummed his way to Oxnard, California, found no action there, and bummed his way back to New Orleans.

Back home, pool playing again proved a dangerous occupation. Morton unwittingly challenged Aaron Harris, one of the city's roughest characters, to a series of friendly games for $2 each to soften him up for a high-stakes kill. Because Morton did not know that he was talking to a man with eleven murders to his credit, he was arrogant with Harris, spewing insolence as he scooped up his money. It dawned on Harris that he was being taken, and he said to Morton that if Morton made the deciding shot and cleaned him out, he would take all of his money back. Morton replied that he carried a .38-caliber pistol, and that if he made his shot, no one was taking anything back. Morton's aim was true: "Into the pocket she went." Aaron Harris was flabbergasted. He had been conned, sassed, bluffed with a pistol, and beaten at pool. Morton grandly threw him a couple of dollars of his money back, and Harris walked away, speechless. Another gambler took Morton aside and told him whom he had been playing. He suggested that Morton "take a little trip to rest Aaron's nerves." Morton saw the wisdom of this and decided "that I should travel for my health." Once again he left New Orleans in a hurry.

Grifting was becoming harder than working. Morton was tiring of scrapes in pool halls, warnings from constables, and jumping freight cars in hasty exits from small towns. He decided to become, if not a full-time musician, at least a full-time entertainer. He teamed for a while with Harry Bernard and Willminor Cook to form a singing trio. By late summer 1913 Ferd Morton was listed in the city directory of Houston ("colored, musician . . ."), where he worked up a "double act" with a woman named Rosa. Billed as "Morton & Morton," they were a typical team of that period in black vaudeville—that is, they were an imitation of Stringbeans and Sweetie May. A photo of Morton & Morton shows a pretty woman in a long dress wagging a finger at a lanky, blackfaced Jelly in tramp garb. A *Freeman* review published in June 1914 called them "a clever pair" and mentioned Jelly's piano playing as a distinguishing feature of the act. As a stunt, he had arranged a classical selection to be played with his left hand alone.

Benjamin "Reb" Spikes saw Morton & Morton in Tulsa late in 1913 and assessed Jelly's talent as a comedian: "my God, he was as funny as a sick baby. He never made nobody laugh." Morton left Rosa to go with McCabe's Georgia Troubadours for a few months, until McCabe disbanded its minstrels in St. Louis. He hung around long enough to dazzle the local pianists (including Artie Matthews) with his playing of "Poet and Peasant" as well as some Joplin rags. Morton was asked to put a band together for a German restaurant in St. Louis, and thus came his first opportunity to create his own orchestrations. His instrumentation was determined by the personnel he could find—clarinet, trumpet, mandolin, and drums, with himself at the piano—but Morton took the job seriously, creating a band book of pop songs and old favorites like "Schnitzelbank."

Morton & Morton reunited to tour the Midwest in the spring of 1914, and it was around this time that Perry Bradford met Jelly in Chicago. Bradford said that Morton's turn "laid an omelette, it was so terrible." Whatever Bradford and Reb Spikes thought of his act, Morton always fancied himself a comedian. Vestiges of vaudeville crosstalk introduce three of the Red Hot Peppers' numbers of 1926: "Sidewalk Blues," "Dead Man Blues," and "Steamboat Stomp." (Morton: "You're so dumb, you should belong to the Deaf and Dumb Society." Johnny St. Cyr: "I'm sorry, boss, but I got the Sidewalk Blues.") And there is tent-show hokum in his "Hyena Stomp" of 1927; it features Lew LeMar, doing rhythmic laughing through several choruses.

◆

Morton & Morton seem to have dissolved their act late in 1914, when Jelly settled in Chicago. He was still at loose ends, but he had acquired salable skills during his years on the road. He knew enough about the band business to become music director at the Richelieu Cafe in August 1914. In November he took charge of a seven-piece orchestra at the new Deluxe Cafe on State Street.

Tony Jackson was back in Chicago that year, after a long sojourn in New Orleans, as the featured entertainer at the Elite Cafe, a large cabaret at Thirty-first and State streets, owned by a man named Teenan Jones. The Elite was so successful that Jones decided to open an Elite Number Two at 3445 South State. The second Elite, another big club, was a quick and utter failure, and it was proving to be a drain on the economy of Elite Number One. Probably at Jackson's recommendation, Jones asked Morton to manage Elite Number Two. He offered Morton $50 a week—big money after his penny-ante vaudeville—and promised him a free hand in running the place.

The new manager began his tenure at Elite Number Two early in 1915. He fired everybody on the staff, including the owner's brother, Give-a-Damn Jones, who had been operating the cash register, and he put himself in charge of the entertainment. He created a five-piece band to be the main attraction. He called the group Jelly Roll Morton and His Incomparables, and he had to do a lot of arranging to keep them in material. The venture was successful, and Morton enjoyed the prestige of his association with the Elite and with the band. He had certainly never created such a stir with his vaudeville music and comedy.

One of the Incomparables' numbers was an old tune of Morton's—written in 1905, he said—that he was now calling "The Chicago Blues." The piece was so identified with him that people asked for it as "Jelly Roll Blues." Morton compounded the flattery by writing a lyric about himself to fit the new title. ("He's so tall and chancy, He's the ladies' fancy. Everybody know him, Certainly do ado' him.") The popularity of "Jelly Roll Blues" inspired him to seek its publication. He took it to Chicago publisher Will Rossiter, who bought it. After arguments with Rossiter's arranger, F. Henri Klickmann, about how to notate the piece, Morton laboriously wrote the score out himself. Klickmann used Morton's version as a model, and "Jelly Roll Blues," issued in September 1915, became the twenty-four-year-old composer's first published work and the first published jazz composition.

There was much to argue with Klickmann. Only a few blues had been published as piano solos before 1915, and "Jelly Roll Blues" was unlike any of them. Except for the length of its two melodic strains—twelve bars each—the piece is hardly recognizable as a blues. (The word "jazz" was not in polite usage in 1915—it referred to sexual intercourse rather than to music—so Rossiter and Morton used the current fad word "blues" in the title.) Even in Klickmann's simplification of it, "Jelly Roll Blues" is a complex piece, and it is a preview of things to come from Morton. He supplies three written variations for his first theme, and he colors them in orchestral sounds: clarinet trills, the sustained notes of a bowed bass, trombonelike breaks for both hands in unison, and smears of triplets in the left hand. The two themes are separated by a four-bar interlude that takes the key from B-flat to the mellower E-flat. Unity is achieved by using the same melody and rhythmic pattern in the final two bars of each statement of both themes. Morton begins one of the variations with an astonishing four bars of shifting chromatics under a succession of twenty-nine repeated B-flats! His melodies beg for more improvisation, and his variations are meant to show the way. Morton was immodest but correct when he said that "Jelly Roll Blues" had "more originality to it" than any other blues of its time.

Morton had more confidence in "Jelly Roll Blues" than Will Rossiter had. The rarity of the 1915 edition indicates that not many copies were printed or distributed. The piece was not recorded until the Original

Memphis Five's version in September 1923, and Morton would make his first recording of it in 1924. "Jelly Roll Blues" did not make its composer rich or famous, but it confirmed his belief that he was doing what he was meant to do. There would occasionally be other occupations for him, some licit and some not, but after his first publication, he knew that, however he earned his living, his heart lay in music.

Another band job came to him in the summer of 1917, and Morton's acceptance of it probably delayed his recognition as a jazz master by five years. He had established himself in Chicago, and he had a strong reputation as a player and as a leader there. Yet when the music industry began to look to Chicago as a source of blues and jazz—after the ODJB's first hits—Morton wasn't there. Instead of being at the center of this first fervent curiosity about jazz, he was twelve hundred miles away. After the year or so of stability in Chicago, his life was complicated once more by a stormy romance, aimless travel, and scratching for a living again.

Morton was asked to come to Los Angeles to take charge of the music at the Cadillac Cafe, on Central Avenue between Fifth and Sixth streets. He knew a couple of Biloxi musicians living in L.A.—the Johnson brothers, Bill and Dink—and they wrote to assure him that he would do well in the movie capital. He traveled by train (with a ticket this time) and, through the courtesy of his Mississippi friends, a brass band met him at the station when he stepped out into the California sunshine.

Morton's engagement at the Cadillac went well from the beginning, and, he said, his music attracted many movie stars to the club. His bassist at the Cadillac was Bill Johnson, and Morton was happy to find that Bill and Dink's sister was also out West. She and Morton had been sometime sweethearts ten years earlier in Biloxi, and he wanted to get back together with her. He had known her as Bessie Johnson, and he was surprised to hear that she was now calling herself Anita Gonzales and that she had become a savvy businesswoman. She was running a saloon she owned in a raunchy little desert town called Las Vegas, but she came quickly to Los Angeles when she learned that Morton was there. Their romance rekindled, and she took Morton home to Vegas. When he became dissatisfied with living in the desert, she gave up her place and returned to L.A. to appease him.

Whether or not Morton and Gonzales were married, as they said they were, they were bound in a volatile union of two strong wills, a psychology-textbook case of the couple who couldn't live together and couldn't live apart. Each was bright and neither was afraid of work, but their tempestuous affair kept either of them from sticking with any venture long enough to make a success of it. They would spend nearly four years running all over the West, either to get away from or return to each other.

Gonzales bought a small hotel on Los Angeles' Central Avenue—which she named The Anita—and Morton opened a gambling club next door. He played in various places around town, organizing bands on a job-to-job basis for clubs in Watts and for a new amusement park on Leak's Lake (now Wayside Park). This arrangement lasted almost a year, until, without telling Morton, Gonzales left to buy a restaurant in Arizona. Jelly abruptly pulled up stakes to join her there, and when the restaurant went broke after a few months, they went to San Francisco, where they became partners in a club called the Jupiter. Anita left again, this time to run a rooming house in Seattle, and Jelly followed her. He got a job in Vancouver, and she followed him there. They celebrated their reunion with a long trip to Alaska together. After their fifth honeymoon, there was a horrendous row in Tacoma, during which Anita broke a steak plate over Jelly's head. She went back to L.A., and he went in the opposite direction, to play piano in bars in Wyoming and Colorado. A bad run of gambling in Denver took all his money.

The tearing around finally stopped when Jelly received a wire from Anita saying that her parents were ill and she needed him. He was broke, so he rode in freight cars from Denver to Los Angeles to be with her. It was a ruse. Her parents were not ill, she had simply wanted him back; and she got him. There were plenty of arguments to come, but the two settled in Los Angeles and tried to make a go of it as partners. Their life together was not exactly peaceful, but they made a detente that lasted about a year.

Morton was playing off and on during this time, but he wasn't writing much. He applied for his first copyright—for "Frog-I-More Rag"—in May 1918, but he seems not to have sought a publisher. (The piece had been written about ten years earlier, and it was named for a young pianist, Benson "Frog-Eye" Moore, whom Morton had met in his southern travels.) And there was a sizable backlog of older pieces that he had chosen not to copyright or publish. He spoke for many an itinerant composer when he told Alan Lomax:

> The fact is that the publishers thought they could buy anything they wanted for fifteen or twenty dollars. Now if you was a good piano player, you had ten jobs waiting for you as soon as you hit any town, and so fifteen or twenty or a hundred dollars didn't mean very much to us. . . . We kept our melodies for our private material to use to battle each other in battles of music. The men who had the best material in these battles were considered the best men and had the best jobs, and the best jobs meant, maybe, a hundred dollars a day. So we didn't give the publishers anything, but they said, "We know where to get tunes," and they would steal our tunes and come out with them anyhow.

However, two acquaintances from Morton's vaudeville days started him thinking about publishing again. Benjamin F. "Reb" Spikes and his brother John Curry Spikes had recently gone into partnership with a man named Carter to open a music store in Los Angeles, at 1203 Central Avenue. Reb dabbled in the entertainment business, as a promoter of the new Leak's Lake park and as occasional saxophonist and singer with Morton in clubs. When Reb and Jelly were playing in Oakland, they began fooling around with an old dirty song called "Tricks Ain't Walkin' No More." Morton showed Reb how to smooth out the melody to make a ballad, and Reb came up with some lyrics that could be sung in mixed company. In December 1919 the Spikes Brothers and Carter Music Company copyrighted the lead sheet of the new number. It was called "Someday Sweetheart," and, with music and lyrics credited to John C. Spikes, the brothers published the tune.

In 1921 they managed to get "Someday Sweetheart" into an L.A. revue, the *Pantages Broadway Follies*, and they reissued the number in September of that year. In 1922 it was bought by a Seattle publisher, Harold Weeks, who issued a revised edition (still attributed to John Spikes). In 1924 Weeks sold the song to the Melrose Brothers company in Chicago. Their edition was credited to Benjamin and John Spikes, and Melrose plugged it heavily. Sparked by Gene Austin's recording and later recordings by Sophie Tucker and Ted Lewis, the song became a standard. Morton didn't make a fuss about his lack of credit or payment, but he learned to keep an eye on the Spikes brothers. He was obviously writing a lot from 1920 to 1922—he had a trove of material when he made his first recordings in 1923—but he did not offer anything else to Reb and John Spikes.

Around midyear 1921, as his wandering subsided, Morton reestablished himself in Los Angeles. He played in clubs and hotels around the city, and he put together a band that worked all over southern California. (He pulled his group off a job at the U.S. Grant Hotel in San Diego when he found that they were being paid only half of what a local white band had received.) He ventured as far south as Tijuana to play in a black-owned place called the Kansas City Bar. He had a good time there, and he wrote one of his happiest pieces, "Kansas City Stomp," to commemorate it. One of the Kansas City's waitresses so charmed him that he wrote "The Pearls" for her.

Count Basie met the becalmed Morton in Los Angeles in 1921. Morton let Basie sit in at a club where he was playing and saved him from embarrassment when a singer called for a song in a key that Basie did not know. Jelly quietly slid onto the piano bench and said, "Don't worry about it. I'll play for her." Basie remembered him as "a great fellow." Ada "Bricktop" Smith, then a cabaret singer, worked with Morton at the Cadillac during this period. Years later, she smiled at the memory of his big talk, but she also recalled his being able to back up everything he said he could do.

Early in 1922 Morton heard that King Oliver's band was coming off a long engagement in San Francisco, and he decided to present them at Wayside Amusement Park in the spring. Oliver's pianist, Lil Hardin, wanted to go back to Chicago after the San Francisco job, so Morton coached a replacement for her in order to get Oliver. The pianist who subbed for Lil Hardin was Bertha Gonsoulin, and she is the only person known to have studied with Morton.

Morton would not have known Oliver well in their New Orleans days, but he surely knew of him as a cornetist. Oliver had been in

Chicago since 1918, and he had been a fixture at the Dreamland Cafe since 1920. He was king of Chicago's jazz scene in the early 1920s, as Morton was king of L.A.'s, but he ruled over a larger realm. Oliver was so well-situated that he could have painted a rosy picture of Chicago in 1922. He must have talked with Morton about the city's thriving dance-halls and of the New Orleans players who worked in them.

And although he had not yet had any of his own compositions published, King Oliver probably knew about the Melrose Brothers Music Company. Walter and Lester Melrose were small-timers, the white Chicago counterparts to the Spikes brothers. In 1920 they became co-owners—with Marty Bloom—of a music store at Sixty-third Street and Cottage Grove Avenue, and in 1922, their company began to specialize in the publication of blues and jazz compositions. Whether or not it was Oliver, someone or something put thoughts of Chicago into Morton's head, and, at about the same time, the Melrose brothers somehow—also perhaps through Oliver—learned of a Morton instrumental called "The Wolverines." They wrote to Morton to ask about it.

Morton said later that the Spikes brothers had intercepted the Melrose letter—it may have been sent to him in care of their music store—and that they had quickly written lyrics (and possibly a lead sheet) for "The Wolverines" to cut themselves in on the sale of it and sent it to Chicago. In any case, the piece, now titled "Wolverine Blues," received its first copyright on February 14, 1923, as a song with words by Ben and John Spikes and music by "Fred Morton." The copyright holder was Melrose Brothers Music Company. Morton became so irate when he learned of this that he decided to go and see Melrose to get the Spikeses' name off of it. "Wolverine Blues," either as a result of its success or because of its theft, was the impetus for his returning to Chicago, where he should have been all along.

Morton held his anger in check to deal one last time with the Spikes brothers. He needed money to go to Chicago, so he sold them the only copyright he owned, "Frog-I-More Rag." He told Anita at the time he left, in early April 1923, that he had a thousand dollars, and some of it probably came from this sale. This copyright was already potentially valuable. King Oliver had chosen the number to record in his first session for Gennett on April 6, just ten days before the Spikes brothers' copyright was registered. The label on Oliver's record spelled it "Froggie Moore," and that is the title that the Spikes brothers filed with the Library of Congress. They wrote words to "Froggie Moore" and submitted them for copyright with the melody, but they never published the number as a song or as an instrumental. In 1926 Melrose issued "Sweetheart o'Mine," a song based on the trio strain of "Frog-I-More Rag," with words by Walter Melrose. The original Morton piano version was never published. Morton promised Anita that, when he made a second thousand in Chicago, he would send for her. She did not see him again for seventeen years.

◆

George Ade's Chicago of 1915 had become Ben Hecht's Chicago by 1923. The overgrown town Morton had known was now a city on a toot, heavily into the manufacture and enjoyment of illegal booze and hot music. Bootleg liquor was available at clubs and parties everywhere in the city, under the aegis of mobsters who regulated the supply. The liquor-jazz link was most firmly forged on Chicago's black South Side, where gangsters controlled most of the clubs as well as the refreshments served and the music played in them. Earl Hines remembered Thirty-fifth Street in those days: "It was lit up like Paris, and there were some of the most dangerous people in the world on it. That's why Jelly Roll Morton carried his pistol and was so loud-mouthed. You had to act bad whether you were bad or not." Morton would never lead a band at a Chicago club, even in his palmiest day in the mid-1920s. His mouth and his swagger made him look like trouble to the mob-connected club owners, and they correctly pegged him as someone who would not have done business solely on their terms.

But Jelly Roll Morton had not come to Chicago to lead a band in the summer of 1923. He had come for a showdown with the Melrose brothers, and he knew he held the upper hand. They had wanted his "Wolverine Blues," had paid good money to the Spikes brothers for it, and they had already got the New Orleans Rhythm Kings to record it for Gennett. The sheet music was in the stores, and it looked like a hit. ("Wolverine Blues" was, in fact, the first hit the company had, and

Melrose would follow it with "Tin Roof Blues" in August 1923 and "Sobbin' Blues" in October. These three numbers, coming within six months of each other, made Melrose the preeminent Midwestern publisher of blues and jazz.)

When he saw the stir that "Wolverine Blues" was causing in Chicago, Morton changed his mind about making a fuss. He realized that Melrose was promoting his work as Rossiter and Spikes had never done. Instead of troubling the waters, Morton decided to fish in the Melrose pond. Wearing a cowboy hat and a red bandanna around his neck, he breezed into the publisher's music store and introduced himself. With a smile broad enough to show the diamond in his front tooth, he said, "Listen, everybody, I'm Jelly Roll Morton from New Orleans, the originator of jazz!" He sat down at a piano and knocked out "Wolverine Blues," then, after he had gathered a crowd, he entertained them for nearly an hour with music and braggish talk about himself. Lester Melrose was dumbfounded. The composer of "Wolverine Blues" had walked into his store, had played like a man possessed, and had promised that there were dozens more hits where "Wolverine" came from. Lester couldn't wait to tell Walter.

The big noise in the cowboy hat wooed the Melroses, and he won them. The company would issue most of Morton's work that saw print, twenty-six instrumental compositions—some of them conceived for band and published in orchestrations only—as well as a handful of songs, from 1923 to 1929. Melrose bought four Morton pieces ("Grandpa's Spells," "Kansas City Stomp," "Mr. Jelly Lord," and "The Pearls") right away and "London Blues" in September. The publisher had ties to the Gennett Record Company, offering the Indiana firm Chicago musicians to record Melrose tunes; Jelly bet that he would soon be in the Gennett studio, too.

Morton had business cards printed proclaiming himself "composer and arranger for Melrose Music Company." Composer he certainly was—although he probably never had a staff writer's contract—but his pieces were prepared for publication by Elmer Schoebel and Mel Stitzel, Melrose's house arrangers, sometimes using the sketches and figures that Jelly made for recording sessions.

One did not have to read the card to know that Morton was the composer of "Wolverine Blues." He talked it up everywhere he went. He played it for Alberta Hunter at the Pekin Cafe, and she fondly recalled him as "a braggadocio and very good-natured." He dropped by to show off at Jones' Music Store on South State Street, where black musicians hung out. Lil Hardin, King Oliver's pianist and Louis Armstrong's wife, heard him there, and she was impressed, too. She said:

> I had never heard such music before, they were all his original tunes. Jelly Roll sat down, the piano rocked, the floor shivered, the people swayed while he ferociously attacked the keyboard with his long skinny fingers, beating out a double rhythm [his trademark 4/4 time] with his feet on the loud pedal. I was thrilled, amazed, and scared. Well, he finally got up from the piano, grinned, and looked at me as if to say, "Let this be a lesson to you."

Morton was too impatient to wait for Melrose to get him into Gennett. He finagled an introduction to J. Mayo Williams, the black producer at Paramount's race record division, and talked Williams into producing the first known Morton recording session. (He claimed to have made two sides in Los Angeles in 1918, playing in a band that included Reb Spikes, Mutt Carey, Wade Whaley, and Kid Ory, but no records nor masters from this session have ever been found.) In early June 1923, Morton took a five-piece pickup band with him into the Paramount studios and cut two numbers, "Big Foot Ham" and "Muddy Water Blues." "Big Foot Ham" is the better side, and it shows Morton's nascent orchestral ideas in a series of breaks taken by various combinations of instruments. The highlight of the number is a duet passage by a clarinet and an alto sax. Morton's piano is under everything, but he takes no solo on either side. The Paramount sound quality is typically fuzzy, but it is clear enough to hear an arranger's mind beginning to work.

About a month after Morton's debut on disc, Melrose arranged for him to be a "guest artist" in two sessions with a popular white band, the New Orleans Rhythm Kings. The NORK featured New Orleans musicians—cornetist Paul Mares, clarinetist Leon Roppolo, and trombonist George Brunies—and Elmer Schoebel, a Melrose arranger, was the band's first pianist. They had built a following during their long stay at Chicago's Friars' Inn, and they had brought Melrose its first two record hits, "Wolverine Blues" and "Tin Roof Blues," in March 1923. It seemed a good idea to pair the company's current hit maker (the NORK) with its next (Morton), as well as to launch some of Morton's tunes with the band. The sessions were scheduled for July 17 and 18 in the Gennett studios in Richmond, Indiana. Because the trip from Chicago involved an overnight stay, the band vouched for Morton as a Panamanian so that he could check into a Richmond hotel. They were about to make the first interracial jazz recording, but it would not do to let the word out before they had secured their rooms. (Richmond had an active Ku Klux Klan at this time, and Gennett occasionally recorded Klan songs for release on its label.)

The Rhythm Kings numbered nine on this trip, not including Morton and another pianist, Kyle Pierce. In their two days at Gennett, Morton played on five tunes with the band, and Pierce played on three. Morton was, of course, featured on his "Mr. Jelly Lord" and "London Blues." A third debut piece, "Milenberg Joys," was co-composed by Morton, Mares, and Roppolo. (The tune's title misspells the name of Milneburg, a New Orleans amusement park. Morton was indifferent to "Milenberg Joys." He said he didn't write much of it, and he made only one other attempt at its commercial recording, a Gennett master that went unreleased in 1924. The piece was published in 1925—with lyrics by Walter Melrose—and in the late '20s it was the most frequently recorded number with Morton's name on it.) The NORK recordings with Morton are the young band's best. His playing obviously inspired Mares and Roppolo, and they responded with vigor and imagination.

The real treasures from those stifling July days at Gennett were the six Morton piano solos. They are the first jazz piano records as well as the first recorded body of a jazz composer's work. Morton had copyrighted and published almost nothing before 1923, but somehow during the previous twenty chaotic years he had amassed a trunkful of fine tunes. The list from his first solo sessions included "New Orleans Joys" (his new name for "New Orleans Blues"), "Kansas City Stomp,"

"Wolverine Blues," "The Pearls," "Grandpa's Spells," and "King Porter Stomp." None of them is a sketch or work-in-progress. All are fully realized compositions, finished to the last detail and brilliantly executed. There had been nothing remotely like them on records before.

The trademark of Morton as composer and player is his great variety of effects, and his first recorded solos are alive with intelligent choices. He was the first to think about musical structure beyond that imposed by the three-minute time limit of a 78-rpm record, and he mapped out his three minutes to show every facet of his tunes. These sides are built around preset (composed) variations on each theme, taken further by performance improvisation at specific places in the overall structure. The unified whole was more important to him than even the cleverest parts. He often uses the rondo form, in which his arrangement, with improvisations programmed into it, returns to and elaborates on his themes as a piece progresses. (In the 1930s, when recorded jam sessions became the in thing, Morton loathed them. They left too much to chance. He wanted nothing hit-or-miss in his music.) The miracle is that, for all his preoccupation with structure, his records sound so loose and relaxed.

Morton was one of the very few jazz musicians to build improvisations on the melody itself, not on the harmony. He said, "My theory is never to discard the melody. Always have a melody going in some kind of way." Paradoxically, his adherence to melody gave him great freedom, and it led him down interesting byways. After a statement of the tune, he would make a variation or two on it, then he would improvise on his variations, keeping the melody as the foundation of it all. (Without listening to several Morton performances of a piece, it is hard to tell the "written improvisations" from the spur-of-the-moment ones.) Within the boundaries of melody, he could recompose a tune at each performance of it and never run out of ideas. Harmonic improvisation, the method of those who came later, does not build nor feed on itself but makes each improvisational flight a separate entity. It is improvising the hard way, and it increases the odds against several players making a cohesive performance of a given piece. It tips the scale in the best soloist's favor.

Morton liked room to play around rhythmically, and his easy, medium 4/4 time gave it to him. Displays of speed did not interest him as much as the capacity to swing did. He sometimes tied a drum stick to his foot to tap out his four even beats on the loud pedal of the piano. It was not unusual for him to use a half-dozen rhythmic devices in a single tune: riffs (repeated rhythmic figures); breaks (dropping the rhythm while the melody continues); his "Spanish tinges" (habanera and tango rhythms); a walking bass that plays on all four beats; and rhythmic interplay alternating between the two hands. And Morton was the only early jazz player who was not afraid of stillness. Some of his passages consist of whole-note and half-note melodies with nothing going on underneath them. The listener can feel the beat that isn't there.

On these first solos, Morton's mature piano sound is there: thick, dark, and wooden. His usual playing territory was the middle register of the piano, and he often played inverted sixth chords with his left hand to give his music its density. When he leaves the middle ground, going into upper octaves or into deep bass figures, the movement is set in stark relief. And more than any other jazz pianist of the 1920s, Morton played *chords* with his right hand rather than single-note melody lines.

Morton's dynamics come from the simplest performing principle: leave yourself someplace to go. He said: "Jazz music is to be played sweet, soft, plenty rhythm. When you have your plenty rhythm with your plenty swing, it becomes beautiful. To start with, you can't make crescendos and diminuendos when one is playing triple forte. You got to be able to come down in order to go up. If a glass of water is full, you can't fill it any more; but if you have half a glass, you have the opportunity to put more water in it."

No pianist of Morton's time had such a distinctive attack: sharp and strong but not loud. The 1923 Gennetts are so subtly shaded that he roars without roaring and whispers without whispering. Right-hand cluster chords in "Kansas City Stomp" give the tune a half-major, half-minor sound, and the shift of accents to the second and fourth beats gives it a solid swing feel. "The Pearls" is built on contrasting melodies, bound together by four-measure interludes that relate them. "New Orleans Joys" has the wildest improvisation of all, a dancing, broken-time figure in the right hand that floats above the "Spanish tinge" rhythm under it. The whole-note/half-note third strain of "Wolverine Blues" weds calmness to animation. "Grandpa's Spells," one of Morton's raggiest pieces—not fast, just bright—has a toddling, reckless-sounding opening and sharp, but not loud, elbow crashes to punctuate the third strain.

And in that first solo session there was "King Porter Stomp," a tune that is, along with "Maple Leaf Rag" and "Royal Garden Blues," one of the most joyous outbursts in all of popular music. "King Porter" has three strains, and Morton always played them in order, escalating the excitement by introducing each one, improvising on it, then barreling ass to the next. The third strain is a kick-out-the-jams riff, swinging and powerful enough to intrigue arrangers for the next twenty years. Morton made six commercial recordings of "King Porter," the most he would make of any of his compositions. (The six include a piano roll and a duet with King Oliver. Oddly, he never recorded the piece with a band.) Fletcher Henderson's band had big-selling records of "King Porter" in 1928 and in 1933. In late 1935, when Morton's fortunes were sinking fast, the Benny Goodman band—using the Henderson arrangement—had one of its biggest hits with "King Porter Stomp." Although the public knew Goodman as the performer and jazz buffs knew Henderson as the arranger, no one seemed to recall who the composer was.

Morton would put all his theories into glorious practice with his Red Hot Peppers, but as these records show, the theories existed long before the Peppers came into being. If he had never recorded solo again or if he had never led a band, his place in jazz history would be secure on the basis of his first Gennett solos alone.

Morton kept tinkering with small bands. He put together a five-piece group called Jelly Roll Morton's Jazz Band for two OKeh sides in October 1923, and his spasm-like Steamboat Four—a kazoo, clarinet, comb, and piano—recorded two numbers for Paramount in April 1924. Nothing came of either group, so on June 9, 1924, Morton went back into the Gennett studios as a soloist. The feat that he pulled off that day was not equaled by another jazz pianist or composer until Willie the Lion Smith's Commodore date in January 1939. No pianist had ever recorded so many solos in a single session, nor had any jazz instrumentalist recorded so many of his own compositions. Morton recorded eleven pieces (nine of which were issued), without repeating any of the numbers that he had recorded the previous year for his Gennett solos. The nine released sides were "Shreveport Stomps," "Mamanita," "Jelly

Roll Blues," "Big Foot Ham," "Bucktown Blues," "Tom Cat Blues" (a reworking of "Wining Boy Blues"), "Stratford Hunch," "Perfect Rag," and "Tia Juana" (by Gene Rodemich).

No jazz figure before Ellington had a body of work to compare with the seventeen Morton compositions—fourteen piano solos and three pieces with the NORK—from the Gennett sessions of 1923-24. There would be about twenty more major Morton compositions, giving him the three dozen or so instrumental pieces that would make him the most recorded jazz composer. (Duke Ellington's songs have had more currency than Morton's, but the Ellington instrumentals were played and recorded almost exclusively by the Ellington band.) A few weeks after his Herculean session at Gennett, Morton made thirteen of his sixteen known piano rolls, for the Vocalstyle company in Cincinnati. Twelve of them were his own compositions.

Morton kept trying to organize a permanent band. In September 1924 he called Lee Collins, a young New Orleans cornetist who had come to Chicago to replace Louis Armstrong in King Oliver's band. When Collins went to Morton's rooming house to discuss recording, he arrived to find the composer in bed but not alone. With a woman lying on either side of him, Morton outlined his plans for the first (and last) recordings by Jelly Roll Morton's Kings of Jazz, four sides for Autograph Records. In the so-so Autograph sessions, Collins emerged as the most agile improviser, and Jelly featured himself hardly at all. Morton the arranger was still outclassed by Morton the composer, but the arranger would soon catch up.

In December 1924, Morton made two duets with King Oliver ("King Porter Stomp" and "Tom Cat Blues"). Jelly let Oliver have the spotlight, as he let the white clarinetist Volly de Faut shine in the Jelly Roll Morton's Jazz Trio recordings of May 1925. (The trio consisted of clarinet, piano, and drums; Morton was the first to use this combination for instrumental jazz.) Morton toured with a second edition of the Incomparables early in 1926, and while they were on the road, they stopped by Gennett to record a side.

Even though Morton had not yet had a hit record, Melrose was still high on him. His songs ("Milenberg Joys," "Wolverine Blues," "Sweetheart o'Mine," and "Sidewalk Blues") were bringing in mechani-

THE RED HOT PEPPERS AT THE TIME OF THEIR FIRST VICTOR SESSION. L TO R: ANDREW
HILAIRE (DRUMS), KID ORY (TROMBONE), GEORGE MITCHELL (TRUMPET), JOHN LINDSAY
(BASS), JELLY ROLL MORTON (PIANO), JOHNNY ST. CYR (BANJO), AND OMER SIMEON
(CLARINET). COURTESY RCA VICTOR/BMG.

cal royalties, so Jelly seemed like a good investment to the publishing
brothers. Late in the summer of 1926, Melrose got Morton a contract to
record for Victor, and the group that he took into Victor's Chicago studio on Oak Street on September 15, 1926, was the first to be called the
Red Hot Peppers. The personnel (and number) of the Peppers varied
over time, but Morton's partiality to New Orleans musicians would
remain constant. He had three of the best on his first session: banjoist
Johnny St. Cyr, trombonist Kid Ory, and his favorite clarinetist, Omer
Simeon. His bassist was John Lindsay, his drummer was Andrew Hilaire,
and his cornetist was a Kentuckian, George Mitchell.

Simeon played on four Peppers sessions—three in 1926 and one in
1928—and two decades later he remembered one of Morton's most startling innovations; rehearsal before recording.

> We used to go to his home for rehearsals. . . .Walter Melrose
> brought all the music down from his music store. Morton was

working for Melrose then and the pieces we played were mostly stock arrangements Jelly had made up and published by Melrose. Jelly marked out parts we liked and he always had his manuscripts there and his pencils and he was always writing and changing little parts. . . . Jelly left our solos up to us but the backgrounds, harmony and licks were all in his arrangements. He was easy to work for and he always explained everything he wanted. We would have a couple of rehearsals at Jelly's house before the date and Melrose would pay us $5 a man. That's the only time I ever got paid for a rehearsal. . . . Melrose spared no expense for a record date—anything Jelly Roll wanted he got. Melrose worshiped him like a king. . . . [Morton] was fussy on introductions and endings and he always wanted the ensemble his way but he never interfered with the solo work. He'd tell us where he wanted the solo or break but the rest was up to us.

Morton's rehearsing and "changing little parts" paid off in the first Peppers session with "Black Bottom Stomp," one of the hottest records ever made and the band's first hit. "Black Bottom Stomp" is in brisk 4/4 time and relentless in its drive, and Morton's arrangement is tight—with every second of sound accounted for. The piece is a kaleidoscope of textural effects, and the stakes are raised with every solo. Simeon is all over the place in his two choruses: the first a high, darting flight and the second low and burbling, in the *chalumeau* style so beloved by New Orleans clarinetists. Mitchell's cornet solos are hard and clear, and St. Cyr's banjo rings under everything. And, in a change from his earlier band recordings, Morton features his own piano, in a whirling solo chorus that swings as hard as the ensemble choruses surrounding it. There is no letup, even during the four-bar interludes that separate the two melodic strains. "Black Bottom Stomp" is not fast (nor does it speed up), but it has the inexorable momentum of a runaway train.

Because he had sounds, not players, in his mind, Morton was ready to change the makeup of the Peppers by their second session, only six days after their first. He wanted three clarinets for passages in "Sidewalk Blues" and "Dead Man Blues," and, although Melrose was probably not happy about the extra salaries, he got them. Simeon was his mainstay, and two other clarinetists joined him to make a temporary trio that was used sparingly but effectively in the two blues pieces. Two months later, Morton modified the Peppers again by using a violinist to solo on "Someday Sweetheart" and by having Omer Simeon double on bass clarinet. An experiment in a December 1926 session that Morton deemed a failure was his own vocal on "Doctor Jazz." It is more shouting than singing, and Morton did not sing again on records until the late 1930s.

With the first three Red Hot Peppers sessions, Morton hit his stride. All of his thinking about how a jazz band should sound came to full fruition. Early in 1927, the Peppers had four hit records from these dates ("Black Bottom Stomp," "Original Jelly Roll Blues," "Doctor Jazz," and "Grandpa's Spells"). After the experience of expanding several of his piano works into band arrangements, Morton began to think in purely orchestral terms. Some of his compositions from this period—such as "Black Bottom Stomp," "Jungle Blues," "Billy Goat Stomp," and "Hyena Stomp"—were first conceived as band works, not as piano solos. (Some record collectors have assumed over the years that all compositions recorded by Morton in the mid-1920s were his own. The Red Hot Peppers' sound was, of course, Jelly's sound, so it all could be mistaken for Morton. But several of the classic Peppers recordings from this time are not his works. "Dr. Jazz" was composed by King Oliver; "The Chant" was by Mel Stitzel; and "Steamboat Stomp" was Boyd Senter's. However, the Peppers' recordings of these numbers remain the definitive performances of them.)

On June 10, 1927, Morton made two sides with a trio at a Peppers date. The numbers were "Wolverine Blues" and "Mr. Jelly Lord," and he chose them to feature clarinetist Johnny Dodds—whose brother, Baby Dodds, was the drummer in the trio. Although he did not play the clarinet, Morton loved its sound, and he used it more prominently—and more often—than the cornet in Peppers recordings. Morton seems to have heard his ballads and his slower blues voiced by reeds rather than by his own piano. The clarinet trios in his 1926 "Sidewalk Blues" and "Dead Man Blues" are sweet and haunting, and his 1929 trio arrangement of "Turtle Twist" (featuring Zutty Singleton's drumming) gets its sensuality from Barney Bigard's winding clarinet lines.

Jelly preferred New Orleans clarinetists, of course, and among those he showcased were Omer Simeon, Barney Bigard, Johnny Dodds, George Baquet, and, in the late 1930s, Albert Nicholas. Simeon, Bigard, Baquet, and Nicholas all had the same teacher: Lorenzo Tio, Jr. (Tio himself claimed to have recorded with Morton in 1930, but this has not been verified.) Morton would use Russell Procope in 1928, and he would team Sidney Bechet—on soprano sax—with Albert Nicholas in 1939. He used a bass clarinet on "Someday Sweetheart" (1926), on the beautiful and neglected ballad "If Someone Would Only Love Me," and on "Fussy Mabel" (both in 1930). Morton's clarinet passages were the most thoroughly written-out parts in his arrangements, and the reed figures in Peppers recordings greatly influenced young clarinetists of the late 1920s.

In the summer of 1927 Marty Bloom, the silent Melrose partner, brought Jelly Roll Morton into the Chicago offices of Music Corporation of America on West Randolph Street. At that time MCA was a small booking agency for bands, successfully representing hotel and cafe orchestras—Don Bestor's, Ted Weems's, and Zez Confrey's among them—in New York. The six-man Chicago office, headed by Bill Goodheart, had recently signed Guy Lombardo and Wayne King, and it was hoping to find a hot band that could draw as well as its sweet bands. Morton was the golden boy of Melrose Music, with hits on sheet music and on records, and Melrose wanted to capitalize on these by sending him out with a touring show built around his band. Melrose chose MCA as the means to get him on the road.

The MCA staffers hardly knew who Morton was, but he told them. He turned their office into his pulpit, preaching his genius and cheerfully denigrating every other bandleader. Karl Kramer, the agency's publicity director, remembered Morton as "the biggest braggart that had ever come down our musical pike," but when the bragging was over, MCA signed him on the spot. Bill Goodheart got on the phone and quickly landed Morton's first engagement, a week at Milwaukee's Alhambra Theatre at $1,500. It was only then, after signing Morton and booking him for a big job two weeks away, that MCA discovered that he didn't have a band. The Red Hot Peppers did not exist outside the studio.

It was Jelly's turn to get on the phone. He called various Peppers, and, for one reason or another, they all turned him down. In a panic now,

MCA pulled in a small black band, the Chicago Blew Blowers, from its summer circuit and presented them to Morton for his approval. He approved, and they began to assemble a revue. A statuesque girl dancer was hired, along with a tap-dance team and a singing-dancing male chorus. Morton pushed to play his own numbers, as Melrose had told him to, but MCA overruled him in favor of pop-variety fare, such as Vincent Youmans's "Hallelujah" and a few spirituals. Opening night in Milwaukee went well enough to satisfy the MCA agents in attendance, and they congratulated themselves for saving the $1,500 they could have lost on the Alhambra's pay-or-play terms.

A few days later, unbeknownst to Morton, more MCA agents dropped in to see the show. They were shocked to discover that their revue had been turned into a Jelly Roll Morton festival: dance numbers had been scrapped, vocals were cut, the Blowers/Peppers played only filler around Morton's piano solos. When his agents confronted Morton backstage, he simply said, "People didn't come here to see a show, they come to hear old Jelly play the piano." MCA knew that he could not be trusted with a stage show again, so the Alhambra was Morton's first and last big engagement through the agency. To salvage the remainder of his contract, MCA booked him for dances, mostly one-nighters in the Midwest. These gigs, which should have been profitable, were put in the hole by Jelly's mismanagement. He would collect his fees from promoters, and, instead of using them for expenses, he would pocket the money and wire MCA for more. When MCA put out the word among promoters not to pay Morton but to pay the agency instead, Jelly was furious. After Morton missed several shows, he and the agency decided to cure their mutual headache by terminating their contract. MCA—along with ASCAP, the musicians' union, Duke Ellington, and W. C. Handy—would be on Morton's enemies list for the rest of his life.

The winter of 1927-28 found Jelly personally and professionally uneasy. The blowup with MCA had dented his ego, and Melrose was doing little to cheer him up. There had been no recordings for him since June, and there were no new Morton publications. Melrose was learning—as publisher Leo Feist had learned with the ODJB tunes—that there was only a small market for jazz instrumentals in sheet music form. The nature of jazz made it impossible for the amateur player to replicate the sound, which would have been the only impetus to buy the sheet music. However jazzy the home player, he was not a band, and he couldn't make his piano sound like one, as Jelly Roll Morton did. (This feeling of futility would become even more pronounced in the rock era, when amateurs realized that buying the sheet music did not make one's piano sound like an electric guitar.)

Melrose had bought Morton's "Ted Lewis Blues" in February 1927 and had given it to Johnny Dodds's Black Bottom Stompers for its first recording in April. Louis Armstrong was Dodds's cornetist for this session, and his solo drew so much attention that Melrose incorporated a rough transcription of it in the published orchestration of the piece that summer. Armstrong's name was added as co-composer on the inside sheet of the published piano version as well as on the parts of the printed orchestration. The title was changed, too, and Morton learned from the Stompers' record label that he and Armstrong—whom he barely knew—had written something called "Wild Man Blues." The tune was not a hit and, therefore, not a big deal, but Melrose's handling of it showed him that the company was willing to meddle with his work (and credit) when a commercial opportunity arose to do so.

Late in 1927 Morton began seeing Mabel Bertrand, a pretty dancer from New Orleans, whom he had met in Chicago's Plantation Club. There was a hasty and ardent courtship, much of it conducted over the telephone, before the November day when he asked her to go for a spin in his Lincoln. He drove her to Gary, Indiana, where a justice of the peace married them. They took a monthlong honeymoon in Kansas City, then they drove north and east and didn't stop until they got to Harlem. With his unerringly bad timing, Morton was turning his life over yet again. If his genius was being undersold in Chicago, it would surely impress New York.

◆

Melrose advertised Morton as "an exclusive Victor recording artist," and Morton advertised himself as a "composer and arranger for the Melrose Music Company," but as soon as he got to New York, he began to flirt with other publishers and with another record label. In April 1928 he sold his "State and Madison" to Denton & Haskins (which had bought his "Windy City Blues" in October 1927). Also in April he placed "Ham and Eggs" (a reworking of "Big Foot Ham") and "Buffalo Blues" with Joe Davis's Triangle Music Company. Morton's first New York recordings were as pianist with Johnny Dunn and His Band in March 1928 for Columbia. Morton was unbilled on the labels for these four sides, but his solos on "Ham and Eggs" and "You Need Some Lovin'" could have identified him to any Victor executive who was paying attention.

By June 1928 Morton was back in the Victor fold, with the first New York edition of his Red Hot Peppers. There were six players, not including Morton, and five of them were drawn from the band he was leading that summer at Harlem's Rose Danceland, a dime-a-dance imitation of Roseland, at 125th Street and Seventh Avenue. The June date was a happy reunion with Omer Simeon—the only non-Danceland player—whose frisky clarinet swings "Shreveport Stomp." Morton made a quartet arrangement for "Mournful Serenade" (a reworking of King Oliver's "Chimes Blues"), and the full band tossed off "Georgia Swing" and "Boogaboo." Jelly's piano permeates the Peppers, as it had always done. (With the possible exception of Count Basie, no other piano-playing leader translated his piano sound into that of his band so much as Morton. Neither Ellington's nor Henderson's band reflected its leader's personal piano style; Morton's bands did, whatever the personnel.)

Morton rented midtown office space, where he moaned to visitors about the terrible state of jazz in New York. He said it was "loud, blary, noise, discordant tones," forcing listeners "to hold their ears to protect their eardrums from a forced collision with their brains." Mary Lou Williams, an admirer of Morton's, was taken to meet him one day, and she got an unasked-for piano lesson. She said:

> I got started on my favorite Morton piece, "The Pearls."
> Almost immediately I was stopped and reprimanded, told the
> right way to phrase it. I played it the way Jelly told me, and
> when I had it to his satisfaction, I slipped in one of my own
> tunes. This made no difference. I was soon stopped and told,
> "Now that passage should be phrased like this."

In July 1929 Morton went to the Victor studios in Camden, New Jersey, to record what would be his last piano solos for nearly ten years.

He played four new numbers: "Pep," "Seattle Hunch," "Frances," and "Freakish." All four were fine performances, but none of them sold many records. Because of his declining sales, Victor was merely riding out its contract with Morton in 1929-30. The company gave him a few more Peppers sessions, as well as orchestra and trio sides, but there were also jobbed-in piano accompaniments for Lizzie Miles and for Billie Young, a sometime blues singer. In December 1929 and in June 1930 Morton played piano (anonymously) on Victor sessions with the Wilton Crawley orchestra. Finally, on October 9, 1930, he made "Gambling Jack" and "Fickle Fay Creep," his last tunes with a Peppers ensemble and the end of the road with Victor. He was still able to command $1,600 a night by taking pickup Peppers on the road, but his recording career had slid away and he knew it. It was around this time that his big talk, which everyone had found so amusing before, began to turn sour.

The truth was that, by the time Morton arrived in New York, the jazz contingent's vote was in, and Jelly Roll, the strict constructionist, had lost. Louis Armstrong, not he, had been elected by fans and players to be the navigator of jazz's ship. Armstrong's brilliance made every instrumentalist want to do what he did: to take center stage and hold it by dazzling solo playing. Because of him, jazz became star-centered, in recording and in performance, and the Morton arrangements that let everybody improvise around the melody seemed to carry democracy too far. With the arrival of other star turns—such as Sidney Bechet, Coleman Hawkins, and Bix Beiderbecke—the soloist's triumph was complete. The typical studio jazz band became as anonymous and inconsequential as the nonentities who played behind Buddy Bolden a generation earlier. And when Armstrong began to sing on records in 1926, he showed untrained singers how to shine, and gave "singer"/instrumentalists a second way to solo.

In 1929 Armstrong brought yet another sea change to jazz with his enormously successful recordings of pop songs. Until that time, he had dealt mostly in original instrumentals, but when he swung pop—"I Can't Give You Anything But Love," "When You're Smiling," "Sweethearts on Parade"—he transformed the jazz repertoire, enlarged it a thousandfold, and the public loved it. Listeners could more easily apprehend what Armstrong was doing to "I'm Confessin'" than they could take in Jelly's multitextured variations on "Burnin' the Iceberg." With each new ad-libbed pop hit of Armstrong's, Morton's composer/arranger craftsmanship of original tunes seemed more old-fashioned.

Morton began to have trouble hiring players for band jobs. Young musicians didn't like to work for "the Roll," as they called him. They found him too demanding ("You'd please me if you'd just play those little black dots—just those little black dots that I put down there") and too preachy ("I'm telling you those white boys are not playing corny anymore. . . . They're getting the idea of how to play hot. Once they get it, they're going to use it. Then they're gonna sell *you* for five cents a dozen"). He called rehearsals for even the dinkiest dates; he wouldn't allow liquor on the bandstand. He took it all too seriously; he was no fun.

Melrose issued its last Morton publication, the orchestration of "Georgia Swing," in June 1929. Jelly sold a handful of numbers to Southern Music Company in the early 1930s, but they went unpublished. By age forty, he was just about over the hill.

Low fortune did not stop his mouth, of course. Morton pontificated through endless pinochle games at Harlem's Rhythm Club, telling anyone who would listen that Duke Ellington was a fraud, that Ellington had stolen his "jungle music" effects from Morton's "Jungle Blues" of 1927, that no New York musicians could play jazz, that Luckey Roberts was the only ragtimer in Harlem worth his salt, and that MCA and ASCAP (which wouldn't admit him to full membership) were in a conspiracy to keep him from working. He found it particularly easy to rile Chick Webb. The beanpole Morton and the short, hunchbacked Webb were a familiar sight, haranguing each other on sidewalks. Barney Bigard remembered that they "would stand on a street corner and argue so bad you could've become rich by selling tickets." Morton had no close friends among musicians, and jam sessions bored him. He made himself known by spouting off in front of clubs rather than by joining in the camaraderie of after-hours playing inside them.

Willie the Lion Smith was one of the few Harlem musicians who did not think Jelly was a crackpot. He said:

Morton was a man with strong spiritual and magnetic forces;
when he sat down to play, he could hold an audience by the

strength of his strong personality. He was a sharpshooter and he always traveled in fast company. He was intelligent, had something to offer, and as far as I could tell, he was always able to back up what he said. . . . It used to make me mad to hear the New York cats who hadn't been out of Harlem making fun of Morton.

Smith ended his reminiscence with a for-the-record reminder that he had once cut Jelly in a piano contest at the Rhythm Club.

However shaky his career, Morton still looked the part of a high-roller. Mabel was totally devoted to him and helped him keep up the facade. Her days were largely given over to the complexities of his laundry. He needed several fresh shirts a day, wanted his suits cleaned overnight, and liked his socks and ties in rows so orderly that he could coordinate colors in the dark. Even though he was not working much, he could still say to any young musician who crossed him, "I got more suits than you got handkerchiefs." Only Mabel knew the quiet side of him. He liked his dinner at home—gumbo was his favorite—with the rest of the evening free to work on music. His idea of a big weekend was an excursion to Connecticut for a Saturday picnic with his wife.

The strain of being the only genius in town—and an unemployed genius, at that—took its toll on Jelly. He came to believe that the shape shifting of his professional life could have been caused by only one thing: he had been jinxed. If the good magic of Eulalie Echo and Papa Sona had helped him in his early days, then bad magic must be responsible for his unending streak of ill luck in New York. A chance meeting with "a frizzly-haired woman" who claimed to see the future sent his mind further down this dark labyrinth. She told him that someone was "working against him," and he began to see evidence of it everywhere.

Morton was sharing a Forty-fifth Street office with a song plugger, whom he often saw in street corner conversations with an odd-looking old man. (When Jelly told this story to Alan Lomax, he never identified his office mate, referring to him only as "my West Indian partner." He may have been Harrison Smith, with whom Jelly shared an office around this time. Although Smith was from Washington, D.C., Morton's nickname for him was "the West Indian.") The plugger told Morton that the old man could cast spells from a book of charms that he owned. When Morton caught the plugger trying to sell his music to publishers without his permission, there was a violent confrontation. Morton got the upper hand in their scuffle, but as "the West Indian" retreated, he said, "Jelly Roll Morton, you will lose everything you have." After that, Jelly's office went haywire. The phone wouldn't work; visitors stopped at the door, seemingly unable to enter; colored powders were found under the rug and in his desk; water from the cooler made his secretary sick. A storage company mistakenly sold his band bus; he lost a trunk of music and personal effects at a Pennsylvania hotel.

Magic had to be fought with magic, so Morton went to fortune-tellers and voodoo women in Harlem. He bought their readings and potions, and he put their high-priced elixirs into his bathwater. He was drawn to a practitioner named Madame Elise, and he began seeing her almost every day. She cooked charm-foods for him, and she scrubbed his office walls with turpentine. Finally she said that in order to lift the spell against him, he must make a supreme personal sacrifice: she ordered him to burn his clothing. Jelly was mad with fear and worry by then, so he did it. He cut his suits and topcoats into pieces, took them out behind his apartment building, and piled them in a stack higher than his head. He soaked them with kerosene and lit a match. The suit man from suit land proved his faith.

Morton's money was gone, and his nerves were shot, and still his bad luck continued. He decided that Madame Elise was part of the conspiracy against him. There was no striking back at her because he could not pay for any more charms and spells. His career shrank away. Even if he had been able to put a band together, he didn't have a bus to get them to a job or arrangements to use when they got there. He lost his last few dollars trying to start a cosmetics company. One day Jelly Roll told Mabel that he had been offered a job as a fight promoter in Washington, D. C. There was nothing to keep him in New York, so she had to let him go. It would be nearly two years before she heard from him again.

Early in 1937 Jelly began to write Mabel—and to send her a few dollars with each letter—and she learned what he was doing. He was in Washington, managing a small club at 1211 U Street, N.W. The place advertised itself as the Blue Moon, but the sign over its door called it the Music Box. (It was currently done up in bamboo, left over from its days as the Jungle Inn.) It was a plain second-story room, heated by an oil stove and by the oven in the diner below it. A woman named Cordelia Lyle was the owner, and Morton was the staff. He was bouncer, host, sometime cook, bartender, emcee, and waiter. He was also the entertainment, except on Monday nights, when a drag show called the "Mummer Revue" was presented. Instead of being jealous of Jelly's partnership with another woman, Mabel went to Washington to help him with the Blue Moon.

Mrs. Lyle bought the occasional newspaper ad, so word trickled out that Jelly was in residence in her dingy club. There were a few traditional jazz buffs in D.C., and they turned out to hear him. They gladly paid the $1 cover charge (which also bought one drink) to sit near the piano and watch his hands. Although he did not like being thought of as an old-timer, Jelly gave them what they came for, long sets of his '20s piano pieces and Peppers numbers, interspersed with gripes about the sorry state of jazz and the lamentable rise of one-handed piano players. One of his fans was an IRS employee named Roy Carew, who had heard Morton years before as a young man in New Orleans. Another was Alan Lomax, who worked for the Library of Congress. Though neither was in the music business, these two men would be instrumental in the brief resurrection of Jelly Roll Morton.

But not all of the Blue Moon patrons came to worship. Some came to snicker. One of these was a seventeen-year-old pianist named Billy Taylor. He recalled:

> When we heard that Jelly had this little club in Washington
> . . . we decided to take a ride down and have a few laughs.
> Even though it was a Saturday night, we had no trouble get-
> ting a booth in the place. Somebody recognized us as part of
> the new crop of jazz pianists; word started to pass around the
> house that some young hipsters had stopped in to have some
> fun with old Jelly Roll. And then Jelly came on. He looked
> shockingly sick and feeble—old and a little mad. But he wore
> his old, Southern-gentleman's suit with dignity, and when he
> smiled, the diamond in his tooth still glittered hard. He played
> a new piece of his called "Sweet Substitute," and then (since
> the grapevine grows quick in little places like this) he looked

Jelly Roll Morton at the Blue Moon/Jungle Inn, in Washington, D.C., c. 1938.
Photo courtesy the Frank Driggs Collection.

straight over at our booth. His eyes had a very personal kind of pride which I had never seen before. His look had the strangely arrogant wisdom of those who know, those who have been there and seen it and at the end realized that nothing very shattering has happened after all. . . Then Jelly spoke only to us: "You punks can't play this." I forget the tune. What I do remember is a big, full, two-handed piano player—a ragtimer modified and relaxed by way of New Orleans and *very* swinging . . . and as I listened suddenly I knew. "Golly, he's right. I *can't* play what he's playing. Just purely technically, I can't play two hands together and separately the way he does." I looked over at the other confident young men who had come with me; I saw that they knew that they couldn't either. Ours was a very quiet booth for the next three hours.

In the summer of 1938 Morton caused a firestorm in the jazz world with a scathing attack on one of its most revered figures, W. C. Handy. When he heard a radio host, Robert Ripley, identify Handy as the originator of jazz and blues, Jelly went berserk. He fired off a long letter to Ripley to set the matter straight. He sent a copy of the letter to *Down Beat*, and the magazine published his diatribe in two parts, in its August and September issues. He called Handy "the most dastardly impostor in the history of music," and said that he could neither write nor play jazz or the blues. Jelly himself was the only originator, he said, of jazz and swing: "I laid the foundation of jazz and am still the flowing fountain."

Handy's answer was published in the September *Down Beat*, alongside part two of Morton's screed. He said,

> Jelly Roll Morton says I cannot play "Jazz." I am 65 years old and would not play it if I could, but I did have the good sense to write down the laws of jazz and the music that lends itself to jazz and had vision enough to copyright and publish all the music I wrote, so I don't have to go around saying that I made up this piece and that piece in such and such a year like Jelly Roll and then say somebody swiped it. . . . If I didn't know him, I would think he was crazy, and it is the act of a crazy

man to attack such fine men who have done outstanding work like Paul Whiteman [and] Duke Ellington.

With what was either a political *non sequitur* or another slur at Handy, Morton signed off part two: "Lord protect us from more Hitlers and Mussolinis."

Even before the dust-up with Handy, Morton had notions of an autobiography, and now he saw it as an historical mandate. He had already pieced out a couple of chapters when Alan Lomax had a better idea. He invited Jelly to tell his story for the Library of Congress. On a May afternoon in 1938 Morton sat at a piano in the Library's Coolidge Auditorium, and Lomax turned on his primitive recorder.

Over the next few weeks, music and talk poured out of Morton, prodded by memories of his Storyville life and his early wanderings. Pianists, pimps, thugs, and madams of forty years earlier jostled their way into his recollection. He described their clothes, shoes, houses, food. He illustrated the playing styles of long-dead sports and game kids who had been known only by nicknames when they were alive. For almost every musical sample, there is the story of a murder or a melee. He illustrates his jazz theories by showing, step-by-step, how he "transformed" the themes and tempos of an old French quadrille into "Tiger Rag." He repeats the experiment by his straight singing and playing of an old tear-jerker, "My Gal Sal," before he turns it into a romping jazz number. He plays a theme from Gounod's *Faust*, and he jazzes the "Miserere" from *Il Trovatore*. And he proved that, during his bleakest times in the 1930s, he had somehow kept writing. The Lomax sessions brought the debut recordings of "Creepy Feeling," "Spanish Swat," and "The Naked Dance." Another number recorded for the first time here was "The Crave," a whorehouse tango that he had written years earlier.

Although no one except a few members of the Library of Congress staff heard the Lomax recordings, the jazz world knew that they had been made. They gave Jelly the imprimatur of history, and, along with the publicity from his flap with Handy, they put his name before the public again. The condition of his career rose from critical to serious. It was enough to give Jelly hope, and he determined to ride it for all it was worth. He was invigorated as he had not been in a decade, ready to write, arrange, and record again. He would set his house in order, nail down his ownership of his recent compositions, then go after the money he was owed from his old ones. In 1938 Roy Carew helped him organize Tempo Music Company. Tempo acted only as a holding company for new copyrights at first, but it would eventually publish ten Morton compositions.

The Library of Congress has never issued the complete Morton interviews. In 1947 permission was given to Circle Records to issue some of the material, which Circle reordered from the original sequence and edited to omit the most vulgar of his blues lyrics. The Circle set comprised forty-five twelve-inch 78s, which were pressed in a limited edition of two hundred copies. Riverside Records, Classic Jazz Masters [Sweden], and Swaggie Records [Australia] all later reissued—and rearranged the order of—the Circle recordings, with some restorations of the blues cut out by Circle. (In 1994, Rounder Records issued unedited and remastered versions of the musical numbers that Morton recorded— including the risqué blues songs—on four CDs.) Alan Lomax transcribed the acetates and added new material from further interviews with Morton and others for his book *Mr. Jelly Roll*, originally published by Duell, Sloan, & Pearce in 1950. Louis Armstrong, when asked to review *Mr. Jelly Roll* for the *New York Times*, said, "Glad to do it. He was my boy." They were acquaintances rather than friends, but Armstrong showed genuine affection and respect for Morton in his rave review.

Morton would not have another long-term contract with a major label, but several small companies issued his work from 1938 into 1940. The first to record him was Jazz Man Records, a subsidiary of a Hollywood record shop, which hired Neshui Ertegun, the son of a Turkish ambassador, to supervise a Morton session in Washington in December 1938. Morton made four piano solos for Jazz Man, including two new pieces that were written to show that he was still up to date. One was a barrage of notes called "Fingerbuster," the other was "Honky Tonk Music," a rare Morton foray into boogie. (He—like Fats Waller— thought that boogie was beneath him, but he occasionally played it, and played it well, in his later years.) "Creepy Feeling" got its first commercial recording in the Jazz Man session, as did the vocal of Morton's old signature tune, "Wining Boy Blues."

Morton's playing on the Jazz Man sides is all the more remarkable considering the fact that he had not yet recovered from a near-fatal attack at the Blue Moon. The trouble started when a drunken customer swore at Morton, and Morton slapped him. As Jelly was sitting down at the piano, the man came up behind him and stabbed him in the head. When Morton turned around, he was stabbed again, just above the heart. Mabel sprang from behind the bar and flattened the man with an ashtray, probably saving her husband's life. After a few weeks of offhand care at a Washington hospital, Morton was released, and he went back to work. Mabel wouldn't have it. She knew that there would always be more mean drunks than jazz fans at the Blue Moon, and she convinced him that, for his safety and his peace of mind, he had to quit. On Christmas Eve 1938, driving through a blinding snowstorm, Jelly and Mabel headed for New York.

New York was not exactly welcoming to Morton, but it was not as indifferent as it had been five years earlier. Not long after his return, he was hired to put together a band for Harlem's Golden Gate Ballroom. As he was dressing for his opening night, he had asthmatic seizures, and he collapsed, gasping for breath. Morton was in the hospital for weeks, and his doctor released him with a warning that he must not play professionally again. The genius knew better than the doctor, of course, and in the last four months of 1939, Morton came back strong, producing some of the best recordings of his career.

All the reminiscing that Morton had done for Alan Lomax put New Orleans back on his mind, and he drew inspiration for his last burst of great work from his Storyville past. In September 1939 he led two sessions for Victor's Bluebird series with a handpicked group that included four New Orleans masters: Sidney Bechet, Albert Nicholas, Wellman Braud, and Zutty Singleton. The eight musicians, called Jelly Roll Morton's New Orleans Jazzmen, sailed into "High Society," "Oh, Didn't He Ramble?," James Scott's "Climax Rag," and King Oliver's "West End Blues." The band is looser than the Peppers had been, but Jelly's joy at being in their company is evident in his playing. On Halloween night, Morton was a guest on Gabriel Heatter's radio program, *We, the People.* He told his story of the "transformation" of "Tiger Rag," and he made the tiger roar again.

The cream of Morton's late recording work was done for General Records on three December days in 1939. He made seven piano solos the first day, including the first commercial recording of "Sporting House Rag" (a reworking of his "Perfect Rag"). Morton's jazz version of Joplin's "Original Rags" is a fascinating example of his "turning every style into his own." He recorded "King Porter" again, but it was not the "King Porter" of 1923 or of 1926. The distinctive "Jelly Roll sound" is there, but every break is a new one and accents pop up where he had never put them before. He made the first commercial recording of "The Crave" that day, and he played and sang "Wining Boy Blues" (not the X-rated version).

New Orleans tunes and memories dominated the other two General sessions as well. In them he played "Naked Dance," and he played and sang "Buddy Bolden's Blues," "Don't You Leave Me Here" (his version of "I'm Alabama Bound"), "Mamie's Blues," and "Michigan Water Blues." This singing is far better than his shouting of "Dr. Jazz" in 1926. The phrasing is easy and sure, and his weary baritone wraps itself firmly around the blues. His playing behind his vocal of "Michigan Water" is spare and bell-like, and, adding stillness to stillness, he puts a breathtaking stop-time into the descending chimes of his piano break. Another superb vocal from this period was a new number, the terse and harmonically edgy "Sweet Substitute," which he recorded for General with Jelly Roll Morton's Seven on January 23, 1940. A January 30 session for General yielded his last four commercial recordings. As was often the case with Morton now, his reward was artistic rather than pecuniary. He was never paid his session fees from General, and he never received any royalties from these classic sides. It was around this time that Jelly tried unsuccessfully to sue for royalties on his Melrose copyrights.

Jelly subsisted on club jobs in New York, but there was occasional national exposure for him. On July 14, 1940, he did two numbers on an NBC radio show, *The Chamber Music Society of Lower Basin Street*. ASCAP finally granted him third-class membership in 1939, and he began to receive small royalty checks for the recordings of his work. (Jelly shared his royalties equally with Roy Carew, who, although he was still living and working in Washington, was acting as Morton's business manager. Carew sent payments, sometimes as low as $5 and under, to

THIS GATHERING OF LEADING BLACK MUSICIANS OCCURRED IN HARLEM IN 1939. FIRST ROW
(L TO R): KAY PARKER, EUBIE BLAKE; SECOND ROW: CECIL MCPHERSON, LUCKEY ROBERTS,
CHRIS SMITH, JAMES P. JOHNSON, PORTER GRAINGER, CLAUDE HOPKINS; THIRD ROW:
JOE JORDAN, TIM BRYMN, WEN TALBERT, HENRY TROY; STANDING IN REAR: ANDY RAZAF,
J. C. JOHNSON, LAWRENCE DEAS, JELLY ROLL MORTON, PERRY BRADFORD, EDGAR SAMPSON.

Morton, representing Morton's half of Victor's quarterly royalties to
him.) Upon hearing of an upcoming Elks' convention in New York City,
Jelly set to work writing a song that he hoped would be adopted as the
organization's theme. He published the tune himself, and began firing off
letters to Elks bandmasters offering them promotional copies. Morton
found takers for a dozen or so free copies, but no one wanted to buy the
others. Unable to recoup even the cost of their printing, he destroyed
them. "We Are Elks" is today the rarest of all Morton publications.

In late October 1940 Morton received word—probably from
Anita—that his godmother had died in Los Angeles. Eulalie Echo was
survived by her second husband, Ed Hunter, who was blind, and Morton
feared that someone would take advantage of him. Jelly knew that Echo
would have left money and diamonds, and he decided to drive out to
help Hunter tend to the estate. He had two old cars, and for some rea-

son, he took them both. He hitched his Cadillac behind his Lincoln and set out.

Morton drove to California by a northern route, in order to stop and see Anita, who had married a lumberjack and was living in Canyon City, Oregon. He met with perilous weather everywhere in the West. He drove through the Rocky Mountains in sleet storms and snow, and he finally had to abandon the Cadillac in Idaho. By November 9 he had made it to Yreka, in northern California, and he was another four days getting to Los Angeles. He took a room at 4052 Central Avenue, and went to see Ed Hunter. His fears for his godmother's estate proved correct. Before Morton arrived, Hunter had signed away everything he owned to an "administrator." Jelly was exhausted from the ordeal of the trip. He sent Mabel $15 for Christmas, but he didn't say when he'd be back.

His letters to Mabel in early 1941 were mostly about his lack of money and his failing health, persistent headaches and shortness of breath. His letters to Carew were about his dreams of forming a big band in L.A. and starting afresh there. He didn't tell Mabel that Anita had come from Oregon to tend him. In February he wrote to say that he was under a doctor's care and that he had been briefly hospitalized after spitting up blood.

That spring Morton sought out David Stuart, the owner of Jazz Man Record Shop (which had issued his D.C. recordings), and the two became friends. Stuart occasionally took him to hear Kid Ory and Mutt Carey when they were playing in town, but Jelly didn't feel up to sitting in with them. The last note to Mabel came in April, a hasty scrawl on a blank money order form, and it said: "Will write soon. Still sick." On July 10, 1941, Morton died of heart failure in Los Angeles County General Hospital.

Morton's death at age fifty was another instance of bad timing. A new interest in traditional jazz, which had been building among musicians and record collectors for several years, was growing into a full-fledged revival on the West Coast, and, had he lived, Morton would have been at the center of it. Late in 1941 the first recordings of Lu Watters's Yerba Buena Jazz Band, a San Francisco group, sent the California revival sound nationwide. Small bands basing their repertoires on the work of Morton and King Oliver sprang up throughout the '40s and '50s, and small record labels were created to record them. Through the ensuing decades, Morton has continued to be the most played and most recorded composer of instrumental jazz.

As the traditionalists increased in number in the '60s and '70s, Morton the pianist—whose playing had influenced none of his contemporaries—began to saturate the styles of young players like Don Ewell, Butch Thompson, Bob Green, Terry Waldo, and James Dapogny. Celebrating the centennial of Morton's birth, in 1990 RCA issued a five-CD set of all of his Victor recordings from 1926 to 1930. A year later, the New Orleans actor Vernel Bagneris first presented his insightful one-man show on Morton in Oslo, Norway. The following year, he impersonated Morton at Michael's Pub in New York City, and in 1994 Bagneris's *Jelly Roll!* —with Morten Gunnar Larsen at the piano—began its long off-Broadway run.

There is not much argument about the origin of jazz anymore, because the creationists have lost to the evolutionists. Most historians now treat jazz as a kind of folk music, invented by everybody who played it a long time ago, and, therefore, by nobody. There is general recognition of Morton, but it is often grudgingly given and usually doled out sparingly. If he cannot be the music's creator, then he must at least be hailed as its Darwin. It is not much, but it is more than he had in his lifetime. If he were here, he would surely try to persuade us to go the rest of the way.

Chapter 8

LOUIS ARMSTRONG

FOR ABOUT THIRTY YEARS, from the early 1940s until his death in 1971, Louis Armstrong was the most beloved entertainer in the world. People smiled when they heard his name and grinned when they heard his voice. He brought a deep and lasting joy that had nothing to do with pop charts or movie stardom; he was loved for his very being. No one, including the three popes who reigned during this period (and who didn't get around as much as Armstrong), received as many warm and extravagant welcomes as he did. Besides the adoration of millions of fans, he owned the unqualified respect of musicians everywhere. And for once, great affection for a celebrity was well placed. Armstrong earned it by his generosity in performance and by his nonstop travels to deliver his gifts. While Santa made his universal rounds in one night, Satchmo took more than three hundred nights a year to make his. Like Santa, Satch knew what everyone wanted, and, unlike Santa, he never disappointed anyone who believed in him.

By the age of twenty-five, Armstrong had been proclaimed a genius, and by thirty, he was recognized as the one who had done the most to advance the art of jazz. But he never talked about "genius" or "art"—his own or anyone else's. He thought of performing as his stock in trade, as what he did for a living. His only aim was to give full value for every record or ticket bought. If he seemed single-minded in his desire to please, it was because he was wholly uncynical about the bargain that entertainers strike with audiences.

For about five years, the music world was in pop-eyed awe of his talent, but because of his utter lack of pretentiousness, his busy-ness, and his taste in material, Armstrong came to be taken for granted very early in his career. After the first two hundred or three hundred recordings and the first thousand or so personal appearances, an Armstrong record or concert, however brilliant, was no more noteworthy than the sun's coming up in the morning. He had relatively few hit records—and no hits among his own compositions—but he had staying power. His first big record came in 1929 and his last (as of this writing) in 1989. No other recording star—not Jolson, not Crosby, not Sinatra—had hit records over seven decades.

And no one influenced the playing and singing of popular music more than Armstrong. Every instrumentalist and singer who came of age in the late 1920s, as well as many who came later, had the same epiphany: the first time he or she heard Louis Armstrong. His effect was so profound that, even as some of his progressive disciples wrote him off as predictable and commercial in the 1950s and 1960s, they still acknowledged their debt to him.

Soon after Armstrong's proclamation as a genius, jazz writers began to ponder the question of how he would husband his great gifts. Would his stewardship take the form of cross-genre experimentation, of flights into serious and extended forms, of recutting his 1920s jewels even more finely? He could have done any of these things, yet he did none of them. Instead of writing jazz cantatas or recreating his masterful solos, Louis spent the last decades of his life leading off approximately three hundred concerts a year with "Back Home Again in Indiana."

Like all geniuses, Armstrong made his own rules, and he chose to satisfy audiences rather than to impress critics or titillate jazz historians.

If highbrows saw his performances as the frittering away of a great talent, too bad. His talent was his coin, and he spent it as he pleased. Instead of chastising him for roads not taken, perhaps those who were disapproving of him should have celebrated the motives and the imagination of a man who could play "Indiana" a thousand different ways and bring delight every time he played it.

◆

Louis Armstrong was born on August 4, 1901, at 719 Jane Alley, a wooden, two-room row house on a blocklong dirt lane between Perdido and Gravier streets in uptown New Orleans. His mother, Mary Albert, was fifteen at the time of his birth, and his father, William Armstrong, was a year or so older. Jane Alley was a shortcut from one bad neighborhood to another, a slum within a slum in the poorest section of the city. The residents of this dilapidated block took what nature brought them: cold in the winter, sweltering summers, and mud when it rained. Jane Alley houses were ugly, with bare cupboards and bare floors, and they shared privies out back.

Willie Armstrong was a day laborer. He shoveled coal into boilers at a turpentine plant, which is to say that he spent twelve hours a day in a place very much like hell. The few dollars a week that Willie brought home didn't go far toward supporting three people, and soon after Louis was born, his teenage parents—who were not married—went their separate ways. Mary Albert, who was called Mayann, moved a few blocks away to live by herself, and, as Armstrong later said, she may have earned her living as a prostitute. Willie's mother, Josephine Armstrong, who was a washwoman, took the infant Louis to live with her. In 1903 Willie and Mayann reunited just long enough to produce another child, Beatrice (whom everyone called Mama Lucy, even when she was a baby), then they split up again.

When Louis was about five, Mayann retrieved him from grandmother Armstrong's care to live with her and Mama Lucy in a one-room house shared by an uncle, an aunt, and several cousins. There was usually something for everyone to eat, but rarely enough for anyone. Everybody's clothes, including the adults', were hand-me-downs. After a year or so,

Louis and Mama Lucy were moved by Mayann again, this time to live with her and her current boyfriend. Despite being shunted from one dreadful home to another, which differed only in degrees of crowdedness and deprivation, Louis was a sunny and outgoing child. He got along well with his mother, his grandmother, his sister, his father's new wife, Gertrude, and his uncle Ike, as well as the various "stepfathers" who passed into and out of his mother's life, and he regarded most of them with affection. The squalor of his early years would have made Dickens shudder, but it never fazed Louis. And as an adult, he recalled his childhood without regret or complaint. He was especially close to his mother, and he admired Mayann's courage and good humor in making her hard way. He said of her: "She was a stocky woman—dark, lovely expression and a beautiful soul. And she instilled in me the idea that what you can't get—to hell with it."

In 1907 Louis was enrolled in the Fisk School for Boys, where he learned to read and where he sang in a choir. But for Louis the best thing about Fisk School was its location: right across the street from Kenna's Hall, a Perdido Street dance pavilion. Commonly known as Funky Butt Hall, Kenna's vibrated with music day and night. Louis was not old enough to go into Funky Butt Hall, but he loved standing outside to listen. And when neighborhood bandsmen took to the streets for Sunday parades, the transforming effect of music became visible to him. Handymen, porters, cigar makers—even laborers, like his father—became grand figures in braided uniforms, marching under elaborate banners, and playing shiny instruments. People who didn't have much to smile about on weekdays smiled when they saw and heard them on Sundays. Barefoot children danced alongside them as they marched; pretty girls waved and called out their names.

Because the cornet was the instrument with the strongest sound, the stars of these neighborhood ensembles were cornetists. There was Manuel Perez, the stalwart of the Onward Brass Band, who was known for his soaring lead in funeral parades; and Bunk Johnson, the player who, Louis thought, had "the best imagination and the softest sense of phrasing"; and Freddie Keppard, whose zigzag figures dominated the Olympia Orchestra. Whatever their weekday jobs, these men were heroes on Sundays, and it was music that conferred heroism on them.

Before he had ever seen a cornet up close, Louis knew that he wanted to play one.

Armstrong said he was not sure whether or not he had heard Buddy Bolden, the first great cornetist-leader in New Orleans, but he could have. Bolden was at the height of his popularity in the early years of the century, and according to local legend, his mighty horn could be heard—and identified—from miles away. (Bolden began having fits of insanity in 1906, and he was confined at East Louisiana State Hospital, an asylum in Jackson, Louisiana, in June 1907. He lived the remaining twenty-four years of his life there.)

By the time he was six or seven, Louis had chosen his idol among the cornetists: a tall, stocky young man named Joseph "King" Oliver. Oliver was more powerhouse than virtuoso, but he had a beautiful tone, especially in the high register. And when he played for dances, he used cups, bottles, and plungers as mutes for his horn, trying to make the sound of a human voice. Oliver was with the Onward Brass Band for a while, playing duets with Manuel Perez, but not even the presence of the great Perez could take Louis's eyes off Oliver. Oliver occasionally chatted with the little boy who was so riveted by his music, and sometimes, when the Onward stopped to rest during the course of a parade, he would let Louis hold his horn. The first cornet that Louis ever had in his hands was probably placed there by King Oliver. When he was an old man, Armstrong recalled the thrill of being befriended by "the baddest sumbitch in Storyville on cornet."

Like the rest of his neighbors, the six-year-old Louis had a living to make. He peddled papers for a while, and then he took a job that would be his mainstay for several years, working on a junk wagon owned by the Karnofsky family. The Karnofskys were Russian Jews who had built a secondhand empire at 427 South Rampart Street out of rags, bottles, iron, and hard work. Their horse-drawn wagons (often with a Karnofsky son, Morris or Alex, at the reins) plied the streets at all hours, collecting and selling their wares. Louis assisted the drivers by retrieving junk to be resold and by honking a tin horn to announce the arrival of the rolling store.

Louis impressed the Karnofskys with his energy and his cheerful nature, and the family practically adopted him. They began to take him home with them at the end of the day, fed him, and gave him clothing.

Morris Karnofsky loaned him two dollars toward the five that he needed to buy a cornet from a pawnshop. Louis paid him back at fifty cents a week, and by the time he paid off his debt, he had taught himself to wring "Home Sweet Home" out of the battered relic. When he was about ten, Louis received a promotion of sorts. He became a runner on the family's coal wagon, jumping on and off all day to deliver the nickel-a-bucket coal as customers called for it. The benefit inherent in this job was that someone occasionally gave him a small tip for lighting a fire with the coal he brought in.

At age eleven, Louis quit school to give himself a longer workday. Through his own diligence and the encouragement of the Karnofskys, he had made it into the fifth grade, but Mayann needed more money than his after-school work could bring in. He stayed with his coal wagon job, of course, and he sang on the streets in a quartet of neighbor boys. He learned that a little extra showmanship, in the form of dancing and making funny faces, pulled in more coins than did singing alone.

One of the passersby who stopped to enjoy the quartet's monkeyshines was Bunk Johnson. Louis liked Johnson's playing, and he was pleased when Johnson noticed him. Johnson became a sometime mentor, taking Louis into cabarets he was not old enough to enter and letting him hang around to watch and listen. Bunk showed him a few things about the horn and taught him the melodies of some pop songs. This was his first glimpse at the life of a working musician, and it confirmed Louis's ambition to become one himself.

Louis's coaching from Johnson was cut short by a prank. On New Year's Eve, 1912, Louis was singing on Rampart Street with his quartet, and he had brought along a noisemaker, a pistol that belonged to a boyfriend of Mayann's. When another boy began to shoot a pistol into the air, Louis decided that it was time to add to the merrymaking by firing off his own. He hauled out his gun and got off a dozen shots before he was nabbed by a policeman. He was put into a wagon and taken to the Juvenile Court building, where he spent a fearful night. On New Year's Day 1913, a judge deemed Louis a menace to public safety and sent him to begin an open-ended sentence at the Colored Waif's Home, a rundown reformatory about five miles outside of New Orleans.

Luckily for its inmates, the Colored Waif's Home was run by an enlightened administrator, a young black man named Joseph Jones. Many institutions for black youth at the time were nothing more than workhouses that exploited the mindless labor of children who were sent there, but Jones tried to bring learning and order to disorderly lives. There was classroom instruction in basic school subjects, and the vocational training included carpentry, gardening, and music—skills that might actually lead to vocations. Discipline was instilled by close-order drill with wooden rifles, and there was swift and harsh punishment for troublemakers. The boys were led through their days by a series of bugle calls that marked the end of one activity and the beginning of another. Because of his strictness and his military style, the Waif's Home supervisor was called "Captain" Jones by his staff and by the 115 boys living under his charge.

After a week or so of unease with institutional living, Louis began to realize that—beginning with regular meals and showers—the Waif's Home had something to offer. What he wanted most was to play in the band, an ensemble of fifteen or so brass instruments and a few percussion players. The director, "Professor" Peter Davis, gave him a try on tambourine, then taught him to play some bugle calls. The boy's gung-ho spirit impressed Davis, and Louis became his prize pupil. Davis moved him up to the cornet and began to teach him to read music. He quickly learned all the cornet parts in the band book. After only a few months, Louis was named the band's student leader. When the Waif's Home ensemble marched in parades and played for picnics, he was the main attraction. His neighbors from "back o' town" thrilled to see him, a minihero in cream-colored uniform and officer's cap, stepping out in front of the band and blowing more horn than anybody else. At one parade, Kid Ory's band was marching behind the Waif's Home unit, and the great trombonist himself complimented Louis's playing.

In June 1914 Louis was pronounced rehabilitated and was sent out from the Waif's Home to live with his father, whom he hardly knew. He was sad to leave, and the staff and the boys hated to see him go. He moved away from the only secure home that he had ever known, back to his old neighborhood, where the only sure thing was hard times. As might have been expected, Willie Armstrong's interest in the boy went only so far. Shortly after his wife, Gertrude, gave birth to their third child, Willie took Louis back to Mayann.

Mayann's family increased by another when Louis, at age fourteen, volunteered to take his cousin Flora's baby for a while. Flora had become pregnant as the result of her molestation by an elderly white man, and Louis's offer of help was the only one she had. Flora died a few months after giving birth, and the baby, Clarence, became Louis's to raise. The young provider was big enough for physical labor now, and he took on a backbreaking job to support his family. He went to work for the C. A. Andrews Coal Company, hauling from 7 A.M. until 5 P.M. His wagon held a ton of coal, and, for fifteen cents a load, Louis loaded the wagon, delivered the coal, and unloaded it at its destination. In the winter he sometimes moved five tons a day. He stayed with it for four years.

Amazingly, Louis had energy enough to play his pawnshop cornet after his days on the coal wagon. His first music job was at Henry Ponce's cafe, a hangout for pimps and whores, where he earned $1.25 a night. King Oliver often came to hear him there, and their mentor-protégé relationship deepened. Oliver was the city's leading cornetist now, and his encouragement meant a great deal, although there was not much that Oliver could do for Louis professionally. (At the height of his local fame, Oliver was making $25 a week leading a band at Pete Lala's cafe and working days as a butler for a white family.) But Oliver gave Louis one of his old cornets, and his wife, Stella, ladled out red beans and rice to him in the Oliver home. Oliver became Louis's "Papa Joe."

The U.S. Secretary of the Navy closed Storyville in November 1917, but this made little difference to any musicians except a dozen or so pianists. Most players worked in the uptown neighborhoods, in the tonks, cafes, and cabarets patronized by those in the black sporting world. A few of the larger saloons on the fringes of Storyville (such as Pete Lala's and Tom Anderson's) hired bands, but even the best players, including Oliver and Armstrong, never set foot inside the grand houses of the district. No whorehouse, black or white, had a band. So, after the shuttering of Storyville, the situation for black musicians was about what it had always been: stringing together enough jobs at parades, picnics, and dances to add up to a living. Although Louis was spending his days on a coal wagon, he was beginning to make a reputation as a musician in the small venues available to him.

There were other rivals to Oliver's throne besides Louis, including

Buddy Petit and Mutt Carey. Although Louis could barely read music and he didn't have much of a repertoire, his imagination was boundless, and even his competition had to admit it. Mutt Carey said in *The Jazz Record* thirty years later:

> I remember once when Louis came out to Lincoln Park in
> New Orleans to listen to the Kid Ory band. I was playing
> trumpet with the Kid then and I let Louis sit on my chair.
> Now at that time I was the "Blues King" of New Orleans and
> when Louis played that day, he played more blues than I ever
> heard in my life. It never did strike my mind that blues could
> be interpreted so many different ways. Every time he played a
> chorus it was different and you knew it was the blues.

Early in 1918 Louis took a job playing in a trio (with a pianist and a drummer) at Henry Matranga's tonk, where his pay was $1.25 a night, exactly what he had earned at Henry Ponce's four years earlier. In June, King Oliver got an offer to lead the band at Chicago's Lincoln Gardens, and he left the cornet chair in Kid Ory's band to take it. When Ory asked Louis to replace his star cornetist, it meant that Louis was now in the first rank. Louis happily accepted Ory's offer. Oscar "Papa" Celestin soon asked Louis to join his Tuxedo Brass Band, and for nearly a year Louis divided his time between Celestin and Ory, two of New Orleans's top leaders.

Louis began seeing a prostitute named Daisy Parker, first as a customer and then as a suitor. Their marriage, late in 1918, put him in another financial bind. He was the provider for five people now (including his mother, his sister, and his "adopted" cousin, Clarence). He and Daisy took Clarence to live with them in a shabby two-room apartment. The marriage was in trouble from the start, filled with bickering, jealousies, and worry over money. When three-year-old Clarence fell off a porch and injured his head, another worry invaded the lives of Louis and Daisy. Doctors told them that he would be mentally disabled for the rest of his life, a child who would grow older but would never grow up. The promise that Louis made at age fourteen became a lifelong obligation.

In the spring of 1919 Louis was playing on the street with the Kid Ory band, when he was heard by Fate Marable, the pianist and bandleader in charge of music for excursion boats owned by the Streckfus family. Marable offered Louis a job in the twelve-piece band on the *Dixie Belle*, which made cruises out of New Orleans every evening. Armstrong took the job, and he quickly saw that he would have to improve his rudimentary note reading to keep it. Marable was a martinet, and Louis worked hard to please him. By the summer his reading had greatly improved, and Marable offered Armstrong $50 a week to join the band on another Streckfus boat, the *Sidney*, which made weeklong cruises back and forth between St. Louis and St. Paul. King Oliver had written Armstrong with vague promises to bring him to Chicago, but without anything concrete from Oliver, there was nothing to do but go with Fate Marable.

The Marable bands played for ballroom dancing, which meant learning pop tunes in middling tempos, short numbers with predictable rhythms. Captain Joe Streckfus demanded decorum on his ships' bandstands, and Marable made sure that he got it. There was no challenge playing, no horsing around, no drinking. In other words, playing for Marable was the exact opposite of playing in an uptown tonk, and any musician who forgot the difference was fired on the spot. As he always did, Louis made the best of it in his three seasons with Marable. He liked being on the boat and making side trips into cities along the river, and the salary was a godsend. He enjoyed the company of the other musicians: drummer Baby Dodds, bassist Pops Foster, banjoist Johnny St. Cyr, and violinist Boyd Atkins among them. In his second season, Louis was even allowed to stretch his solos a bit. But when he wanted to play hotter, Marable reined him in.

Finally Louis got fed up with the constriction of Marable's music, and he turned in his resignation. Armstrong's leaving Marable was a bold move, and it implied more than feeling his oats. A job with the Streckfus line was the best that a New Orleans musician could have in the early '20s—steady, well paying, and prestigious—and Louis's walking away from it showed how serious he was about his development. He preferred to take his chances than to have a secure job that held him back as a player.

On his return to New Orleans, Armstrong found regular work at Tom Anderson's Cafe on Rampart Street and some dates with Papa Celestin for Sunday picnics and dances. His marriage had disintegrated during his time away, and Daisy had taken a lover (another cornetist, Kid Shots Madison, who had been in the Waif's Home band with Louis). His sister, Mama Lucy, had moved to Florida with her boyfriend, and Mayann was working as a laundress and looking after Clarence. Louis settled into the role of local star, always in demand but not really breaking any professional ground.

Then, one day in early August 1922, Louis got the telegram that he had almost stopped dreaming would come: King Oliver was offering him a job with his Creole Jazz Band at the Lincoln Gardens Cafe in Chicago at a salary of $52 a week. The men in the Tuxedo Brass Band tried to talk him out of it, but there was no question of what Louis would do. If Oliver had summoned him to the moon, he would have found a way to get there.

There was one more job for Louis to play, a funeral on August 8, the day he was to leave for Chicago. The trombonist Eddie Vincent's father had died in Algiers, across the river, and Papa Celestin's band was hired to lead the parade from the house to the cemetery. They played "Flee As a Bird to the Mountain," and, since it was known by then that Louis was leaving, not all of the tears shed that day were for the departed Mr. Vincent. Louis hurried home from Algiers to pack and to catch a 7 P.M. train. Mayann made him a fish sandwich to take along, and when Louis arrived at the L & N station, the place was crowded with well-wishers, neighbors, and musicians, including Papa Celestin and his Tuxedo Brass Band. There were sobbed farewells, and there were loud hellos from the porters and waiters on the train who recognized him and wished him luck in Chicago. The roar of Louis's departing train drowned out the shouting of those who loved him, and he was gone.

◆

It was nearly midnight when Louis's train arrived at Chicago's Illinois Central Station. Because there was no one to meet him, a policeman helped him get a taxi to the Lincoln Gardens, at Thirty-first Street and Cottage Grove Avenue. The long ride through the strange city unnerved him, and as the car pulled up in front of the club, Louis was awed by its size and splendor. He had been a hotshot in New Orleans dives, but this big club in this big city was something else. He suddenly felt like a hick. Too intimidated to go in, he stood outside listening to the Creole Jazz Band wailing away. The next thing he knew, King Oliver was bustling out to greet him. Oliver ushered him inside, presented him to the band, and seated him to hear the end of their set. When the band had finished for the night, Oliver took him to his apartment for a late dinner of Stella's red beans and rice. After much talk of old times, his boss escorted Louis to the boardinghouse where a room had been reserved for him. A few hours in Oliver's warm company reassured Louis that perhaps he could make his way in Chicago after all.

Oliver had not used a second cornetist in his Creole Jazz Band before. He created the chair for Louis, and, in doing so he was not only sharing his spotlight with an unknown, he was tinkering with the sound that had brought him great success. No one knew exactly what Louis was to do or how he would fit in. During the several days of rehearsals before Louis's first night at the Lincoln Gardens, he concentrated on his leader intensely. He not only listened to Oliver, he watched him and he read him, figuring out how to walk the tightrope. He had to support Oliver, to add to what he was doing, but he must not take anything away from him.

Louis knew four of the five members of Oliver's band from New Orleans. The clarinetist Johnny Dodds had worked for Kid Ory, and his brother Baby Dodds had played drums for Fate Marable during Louis's time on the Streckfus boats (and had resigned in disgust on the same day that Louis did). The trombonist Honore Dutrey had been in Buddy Petit's orchestra, and Bill Johnson had played tuba in marching bands, as well as string bass and banjo for various ensembles.

The ringer in the Oliver band, and the player Louis had not met before, was the pianist, a petite young woman named Lil Hardin. Hardin was from Memphis, and she had spent a year or so at Nashville's Fisk University before moving to Chicago with her family in 1918. She was working as a sheet-music demonstrator in Jones' Music Store where she caught the eye, if not the ear, of Lawrence Duhé, the New Orleans clarinetist who was the original leader of the Creole Jazz Band. He was impressed with Lil's ability to read music, and he hired her to play with his band at the DeLuxe Cafe. Duhé gave up the band not long after hiring her, and Mutt Carey took it over briefly. When King Oliver succeeded Carey as director of the Creoles, he inherited Lil as his piano player.

Lil was not a very good pianist, but she could play enough to suit the Creole's three leaders, all of whom kept her on. They were all bred in New Orleans, and they shared the New Orleans bandsman's typical indifference to pianists. They had played outdoors more often than they played indoors, and the piano was not used on outdoor jobs. And because the city's best pianists were always occupied in whorehouses—which paid better than the places the bandsmen played—the piano was an afterthought in most New Orleans dance ensembles as well. Most local leaders had never worked with a good pianist, and, beyond filling out the rhythm section, they rarely saw the need for a pianist at all. Lil's vaunted reading ability meant little to the Creole Jazz Band, because they used "head arrangements." She was there to add density to the rhythm, to take the occasional break, and to add a touch of sex to the band's publicity, to be advertised as "The Hot Miss Lil."

Armstrong learned to walk his tightrope very well in the winter of 1922-23. He played harmony under Oliver's lead and discreet fills after phrases, never outplaying his boss but always complementing him. He occasionally cut loose, but only in his own solo choruses. His soloing was so spectacular, however, that he quickly acquired his own following among musicians, black and white.

Word got out that there was a young man with unbelievable chops at the Lincoln Gardens, someone of great agility, who could hit two hundred high Cs in a row! Two cornetists, Johnny Dunn and Freddie Keppard, came by to check him out and challenge him, and he blew each of them off the bandstand. Members of the Paul Whiteman and Isham Jones bands dropped in to marvel at him after their Chicago concerts. Jimmy McPartland, Frank Teschemacher, and Bud Freeman—goggle-eyed white boys from Austin High School—risked the fury of their parents by sneaking off to the South Side to listen to Armstrong.

Hoagy Carmichael drove up from Bloomington to visit his friend Bix Beiderbecke, and Bix took him immediately to hear the New Orleans wonder. Carmichael's recollection, in his autobiography *The Stardust Road*, catches the near-religious ecstasy of those who discovered Louis at the Lincoln Gardens. Hoagy and Bix, packing their own bathtub gin and a handful of "muggles" (marijuana cigarettes), settled at their table to listen, when Armstrong

> slashed into "Bugle Call Rag." I dropped my cigarette and gulped my drink. Bix was on his feet, his eyes popping. . . . "Why," I moaned, "why isn't everybody in the world here to hear that?" I meant it. Something as unutterably stirring as that deserved to be heard by the world. Then the muggles took effect and my body got light. Every note Louis hit was perfection. I ran to the piano and took the place of [Lil]. They swung into "Royal Garden Blues." I had never heard the tune before, but somehow I knew every note. I couldn't miss. I was floating in a strange deep-blue whirlpool of jazz. It wasn't marijuana. The muggles and the gin were, in a way, stage props. It was the music. The music took me and had me and it made me right.

Oliver and Armstrong devised a stunt that made it look as if Louis had supernatural powers. As Oliver improvised breaks, Louis took the same breaks in harmony with him, seemingly reading Oliver's mind as they invented music in perfect unison. Years later Armstrong explained how they did it: "While the rest of the band was playing, Oliver'd lean over to me and move the valves on his cornet in the notes he would play in the next breaks or a riff he'd use. So I'd play second to it." The feat is impressive even after the trickery is revealed, because it shows Armstrong's enormous powers of concentration. He could figure out and remember harmony to an unheard melody (by "seeing" it) while the band was playing something else entirely.

As Armstrong's South Side fame grew, he became something of a city slicker. He traded his boxy, threadbare suits for snappier ones, and he began to squire Lil around the city in her secondhand Hudson. He changed his bowl-cut hairstyle to a sharper "natural," and he lost some weight. He started attending the theater, and he became a great admirer of Bill Robinson. He moved out of the boarding house and took an apartment—with a shower—at 459 East Thirty-first Street. He bought a typewriter and he found that it relaxed him to type long letters to his New Orleans friends.

King Oliver's Creole Jazz Band, Chicago, May 1923. L to r: Honore Dutrey (trombone); Baby Dodds (drums); King Oliver (cornet); Louis Armstrong (slide cornet); Lil Hardin (piano), Bill Johnson (banjo), Johnny Dodds (clarinet). Courtesy the Frank Driggs Collection

On April 6, 1923, King Oliver's Creole Jazz Band took a four-hour train ride from Chicago to the Gennett studios in Richmond, Indiana, to make their first recordings. The session was probably arranged by the publisher Walter Melrose, who had begun sending artists to Gennett to record his company's songs the previous year. Melrose Music had already published a Lil Hardin song, and the company would soon add King Oliver to its roster of writers. Because no hotel in Richmond would accommodate blacks, the Creole Jazz Band would have a few hours in the studio, then would take the train home.

Oliver's band was rehearsed and ready, but the primitive conditions at Gennett frustrated even the best-prepared performers. The studio was a long, narrow box in a converted factory building on the grounds of the Starr Piano Company. There was a railroad track a few feet from the front door, and in an attempt at soundproofing, the walls had been filled with sawdust and hung with heavy draperies. The result was an oppressively hot, sound-dead room, wherein the rumblings of passing trains could be heard but musicians standing a few feet apart could barely hear each other. The acoustic recording process involved catching sound in two megaphone-shaped cardboard horns hung from a pipe on the wall. The sound passed to a stylus behind the wall that etched its vibrations onto a soft-wax master disc.

A Gennett session always began with the near-hopeless search for balanced sound. Under the direction of engineer Ezra Wickemeyer, the performers had to move themselves about the room, standing in various groupings at various distances from the immobile sound-catchers, until test pressings yielded some tolerable standoff between the instruments that would carry the melody and those that would supply the rhythm. For the Creole Jazz Band, all of whom were new to studio work, the process was tiresome and confusing. Only Lil was stoic during all the moving around and starting and stopping.

It was finally decided that Oliver would be nearest the megaphones, and that Lil's piano, Bill Johnson's banjo, and Baby Dodds's drums would be close to but slightly behind him. Johnny Dodds's clarinet and Honore Dutrey's trombone would be further away. And to keep a balance of power, literally and figuratively, Louis would stand completely apart, off in a corner about fifteen feet from the rest of the band.

Gennett's reputation for imperfect sound was upheld that day, but the nine sides made by the Creole Jazz Band show them to be a lively bunch. They were an ensemble, first of all, with the rowdy, cheerful group ethos that has always characterized New Orleans band recordings. Oliver is first among equals, driving the tunes with frequent solos but also providing countermelodies for those who take up the lead after he is through with it. He chose to use a mute on several numbers, so the clarinet is often the dominant instrument in terms of pure sound. (Lil's piano is almost inaudible except on her solos, and, in order to be heard at all, Baby Dodds played woodblocks rather than drums.) Oliver's muted solo on "Dippermouth Blues" is his loosest and best of the day, and "Snake Rag" and "Weather Bird Rag" are studded with the Oliver-Armstrong duet playing that demonstrates the perfect unison they were renowned for.

Amid the ensemble camaraderie, Louis bursts in with two brief solos, and they are startling to hear. The first comes late in "Chimes Blues," after a heavy-handed imitation of chimes by Lil. What he plays is not a jazz improvisation at all, but the embellishment of a rag theme, making an eight-measure melody out of a simple rhythmic figure. Louis plays with the five-note phrase like a puppy with a sock, collaring it for two strains and shaking it every raggy way but loose. The second solo is Louis's searing treatment of the trio of Jelly Roll Morton's "Froggie Moore." His tone is big and brilliant, more powerful than Oliver's. He does more than drive the tune, he swings it. No cornetist before him had ever shown such authority and imagination on a recording. The total time of both solos is just under two minutes, but they are like heat lightning. Suddenly and briefly, Armstrong illuminates the landscape around him.

Louis would make thirty-seven sides with Oliver's band—six more for Gennett, four for Columbia, three for Paramount, and fifteen for OKeh—all of them in 1923. Possibly protecting his own reputation, Oliver rarely let Louis solo on records after that first session (with the notable exception of two choruses of "Riverside Blues," made in late October for OKeh). If Louis felt slighted, he never mentioned it.

Lil, however, talked of nothing except Oliver's slights. She and Louis were live-in lovers by this time, and she complained incessantly about his hero's treatment of him. She knew that Louis was the better cornetist, and she knew that the crowds who packed the Lincoln Gardens every night were there to hear Louis, not Oliver. She thought that he deserved, at least, featured billing, and she suspected that he would never get it. She was dismayed to learn that Oliver was withholding part of Louis's salary and was giving him an "allowance" every week instead of his full wages. She had written tunes with Oliver and had seen herself credited on copyright forms as "arranger." She tried to head off any tune theft from Louis by showing him how to copyright his own compositions. (There were nine copyrights registered in Armstrong's name in 1923, the most he would ever register in a single year. Lil's name is on five of them as arranger, on one as lyricist, and on three as co-composer.) However uncomfortable Louis was with Lil's harping about his benefactor, he was grateful for her coaching him in sight-reading and for the informal "music appreciation" course that she devised to introduce him to the classics.

On February 5, 1924, Louis and Lil were married. She bought an eleven-room house for them at 421 East Forty-fourth Street, and the place soon filled up. Lil's mother moved in, and Louis sent to New Orleans for Clarence. Louis's mother, Mayann, moved to Chicago and lived nearby for a time. She was a frequent guest, as was Louis's best friend, the drummer Zutty Singleton. Louis bought Lil a new piano, and Jelly Roll Morton sometimes dropped by to play it.

Lil was not the only source of dissension in Oliver's band in the spring of 1924. The other players found out that their boss was shorting them on payday, and they suspected that he was withholding record royalties from them. (Of the four labels for which they recorded, only Gennett had a royalty agreement with its artists. However, Gennett's distribution was so poor that there were probably no royalties owed to the Creole Jazz Band.) The hostility toward their leader became so open and so intense that Oliver began packing a pistol on the bandstand. When Oliver booked a short tour in midyear, the entire band, except for Louis and Lil, refused to go. The boss hired replacements and went without them.

But during the tour Lil's unceasing complaint finally had its effect. When they came home, Louis reluctantly gave Oliver his notice. Because Louis did not have a job to go to, Lil thought she had better keep hers. After all her rabble-rousing about leaving Oliver, she stayed on as the only original member of the group that had come to fame at the Lincoln Gardens. After a few uneasy weeks without work, Louis took the first offer he got, to play first cornet in the band being organized by a Chicago singer named Ollie Powers.

Louis did not stay with Powers long, because he was soon invited by Fletcher Henderson to join the Henderson orchestra in New York. When he was passing through New Orleans on tour with Ethel Waters in 1921, Henderson had heard Louis and had offered him a job then. But Louis didn't want to leave New Orleans by himself. He told Henderson that if there were also a job for his friend Zutty Singleton, he would go. There wasn't, so Louis stayed home. There was no turning down Henderson this time. He was the best-known and best-connected black bandleader of the day, and he was an established recording artist. He had recently been chosen to provide the house band for Broadway's most prestigious ballroom, Roseland. Even with such an opportunity beckoning to him, Louis felt that he had to explain to King Oliver why he was leaving Chicago. He asked Oliver for his blessing, and, however cool the blessing may have been, he got it. By the end of September 1924, Louis was in New York, rehearsing for Roseland.

Fletcher Henderson led the first large band—eleven men, including Henderson as pianist and Armstrong as third cornetist—to play jazz, and, although he was not as priggish as Fate Marable, he, too, played "refined" jazz for dancing. In the Henderson band book of 1924, "By the Waters of Minnetonka" and "Where the Dreamy Wabash Flows" shared space with "Charley, My Boy" and Tin Pan Alley blues. Armstrong's reading skills came in handy as he picked his way through the arrangements by Henderson and his reed player, Don Redman. Only a day or so into rehearsals, Henderson decided that he didn't like the sound of Armstrong's cornet and advised him to switch to the trumpet, which had a mellower tone. Louis, ever the loyal employee, unquestioningly went out and got a trumpet. He quickly adapted his fingering and embouchure to the new instrument, and began to do the same dazzling things he had done on the cornet. (He would alternate between the two for about three years, before finally settling on the trumpet in mid-1928.)

Chicago had daunted Armstrong, but New York did not. He had a reputation now, and he had no qualms about going into Roseland. The band was a hit, and Louis was the hit of the band. He was a solid section player when an arrangement required it, and his solo flights were unlike anything ever heard in New York. His effect on musicians was the same as it had been in Chicago: initial disbelief at his technique that melted into reverence for the feeling behind the technique. The cornetist Rex Stewart remembered catching Armstrong fever when Louis first hit New York:

> I went mad with the rest of the town! I tried to walk like him,
> talk like him, eat like him, sleep like him. I even bought a pair
> of big policeman shoes like he used to wear and stood outside
> his apartment waiting for him to come out so I could look at
> him. Finally, I got to shake hands and talk with him.

In five years or so, after Armstrong's vocalizing had become familiar, singers would be hanging their heads out of car windows on their way to jobs, trying to make themselves hoarse, so that they could sound like him.

Within a week of his arrival in New York, Louis was in the Columbia studios with the Henderson band. The two sides that they made include tantalizing patches of Armstrong, but there is not enough of him. They set the pattern for the forty or so sides that he made with Henderson: the music comes alive when Armstrong is out front, and it is ordinary when he is not. Henderson allowed Louis to record one vocal ("Everybody Loves My Baby" in November 1924), but he thought Louis's singing too odd to be featured again. Armstrong could stretch further at Roseland than he could on the Henderson recordings. Every night he broke up the place with his extended solos, his high notes, and his vocals. He even did some improvised comedy with a character he created, the Reverend Satchelmouth, a hypocritical preacher. Henderson did not keep him in a straitjacket, but he did not let him roam free either at Roseland or in the studio.

During his thirteen months with Henderson, Armstrong was in great demand as a sideman and as an accompanist for blues singers, and it was in these non-Henderson sessions that he made his best recordings of the period. Clarence Williams got Louis into the studio often and, even when using him as an anonymous sideman, let him play. In the last three months of 1924, Louis mixed it up with Sidney Bechet (his only rival as an improviser) on "Texas Moaner Blues" with Clarence Williams's Blue Five, and he accompanied blues singers Alberta Hunter, Eva Taylor, and Sippie Wallace (when each was backed by the Blue Five). And, along with Fletcher Henderson and five other Henderson band members, he played on Ma Rainey's classic "See See Rider." Before 1925 was half gone, Louis had accompanied Clara Smith and Trixie Smith, and he had made nine sides with Bessie Smith, the "empress of the blues" herself. Although he was not the star of any of these sessions, he performed brilliantly. He was a good team player, but he could also carry the ball.

Lil came to New York to check on Louis several times. During her first trip, in November 1924, Clarence Williams invited her to play with his Red Onion Jazz Babies, a studio group created to feature Armstrong. The eight Red Onion sides (five of them featuring Alberta Hunter's vocals), along with the Armstrong-Bechet Blue Fives, were hotter than any jazz recorded in New York before. What they had in common was Louis Armstrong and Clarence Williams, the producer who showcased him.

As Lil assessed Louis's situation in New York, she didn't like what she saw. With one exception, every musician in town was declaring him a phenomenon, and the holdout was Fletcher Henderson. Louis was packing Roseland as he had packed the Lincoln Gardens, yet Henderson had not given him featured billing, nor was Louis mentioned in the band's publicity. Louis's $55-a-week salary was augmented a bit by his studio fees, but he was not earning what he should, Lil thought. She urged him to leave Henderson and come back to Chicago. She was putting together a band for the Dreamland Cafe, and she offered him $75 a week and promised to bill him as "The World's Greatest Cornet Player."

Whether Lil's offer indicated possessiveness or generosity on her part is hard to tell. She was right about Henderson's underusing Louis, but, if her interest was solely in his career, why did she not peddle him to other bandleaders in New York? Any band in town could have had him for $60 a week. And given the shaky state of their marriage, why did she want him back in Chicago? She had been seeing someone else, and he had begun an affair with a Cotton Club dancer. Louis said he'd wait and see what happened with Henderson.

The Roseland job lasted through May 1925, then Louis went on a four-month tour of New England with the Henderson band. Still waffling over Lil's offer, he started the new season at Roseland in early October. Finally there was an ultimatum from Lil: come back to Chicago at once or don't come back at all. Louis gave Henderson his notice. He made two more sessions with Clarence Williams's Blue Five in late October (probably for the money) and one session with Perry Bradford's Jazz Phools on November 2 (two sides that sound like they were made for the fun of it). Then he went home to his wife in Chicago. Within a week or so of his arrival, Lil delivered what she had promised: star billing and $75 a week at Dreamland.

Louis got a studio job almost immediately after his return, on November 9, to work for Richard M. Jones, the black pianist who was recording director of OKeh's race series. Jones himself often provided piano accompaniments for his blues singers, and he asked Louis to play cornet with him as he backed Blanche Calloway and Chippie Hill in separate sessions on the same day. Jones, of course, knew Louis's work before these sessions, but it was these accompaniments that caught the attention of Jones's boss, Elmer A. Fearn. Soon after the day with Calloway and Hill, someone at OKeh—either Jones, Fearn, or the New York boss, Tommy Rockwell—had an idea for Louis, and the company acted on it quickly. It was decided that Armstrong and a few musicians of his choice should record some small-band jazz. Midmorning on November 12, Armstrong walked into the OKeh studios to make his first records with a group he called the Hot Five.

There would be twenty-four succeeding dates, yielding a total of sixty released sides by Louis Armstrong and his small bands, the Hot Five and the Hot Seven. Not one of them is less than good, and most are brilliant. Armstrong was already the best improvisational player alive when he began the series—and he had already made more than 150 recordings—and by the time the series ended, he had taken his playing to unimaginable heights. The Fives and Sevens document Armstrong's three-year exploration of his awesome gifts. Because they were issued on a race label, there were no big hits among them, but there were enough good sellers to keep them coming. They remained in OKeh's catalog for years, and by the end of the 1920s even white record buyers knew of them and wanted them.

Four members of the original Hot Five were New Orleans cohorts: Armstrong, cornet; Kid Ory, trombone; Johnny Dodds, clarinet; and Johnny St. Cyr, banjo. This group, with Lil at the piano, would remain constant for a year of Hot Five recordings (twenty-four sides). The band jelled immediately. Their earliest recordings were made in the New Orleans style: everyone played together most of the time, with individuals featured on breaks more than in extended solos. But this is ensemble playing with an extra ingredient: the open and instantly likable personality of Louis Armstrong. There was not much music on paper: only sketches that roughed out the introductions, the order of breaks or solos, and the return to ensemble playing that ended the tunes. Armstrong's personal style was not written into anything that could be called "arrangements" (as Morton's was with the Red Hot Peppers), but it permeates everything.

Kid Ory later recalled the Hot Five records as "the easiest I ever made," and he described Armstrong's laissez-faire style as a leader:

When we'd get in the studio, if we were going to do a new number, we'd run it over a couple of times before we recorded it. We were a very fast recording band. . . . We spoiled very few records, only sometimes when one of us would forget the routine or the frame-up, and didn't come in when he was supposed to. . . . After we'd make a side, Louis would say, "Was that all right?" And if one of us thought we could do it over and do it better, why, Louis would tell them we wanted to do it again, and so we would do it over. I think one reason those records came out so well was that the OKeh people left us alone and didn't try to expert us. Another reason was, we all knew each other's musical styles so well from years of working together. And then, of course, there was Louis himself. You couldn't go wrong with Louis.

One of the three numbers recorded by the Hot Five on November 12 was an Armstrong composition called "Gut Bucket Blues." It is an ordinary twelve-bar blues tune, made as an ordinary circle of soloing, but in it Louis does a very natural—and as yet unheard-of—thing: he introduces the band. He shouts encouragement to each of them—and calls three of them by name—as his or her solo begins. The last solo is Louis's, and Ory does the honor for their leader, calling on him to "Do that thing, Papa Dip" (short for "Dippermouth," his New Orleans nickname). Louis's shouted introductions—"Play that thing, Mr. St. Cyr"; "Whip that thing, Miss Lil"; and "Mr. Johnny Dodds, do that clarinet, boy"— show him, in their first session, leading his band out of the anonymity of the New Orleans style that was their model. By telling us who is playing, he asserts his claim that music is made by individuals, not units.

There was a short session for the Hot Five on February 22, 1926, which yielded only a single side. But at their third session, on February 26, momentous things happened. One of them was the premiere recording of Kid Ory's "Muskrat Ramble," which would remain a Dixieland standard for decades. More immediately significant was Louis's playing of "Cornet Chop Suey." Except for a piano solo in the middle, it is all Louis—on extended cornet solos that begin and end the tune. It was the longest solo that Armstrong had done on a recording up to that time, and if there were any doubt remaining in February 1926 as to who the boss cornetist was, "Cornet Chop Suey" settled the matter. It opens with Louis's raggy improvisation on a bugle call, after which he begins taking potshots at the melody, darting among the harmonics as he blasts, pings, and glances off it. A hint of vibrato on the tail of his notes gives warmth to the fierce playing. After Lil's feature, he attacks the tune again, with a long series of tricky configurations over a stop-time accompaniment. When it seems that his ideas will spill out forever and will lead him God knows where, Armstrong ends the piece with a paraphrase of his paraphrase on the opening bugle call, wrapping it all up with a unity that is both surprising and satisfying. Louis's pyrotechnics are so effortlessly displayed that he doesn't give the impression of showing off. He sounds like someone playing the cornet wonderfully, rather than a cornet machine.

The other landmarks of that February day were two vocals, the first that Louis made with the Hot Five. One of them has been justly celebrated over the years, and the other has been unjustly neglected. The neglected one is his masterful singing of two choruses of "Georgia Grind." After a starchy vocal by Lil, Louis slips into the song, doing a "straight" reading of the lyric, but playing with the melody and tweaking the beat as he subtly bends and smears the words. It is an easy and charming performance that vastly improves a so-so song, and there had been no recorded singing quite like it. As good as it is, "Georgia Grind" was left in the dust that was stirred up by his second vocal of the day.

The second song of Armstrong's was Boyd Atkins's "Heebie Jeebies," a dance song celebrating a nonexistent dance, with a vague and banal lyric that never says what the "heebie jeebies" is/are. After cornet and clarinet solos, Louis takes two vocal choruses back to back, his gravel voice set against Johnny St. Cyr's banjo, the only accompaniment. In the first chorus he begins to break free of the words as well as the melody and the beat. He slurs some words and omits others altogether, carving up phrases until the original near-senseless lyric makes no sense at all. Then, in the second chorus, he leaves language altogether, singing an astonishing variety of nonsense syllables: growls, deedles, grunts, and moans. Of course, behind his vocal gobbledygook was the same rhythmic imagination that fired his cornet playing, and the effect is eerie and liberating, as if he were floating in space with nothing tying him to a moribund tune. The novelty of Armstrong's vocal made "Heebie Jeebies" the Hot Five's first big record, racking up a sale of forty thousand copies a few weeks after its release. (A race record that sold twenty thousand copies was considered a smash.)

What Louis did to "Heebie Jeebies" would come to be known as scat singing. It was an old device, a kind of humming-while-singing that went as far back as early black vaudeville and perhaps further. Although Armstrong was not the first to do it, he was the first to do it on a record. As his cornet playing expanded the minds of instrumentalists, his scatting showed singers the uses of abstraction. Scatting requires great nerve (to leave words and thought, trusting that something better will be improvised to replace them) and great technique (to invent a variety of sounds and to combine them in a way that makes musical sense). Only a few singers have put scatting at the center of their styles—Armstrong, Ella Fitzgerald, Betty Carter, and Mel Torme are the major ones—but almost every singer since Armstrong has used it to set a casual mood or to make a rhythmic showpiece of a familiar number.

Louis had worked for Lil at Dreamland for about a month when Erskine Tate made him an offer to play trumpet in his twenty-piece orchestra at the Vendome Theatre, a huge silent-movie house at Thirty-first and State streets. With the understanding that Louis would still put in late evenings at Dreamland, Lil encouraged him to go. The Vendome's "Little Symphony" played film accompaniment—from cue sheets prepared for each film and distributed by the producing company—and it performed overtures and light classics between showings of the film. Although he was at first nervous about reading the symphonic scores, Louis was soon in command of them all, not only able to play "Cavalleria Rusticana" but able to bend it to his will. The barrage of high notes from his trumpet, the usual big finish for his classical numbers, caused pandemonium at the Vendome. (At this time he was using the trumpet for live performances and the cornet for recordings.)

One of Louis's fans at the Vendome was a pretty girl named Alpha Smith, who used her housemaid's salary to purchase front-row seats several times a week to hear him. After a flirtation across the footlights, they began seeing each other. They had become so involved by the spring of

1926 that Louis (and Clarence) moved out of Lil's house to live with Alpha and her parents. Louis's leaving Lil meant that he also had to leave his job at Dreamland. He would continue to record with Lil, but he did not want to see her every evening. Thanks to Carroll Dickerson, he didn't have to.

Dickerson led the band at the Sunset Cafe, a large "black and tan" (a club with a racially mixed clientele) managed by a small-time hood named Joe Glaser. At the urging of his pianist, Earl Hines, Dickerson asked Louis to play in the Sunset's late-night floor shows. So Louis juggled two jobs, playing four shows a day with the Vendome Orchestra, then rushing a few blocks away, to Thirty-fifth and Calumet, to play at the Sunset beginning at midnight. He was a trumpet star at both places, and he was a singer and comic presence in the Sunset's floor show. His feature song was "Big Butter and Egg Man," which he used as an excuse for horseplay with his singing partner, May Alix. (Their performance was preserved at a Hot Five session in November 1926.) Not long after Louis joined the Sunset band, Dickerson's drinking began to get on Joe Glaser's nerves. Glaser fired Dickerson and put Louis in charge of the group, renaming them Louis Armstrong and His Stompers.

As busy as Armstrong was with the Hot Fives, the Vendome, and the Sunset early in 1926, he kept up his freelancing in OKeh's studios. The company's singers—including Chippie Hill, Hociel Thomas, and Sippie Wallace—brought out the best in Louis as a collaborator, as these records prove. He never dominates the vocalists or competes with them: he supports them as they lead the way. With Columbia Records' purchase of OKeh in 1926, all of Armstrong's recordings, as star or sideman, began to get better distribution.

On May 28, 1926, Armstrong had two sessions that produced two gems each for Vocalion. With a twelve-man edition of Erskine Tate's Vendome Orchestra, he played fiery figures around the intricate chord changes of "Static Strut," and on "Stomp Off, Let's Go" he showed that, even with a muted trumpet, he could swing an ensemble of eleven men. Both of these Vendome sides feature the bounding piano of Teddy Weatherford, the best pianist with whom Louis had worked so far.

In a blatant act of disloyalty to OKeh—if not outright breach of contract—Lil went into the Vocalion studio, also on May 28, with the original members of the Hot Five to record under the name of Lil's Hot Shots. They produced two loose and swingy numbers, "Georgia Bo-Bo" and "Drop That Sack," both featuring Louis's highly recognizable cornet. The identity of Lil's chief Hot Shot could not have puzzled record buyers, nor was it a mystery in the offices at OKeh. It was said that Louis got called on the carpet by an OKeh executive, who played the Vocalion recording of "Georgia Bo-Bo" and asked him who he thought was singing. He replied, "I don't know, but I won't do it again."

The large bands at the Vendome and the Sunset gave Louis the idea to expand his Hot Five. In May 1927 he added Pete Briggs's tuba and Baby Dodds's drums to make the first recordings with his Hot Seven. Briggs's tuba boots the band along, and Dodds's weight in the rhythm section gives the group a fuller sound. The band's personality is essentially unchanged because Louis is still at its center. Armstrong liked having the extra instruments around him, and over the next year and a half, there would be more Hot Seven sessions, as well as some Hot Fives with six players.

By 1927 cornetists had stopped challenging Louis in clubs. There was simply no point, and everyone knew it. He could outplay anyone else, and there was no weakness in him. He had the most agile imagination of any instrumentalist, and whatever his mind could conceive, his fingers and embouchure could instantly execute. He could put a dozen shadings into the dynamics of a single phrase, and he could swing a quarter note. In a time when a high B-flat was considered the stratosphere for a cornetist, Armstrong could easily hit the C above it (and he eventually worked his way up to high Fs). Best of all, despite his mighty technique, he never gave the impression that he was bombarding the listener with tricks or bullying the ensemble around him. His most spectacular fireworks were lit in the service of music, to freshen the tune, to show how many facets it could have if one only turned it at enough angles to see them all. His blazing sound had warmth as well as light.

Armstrong's sound could be caught on recordings but not on paper. At the request of publisher Walter Melrose, Louis went into a studio and noodled some figures on his horn as the recording apparatus ran. A staffer copied them down to make the contents of two 1927 Melrose folios: *Louis Armstrong's 125 Jazz Breaks for Cornet* and *Louis Armstrong's*

50 Hot Choruses for Cornet. Although these folios became the old and new testaments for young cornetists in the late 1920s, the study of them produced no more Louis Armstrongs.

The latter half of 1927 brought bumpy times to Louis. His stint with the Vendome Orchestra ended in April, and the Sunset Cafe closed a few months later. Suddenly at loose ends, the hottest trumpeter in Chicago began to take one-shot jobs with various theater and club bands—with Clarence Jones's Metropolitan Theatre Orchestra, at Blackhawk's Restaurant, at the Persian Palace—all good gigs, but no more than gigs. His mother, Mayann, died, and her passing (at age forty-one) stunned him. Armstrong put the money he had saved into a $4,000 advance for a year's lease on a building that he wanted to turn into a dance hall. His planning and management were so inept that the project foundered immediately, and he was stuck with an ironclad lease on a shuttered club. On the night that his club closed, someone stole his Hupmobile. He could always make records, of course, so he did. But in late 1927 the $50 session fees were no longer pocket change, they were his main income.

In December 1927 Armstrong took the original members of the Hot Five into the OKeh studios for what would be their last three sessions together. The guitarist Lonnie Johnson was added to the Five for two numbers, "I'm Not Rough" and "Hotter Than That." Johnson's playing sparked Louis's all-scat vocal on "Hotter Than That," which also has a guitar call- and scat-response section. In "Struttin' with Some Barbecue" and "Once in a While," Armstrong bites off cornet phrases so ferociously that they sound, at least in hindsight, like flashes of impatience. Given his doleful state of mind in late 1927, he may have been fed up with his band, as with so many other things. His playing seems to say, "If you won't swing, by God, I will."

Whether or not Louis felt constricted by his ensemble, it is obvious from these records that he had continued to mature and his Hot Five had not. The Hot Five records had been vehicles for Louis since their inception, but by this time no vehicle built on the New Orleans model could carry or contain him. Although they were well executed, the ideas of Dodds and Ory were beginning to sound a bit old-fashioned, and Lil's thump-thump piano was no fresher than her shouting of the vocals she shared with Louis. Unlike the rest of the Five, Louis had gone places and done things beyond New Orleans and Chicago. He had met the challenges of playing with symphonic bands, as well as show bands and dance orchestras. He had backed the best blues singers in the world, and he had thrusted and parried with Sidney Bechet. He had come a long way out of the corner of the Gennett studio, and he was capable of going further. He needed people around him who, if they weren't capable of evolving with him, could at least nurture his own evolution. He did not fire the first Hot Five—he just never hired them again.

In March 1928 Carroll Dickerson took Louis into the group he had formed as the house band for a new dance palace, the Savoy Ballroom. The club was the current hot spot for Chicago dancers, and live radio broadcasts of its dance music sent the sound of the Savoy around the Midwest. Dickerson had reassembled many of the players from his (and Louis's) old Sunset Cafe band, with the exception of his former pianist, Earl Hines. When Louis had taken over the Sunset band early in 1926, Hines, at age twenty, was its most advanced player. The two became friends, and Hines was an investor (and co-loser) in Louis's ill-fated venture as a club owner. However, Hines was unavailable for the Savoy job because he had recently been hired by Jimmy Noone to play at the Apex Club.

Louis enjoyed playing with Dickerson's band at the Savoy, and when the next call came from OKeh, he chose four of them to be in the new edition of the Hot Five. But he passed over the Savoy's pianist in favor of the player he had longed to work with, Earl Hines. Their association in the recording studio would last only six months, but it spurred Louis's playing beyond anything he had ever done.

On June 27, 1928, Louis and the revamped Hot Five went into the OKeh studios for the first time. Besides his new players, Louis also had a new instrument that day, the trumpet. He had never used the trumpet for his small-band recordings before, but he would play it exclusively from now on. Partly because of the trumpet, but mostly because of Earl Hines, the new Five had a sound that was very different from the old: it was brisk, airy, and clean. Armstrong's playing was not only held aloft by the new ensemble, it was sent soaring. Hines was a highly rhythmic pianist, and his touch was so nimble that he could join Louis in his dizzy orbit as Lil never could.

The new Five made three tunes in their first session. Hines's piano solos in the two instrumentals, "Fireworks" and "Skip the Gutter," with their daring runs and stabbing single-note melody playing, show that Armstrong had influenced him well before they got into the studio. Writers would characterize Hines as a "trumpet-style" player, and the trumpet he had in mind was Armstrong's. The highlight of "Skip the Gutter" is a Louis-Hines duet, minus the rhythm section. It is a tradeoff of call-and-response phrases, but it doesn't sound like a contest. It is more like the gossiping of two excited friends.

The third side of the day was a Hines composition called "A Monday Date," a pretty song that prompted Louis' first attempt at singing a ballad. The band takes the number in a brisk 4/4, but Armstrong croons his vocal. He not only aims at the melody notes, he hits them and he holds them. His voice is sandpaper, but his phrasing is smooth. He sounds as though he believes the words he's singing. He ends with a fillip of scat as if to say "I was only kidding," but he wasn't kidding. Within a couple of years, he would be among the most affecting of ballad singers.

At the new Five's second session, on June 28, they produced what is arguably the best jazz record ever made. It was a King Oliver tune called "West End Blues," and it is wonderful because it is mostly Louis, delivering everything he knows about the dignity, sorrow, and grit of the blues. The dignity comes first, with an opening cadenza that climbs and descends a cubist's ladder made of the twelve notes of the chromatic scale. The descent leaves him in the middle register, where, over the band's plodding rhythm, he begins a mournful statement of the melody. By the end of his first solo, Louis is adding tension by providing his own fills at the end of phrases, with the last fill a handoff to Fred Robinson's doleful trombone. The clarinet enters next, and Louis scats a rough vocal obbligato to the clarinet line. Hines follows, parsing the melody out in piano runs, then Louis is back, holding a high note for four full measures while the rhythm moves implacably beneath him. Louis stirs from his one-note reverie to end the tune in a pensive and unspectacular way. Hines plays a bell-like tag, and Louis answers it with a short, sighing cadenza. In three minutes Armstrong has said everything that could possibly be said with "West End Blues," and his performance is perfect in its conception and completeness.

Other treasures from the Hot Five's late-June and early-July sessions included "Sugar Foot Strut," "Two Deuces," and "Knee Drops." On June 29 Louis made a vocal experiment out of Fats Waller's "Squeeze Me" by wordlessly singing over the harmonized humming of Hines and banjoist Mancy Carr.

Louis played at the Savoy through the end of 1928. In December, when OKeh scheduled more Armstrong dates, the company attempted to capitalize on his radio fame by renaming his group. There were two sessions by Louis Armstrong and His Orchestra (a group of six, including Armstrong) and two by Louis Armstrong and His Savoy Ballroom Five (seven, including Armstrong). The orchestra made three sides, including "Muggles," a bluesy meditation on pot, which Louis had recently discovered. The Savoy Five had a tighter sound than the orchestra because, for the first time, Louis used actual arrangements in his small-band work. Alex Hill arranged the scuffling "Beau Koo Jack," and Don Redman charted the other five sides. Both arrangers left plenty of room for Louis and Hines to solo.

On December 5, 1928, Louis and Hines recorded a duet without the band. They chose an Armstrong tune called "Weather Bird," and the record is remarkable for the full sound achieved by only two instruments. It is a busy number that shows both players flirting with abstraction, often skipping notes in three-over-four figures and taking great departures from the melody. There is an exciting break in the middle, with Louis and Earl in a tussle between two intricate syncopations. When "Weather Bird" was made, neither of them knew that it would be their last major collaboration.

Early in 1929 Louis was summoned to New York by Tommy Rockwell, the head of OKeh records. OKeh's investment in Armstrong and his various groups had paid off, and Rockwell, acting as Louis's de facto manager, had some ideas about expanding his career. Rockwell knew that Armstrong was beginning to attract white fans, and he wanted to hasten white acceptance of Louis by getting him into a Broadway show. Before Louis arrived in New York—with several members of his Chicago studio band in tow—Rockwell had talked Vincent Youmans into using him in his forthcoming musical, *Great Day*. Louis eagerly went to Philadelphia to join the cast in rehearsal, but he—along with several other black musicians—was fired soon after he joined the company.

Rockwell began looking for club jobs for Armstrong. He booked Louis and his band into the Audubon Ballroom in the Bronx as replacements on a date that had been canceled by Duke Ellington. Their success at the Audubon led to a stint at New York's Savoy, where they made an immediate hit. Rockwell used their Savoy publicity to get them an audition for Florenz Ziegfeld, who was looking for a jazz band for George Gershwin's *Show Girl*, but Ziegfeld chose to use the Duke Ellington band, a better-known commodity in New York. In late June 1929 Louis and his band began another club engagement, and it was this job that would finally put Louis on Broadway.

He was hired by Connie Immerman to lead the floor show at his Harlem club, Connie's Inn. Immerman was lately riding high as producer of a simulated club revue called *Hot Chocolates*, which was running at the Hudson Theatre on Forty-fourth Street. The show's songs were by Fats Waller and Andy Razaf, and it was enjoying glowing reviews, as well as the best word of mouth on Broadway. With the success of *Hot Chocolates* assured, Immerman had an idea worthy of an Escher drawing. He would put his clublike Broadway revue into his uptown club, which had been its genesis, while simultaneously maintaining its downtown run. He could use the same cast to play the show in two venues per night. Immerman's first step toward this morphing of his shows was to add Louis Armstrong to the Broadway company. The biggest hit, "Ain't Misbehavin'," was performed several times during the evening, but it received its best treatment by Armstrong, who played and sang it in a feature spot. After the curtain fell at the Hudson, the cast dashed uptown to do an abbreviated version of *Hot Chocolates* at Connie's Inn. Even though he shared Connie's stages with the scene-stealing Fats Waller, Louis was the hit of both editions of *Hot Chocolates*.

Louis's feature number in a hit show was the break that Tommy Rockwell had been looking for. On July 19 Rockwell arranged an OKeh session for Louis and his Chicago band to record "Ain't Misbehavin'." It was a perfect match of artist and material, and it produced Armstrong's first crossover hit. It is Louis at his best: his trumpet shimmers, and his vocal is a gem of jazz singing. He has fun with the tune and the lyric but not at their expense. He plays with harmonies in his vocal, finding new places to land around the familiar notes, and he scats the end of his lyric phrases. His trumpet solo quotes *Rhapsody in Blue* before dancing away into the ether, and he ends on a long high note hit squarely in its center. It is a wonderful performance that combines the grand (his trumpet) with the funky (his singing), the amalgam that was the core of Armstrong's art.

Armstrong's recordings were still being released in OKeh's race series, but whites bought copies of "Ain't Misbehavin'" by the thousands. With this song, Louis transcended the (literal) label that a segregated industry had put on him, and its success pointed him toward new vehicles for his rough voice and his steely trumpet. He would record pop songs almost exclusively for nearly twenty years after his first hit. He stiffened the spines of hundreds of Tin Pan Alley products, reforming bad songs and making good songs great.

Only two months after "Ain't Misbehavin'," Louis scored again for OKeh with "Some of These Days" and "When You're Smiling." He was on his course now. Before the year was out, he made definitive recordings of "I Ain't Got Nobody," "After You've Gone," and "Rockin' Chair" (sharing a vocal with composer Hoagy Carmichael). Tommy Rockwell knew that Louis was bookable as a single now, that the band behind him didn't matter. He could be jobbed in with any group, good or bad, and prevail over it, so why bother to keep a band together? When Louis and his Chicago band finished at Connie's Inn early in 1930, Louis, on Rockwell's recommendation, let the last of the Hot Five alumni go.

As Armstrong began his meteoric rise in New York, King Oliver was also in town, drawing his last breath of fame and, mostly, looking for work. He had come in the fall of 1927 to record for Vocalion, and his fortunes had gone steadily downhill ever since. He was offered the chance to install his Dixie Syncopators (a ten-piece group) as the house band at the newly renovated Cotton Club for its reopening in December 1927, but he thought the salary too low, so he turned it down. (Duke Ellington's band took the job and stayed at the Cotton Club for three years.)

Oliver suffered from pyorrhea, and the loss of several teeth had severely affected his playing. He was still recording the Chicago repertoire of the early 1920s ("Tin Roof Blues," "Farewell Blues," "Sobbin' Blues"), and his records weren't selling. He managed to land a contract with Victor in January 1929, and somehow held onto it until September 1930. The King Oliver Orchestra on the Victor label was an impermanent group whose members drifted in and out of studio dates. Oliver survived in the late '20s by taking pickup bands out of town to play dances and club dates in the Northeast. As his fame dwindled, it became harder to put together tours, so in mid-1931 he decided to go where he might still be remembered: the South. As he struggled to keep a band together in the mid-Atlantic and southeastern states in the early '30s, he would find that, even there, nobody remembered him very well.

In the spring of 1930 Armstrong went to Los Angeles for a booking that Rockwell had gotten him at Frank Sebastian's New Cotton Club, near the MGM studios in Culver City. He was not the leader there, but he was so popular with the movie crowd who patronized the club that its house band was given a clumsy new name, Louis Armstrong and His Sebastian New Cotton Club Orchestra. The ten-piece band (including two promising youngsters, trombonist Lawrence Brown and drummer Lionel Hampton) made its first recordings at L.A.'s OKeh studios in the summer of 1930, and over the next few months they turned out some especially fine ballads: "Confessin'," "If I Could Be with You One Hour Tonight," "Body and Soul," and "Memories of You." Armstrong was a real singer now, choosing the most sophisticated pop songs and building phrases with words as intricately as he deconstructed melodies with his trumpet. His own vocal successes did not make him less cooperative with other singers. In mid-July 1930 his cornet lent support to country bluesman Jimmie Rodgers's "Blue Yodel #9," at Victor's Los Angeles studios. Things were going so well for Louis in L.A. that he stayed. He landed a bit role—as a musician—in his first movie, MGM's *Ex-Flame*, early in 1931. (No print of the film survives.)

The only cloud over Armstrong's early days in the movie capital came in November 1930, when he got busted for smoking pot in the Cotton Club parking lot. This jam would have enormous consequences for his career because of the man who stepped in to get him out of it. Louis stayed in the city jail nine days awaiting trial, and, because he had fans among the prisoners there, as well as among the detectives, the experience was more embarrassing than frightening. If Louis was embarrassed, Tommy Rockwell was mortified. The story of the arrest was all over the papers, and, fearing for Armstrong's career, Rockwell sent a goon named Johnny Collins to L.A. to do what he could toward containing the damage. Whether he used sweet reason or hard cash, Collins did the job. Louis received a suspended sentence and went back to work and back to pot. He never smoked it in a public place again, but he would smoke it virtually every day for the rest of his life.

Johnny Collins felt that he had saved Louis's career, and, without consultation with Louis or Tommy Rockwell, he began acting as Louis's manager. Collins had been sent to L.A. to act for Rockwell, but when he realized how lax the Armstrong-Rockwell business relationship was, he simply took over Armstrong's affairs. At first, when Louis didn't know whether Rockwell or Collins was speaking, he followed Collins's orders. Later he would question Collins's decisions and argue with him if necessary. But later was too late. By default, the brightest star in jazz had the worst manager in show business.

Collins was, to say the least, in over his head making decisions about Armstrong's career. He was a crude article, a bully who cared nothing about Louis's gifts but, like so many others, merely wanted a piece of him. He was prone to drunken displays of temper, and he was as likely to hurl a racial insult at Louis as he was to strong-arm a theater owner. His idea of negotiation was gimme-the-dough-or-he-don't-play, and he would never admit that it was Armstrong's talent, rather than his own tantrums, that landed the jobs.

Johnny Collins took his new client back to Chicago and found him a band, a nine-piece group organized by trumpeter Zilner Randolph. They played sweet rather than hot; nonetheless, it was a sound that Louis loved. (He was a lifelong fan of Guy Lombardo.) As would be the case with his other bands of the 1930s, Louis didn't lead the Randolph band, he "fronted" them, which is to say that he stood in front of them and played. He rarely joined in section parts, and there was no interaction with other soloists. In the big band era, Louis would front bigger bands than Randolph's, but he never explored their possibilities. He wasn't interested in give-and-take among sections, and he was indifferent to the intricacies of big-band arranging. He had no theories to propound, and he had no desire to mold a group and develop a sound for it. He just wanted to play, and all he needed was a wall of sound to play against. A second-rate band was good enough to serve as the wrapping for the presents he delivered nightly. His job was not to build bands but to be Louis Armstrong. His talent could override whatever was behind him: out-of-tune reeds, clunky rhythms, odd instrumentation. Whatever his bands might be doing, *he* played jazz and sang magnificently, and that's what the people had come to hear.

The Armstrong-Randolph band had eleven recording sessions at OKeh in Chicago between April 1931 and March 1932. There were hits among them—notably "I'll Be Glad When You're Dead, You Rascal You," Earl Hines's "You Can Depend on Me," and, the biggest, in early 1932, "All of Me"—but a song made in their first session would outlast them all in Louis's repertoire. It was "When It's Sleepy Time Down South," written by two brothers from Louisiana, Leon and Otis Rene, and an actor named Clarence Muse. The song has an interesting chord structure and a lyric that is nonstop cliché, about darkies and their mammies, steamboats, and banjos. Louis liked the song and saw nothing wrong with its stereotypical picture of contentment. He began to use "Sleepy Time" in performance, and by the mid-1940s it had become his signature song. Counting the records made at live concerts, it appeared on more than a dozen Armstrong discs. When people began to complain about the song in the 1950s, he defended it by saying that it was written by blacks, but, after a year or so of hassling about it, he substituted "folks" for "darkies" and kept on singing it.

Johnny Collins got Armstrong a job at the Showboat, a large white club in Chicago's Loop. Like the clubs he had played on the South Side, the Showboat was crawling with gangsters, and Louis became a target for extortionists, in person and over the telephone. Men he did not know came to his dressing room, demanding that he pay them thousands of dollars for the dual privilege of staying alive and working at the Showboat. Connie Immerman sent a stooge bearing a pistol to persuade Louis to leave Chicago and come back to Connie's Inn in Harlem. And Louis was caught in the middle of bad feelings between Collins and Rockwell. Each wanted Armstrong's management contract, and either of them, if he lost it, was capable of hurting Louis to get revenge on the winner. Collins was also feeling the heat, so in the late spring of 1931, he booked the band on a tour of the Midwest to get Louis (and himself) out of Chicago.

After several weeks on the road, the band headed to a job that Louis couldn't wait to start: a three-month booking at New Orleans's Suburban Gardens. Louis's homecoming, after nine years away, was glorious. Eight bands met his train. He was put into a convertible and paraded down Canal Street, which was lined with his fans, white and black. The next day he visited the Waif's Home, where, after posing for photos with Captain Jones and his old bandmaster, Peter Davis, he presented radios to all the boys. He ate in the Home's kitchen, and on a ceremonial tour of the barracks, he flopped down on his old bunk and promptly fell asleep.

Louis had a joyful reunion with Mama Lucy and, after some coaxing, he convinced his sister to let him help her out with some cash. He was a soft touch for strangers as well as friends. He kept his pockets full of coins and doled them out as he walked around "back o' town." A neighborhood baseball team hit him up for uniforms, and he bought them. The team wore his name stitched across the new shirts, and throughout the playing season of 1931 they were known as "Armstrong's Secret Nine." A local tobacco company named a cigar after him, the "Louis Armstrong Special."

There were flashes of racism that marred Armstrong's homecoming, however. On his opening night at the Suburban Gardens, a live radio broadcast was planned. Along with an audience of several thousand people, Louis and the band waited for the white announcer to introduce the show. The man hesitated for a bit and then said, "I just can't announce that nigger." So Louis strode to the microphone and announced himself, giving New Orleans its first chance to hear an African-American voice on live local radio.

Another incident was more insidious, and Louis was not able to deflect it. He wanted to do a concert for his black fans, who were not allowed in the segregated Suburban Gardens. A date and time was set for Louis and the band to play at a local military base, and blacks were to be given free admission. The musicians arrived to find hundreds of people clustered around the locked gate to the grounds. An officer was telling them that, because dancing was not permitted on military property, the band would not be performing there. When protests began, National Guardsmen moved in to disperse the crowd. The band was leaving town the next day, so there was no rescheduling, and there was no way to remedy the situation. Armstrong and his hometown fans had been denied the communion that they needed. He had seen racism before, and he had his ways of coping with it, but this was the first time that it broke his heart. The band stayed on the road in the South through the end of the year, and they endured other slights in other places. But the faces behind the big wire gate with the lock on it stayed in Louis's mind all of his life.

Back in New York early in 1932, Armstrong made two films, a Betty Boop cartoon and a live-action musical short called "Rhapsody in Black and Blue." In the Max Fleischer cartoon, Armstrong's head (in live-action) flies through the air, singing "I'll Be Glad When You're Dead, You Rascal You" as it chases the animated figure of Koko the Clown through animated underbrush. In the nine-minute "Rhapsody," a man gets conked on the head by his wife, and in his unconscious state, imagines that he has gone to Jazz Heaven. Armstrong appears in heaven, incongruously dressed in a leopard skin, and plays "Shine" on his trumpet. Amazingly, Louis transcends the degrading getup and commands attention by his glorious music alone. Armstrong would appear, mostly on the periphery, in two dozen commercial films (from *Ex-Flame* in 1931 to *Hello, Dolly* in 1969). His roles were usually mere setups for his musical numbers, and, over and over, his musicality turned incidental scenes into memorable ones.

In midsummer 1932, Louis, Alpha, and Johnny Collins and his wife sailed for England on the S.S. *Majestic* for the July 18 opening of a two-week engagement at London's Palladium. The leading British jazz magazine, *The Melody Maker*, went into palpitations over his arrival, and jazz fans across the Continent were thrilled that they could see him at last. The Palladium was packed on his opening night, and he was greeted with great applause. Surrounded by a band of black musicians imported from Paris, he launched into his opening number, "Them There Eyes." This was met with less enthusiasm than his entrance was, and as he gave them his standards—"When You're Smiling," "Chinatown," "I'll Be Glad When You're Dead"—the applause lessened by degrees after each one. Before the end of his half-hour set, people had begun to leave the theater. It was during this half-hour that Louis learned of the existence of what was, to him, a new breed of cat: the jazz purist.

Those who walked out on him were the aesthetes of jazz, record collectors and superfans, whose catechism began with "Heebie Jeebies" and ended with "Weather Bird," and who knew his every matrix number, every note, and every intake of breath in between. They were appalled that he would fritter away his talents on Tin Pan Alley songs, when he could best please connoisseurs by re-creating his 1926 solo on "Oriental Strut." His singing, which brought him acclaim in America, repulsed the priesthood at the Palladium because their jazz had narrow parameters. Louis had moved from the New Orleans repertoire to a broader style, and they weren't about to go along with him. They would never understand that, if he had stayed with his 1926 sound, he would not have even been at the Palladium in 1932. He would have been, like King Oliver, hoping his bus got fixed in time to get to Raleigh.

Because there were no jazz critics except those at *The Melody Maker*, Armstrong's appearance was reviewed by English classical music critics, and their responses to him ranged from puzzlement to insult. His singing was called "savage growling," his trumpet solos were called "screeches." They said that his genius was "barren" and that he looked, and behaved, "like an untrained gorilla." Armstrong had never provoked such tirades in America—he had seldom been reviewed at all—and the viciousness shocked him.

Audiences liked him, though, and many local musicians made a point to see every one of his London shows. And *The Melody Maker* remained loyal. The magazine's staffers helped Johnny Collins organize a tour to provincial theaters, and they found a ten-piece (white) British band who were thrilled to back him. Armstrong kept busy in England until October, then he and Alpha took a week off in Paris before returning to America.

In November Armstrong went into Harlem's Lafayette Theatre, and the professional entanglements that he had left behind four months earlier came back to haunt him. Connie Immerman hounded him, simultaneously threatening to sue him for an alleged breach of contract at Connie's Inn and begging him to come back to work there. Collins got Armstrong a Victor contract in December 1932, and OKeh tried to stop him from taking it. His five Victor sessions were done at the company's

Chicago studio, because it was handiest to him during his tour of the Midwest with the Zilner Randolph band.

In July 1933, while Louis was playing at a black theater in Philadelphia, mobsters began harassing him again. They were selling "protection," and Louis was not buying. They lurked everywhere he went—in his dressing room, in restaurants, on the street—and their presence was a silent reminder that he could be harmed if he didn't start paying them off.

Armstrong was afraid, and Johnny Collins didn't know what to do except send him back to England. Collins hastily booked shows at the Holborn Empire, and in late July 1933 Louis, Alpha, and Collins sailed for London on the S.S. *Homeric*. During the voyage, Louis had near-violent quarrels with his manager. Collins's boozy rages had become more frequent, and Louis's patience with him had run out. It was the answering back that Collins could not stand, and now Louis was answering back every time.

Not long after they arrived in London, Collins pitched one final, epic drunk and went home, leaving Louis stranded. Left in a situation that might have frightened him, Louis was elated. Not only was he beyond the reach of the midwestern gangsters who had made his life miserable, he was free of the gangster who had been running his career.

His British admirers came to his rescue. The bandleader Jack Hylton got him bookings in England for the early fall, after which arrangements were made for him to play in Denmark and Sweden. Jobs led to more jobs. A French promoter got him dates in France, Belgium, and Italy. Armstrong's getaway turned into a well-paid vacation. There were frequent side trips to Paris, where he and Alpha ate at fine restaurants and visited with Bricktop and Josephine Baker. And there was also a working trip to Paris in October 1934, when he recorded six tunes for Brunswick. Even the "art" nonsense of the previous trip had subsided. Everyone knew what to expect from him now, and audiences were happy to see him. Louis and Alpha would not come home for a year and a half.

◆

In January 1935, Louis Armstrong returned to America to find that his old problems had not diminished but his career had. He had made his last American recordings in April 1933, and the swing era was well under way without him. He was almost broke after his high living in Europe, and he had no record deal. Columbia was resentful because he had left OKeh (Columbia's subsidiary) for Victor, and Victor was resentful because he had made no records for two years. He was also besieged by lawsuits: two of the European managers who had booked him were suing for breach of contracts—he canceled several bookings to return to the United States—and Lil wanted $6,000 in back royalties from the old Hot Five records. He and Alpha laid low in Chicago for a few months while he assessed his situation.

Louis obviously needed management, and there were several companies he could have called, companies with offices full of band bookers who would have been happy to have Armstrong as a client. But he didn't want a company, he wanted a person, someone smart and tough, someone who would look out for him and give undivided attention to his career. Louis searched his past, recalling employers at various clubs and record companies, until he remembered a man who had impressed him. The candidate was not even in the management business, but Louis knew he was the one. He picked up the phone and called his old boss from the Sunset Cafe, Joe Glaser.

Glaser had not heard from Louis since the Sunset had closed, nearly ten years before. He had had a checkered career since then, most of it on the wrong side of the law. He had run a brothel, done some bootlegging, flunkied for the Capone syndicate, fixed some prizefights, and he had dodged a morals charge by marrying his fourteen-year-old girlfriend. Louis did not know nor would he have cared about any of this. He asked Glaser to manage him, and Glaser said yes. It was the beginning of the tightest artist-manager relationship in show business, and it would last until Glaser's death thirty-four years later. Glaser proved to be as smart and tough as Louis remembered him, a bulldog who was devoted to his client. Few people could abide Joe Glaser, but Louis worshiped him. He always spoke of him as "my best friend," and he said, "I love that man . . . God bless his soul."

When he took over Louis's management, Joe Glaser knew little about the band business, but, like the hedgehog, he knew one great thing: Louis needed the stability of a permanent band and a permanent record label. Live performance and recording, if Glaser could get them in synch, would keep Louis in demand. On this simple duality, Glaser rebuilt Armstrong's career.

The first thing was to find a band. Glaser went to New York to see the Panamanian-born pianist and bandleader Luis Russell. Russell's band comprised thirteen pieces, and it was absolutely ordinary. Glaser thought the Russell band was just right, a beige palette upon which Louis could splash his colors. The two entered into an agreement whereby Russell would tend to the day-to-day running of the band—hiring and firing, commissioning of arrangements, tending to the payroll and expenses of the organization—and Glaser would book the band as "Louis Armstrong and His Orchestra." By late October 1935, Glaser was ready to show the combination in New York, and he chose as his platform Connie's Inn. (Connie Immerman was dead by this time, and his lawsuits against Armstrong had died with him.) Armstrong's playing there, after a two-year absence, proved that he was still peerless. In his four months at Connie's Inn, Louis rejuvenated his old fans and won many new ones.

In the late summer of 1935, Glaser achieved the other half of his plan by finding Louis a record label. Knowing that Louis was *non grata* at Columbia and Victor, Glaser peddled him to Decca, an upstart giant that had been in business for under a year. Decca's boss, Jack Kapp, by poaching other labels' artists, had amassed a solid roster of stars, including Bing Crosby, Guy Lombardo, and the Mills Brothers. Kapp was collecting swing bands as well, issuing records by Jimmie Lunceford, Chick Webb, and Fletcher Henderson. Kapp was delighted to take Armstrong into the Decca fold, and he did not balk at the Russell band as Louis's backing. Best of all, he wanted Armstrong for Decca's general series, not for race records.

On October 3, 1935, Louis Armstrong and His Orchestra made a hit record in their first session for Decca. It was "I'm in the Mood for Love," a Jimmy McHugh-Dorothy Fields song from a current film, *Every Night at Eight*. Another song made that day, "You Are My Lucky Star," did almost as well, giving Louis a great kickoff at his new label. He would record exclusively for Decca for eight years and intermittently for another sixteen years after that. There were no Number 1 hits for him, but he gave the company about two dozen big records. Over the years he was occasionally teamed with other Decca artists (Bing Crosby, the Mills

Brothers, Billie Holiday, Louis Jordan, and Gary Crosby) and with other Decca bands (Jimmy Dorsey's, Andy Iona and His Islanders, and the Casa Loma Orchestra). He sang spirituals with the Decca Mixed Choir, and he recorded Bert Williams's two "Elder Eatmore" sermons. His popular 1935 composition, "Ol' Man Mose," got several recordings by other artists, but Louis's Decca record came first. (The song is a minor-keyed riff that goes into a happy major as the chorus tells us that "Mose kicked the bucket and Ol' Man Mose is dead." Its success prompted other writers to pen an "answer" song, "Missus Mose Has a Million Beaus Since Ol' Man Mose Is Dead.")

Louis began to get small film roles, and he dutifully plugged his movie songs on Decca records: "The Skeleton in the Closet" (*Pennies from Heaven*, 1936), "Public Melody #1" (*Artists and Models*, 1937), "Jubilee" (*Every Day's a Holiday*, 1938), and "Jeepers Creepers" (*Going Places*, 1938). He also sang his movie songs as a frequent guest on radio shows, and when he occasionally hosted *The Fleischmann Hour* in 1937.

There was even a record tie-in with a book in 1936, when Louis recorded a song to plug his pastiche of memoir and defense of swing. Although *Swing That Music* was probably ghost-written, it is the first autobiography of a jazz musician. (Armstrong's recording of his book's title song ends with a barrage of forty-two high Cs.) With Decca as Armstrong's anchor, Joe Glaser's theory of interlocking media worked beautifully. Louis came at his public from several directions at once in the late 1930s, and he always had a new record to sell.

With Louis's career on the upswing, Joe Glaser added another tenet to his management philosophy: never turn down a job. Armstrong was in great demand now, and Glaser booked him constantly—overbooked him, some said. Louis loved performing for live audiences—for dancers as well as listeners—and he was not averse to hard work, so he pitched in. His life became a perpetual tour, interrupted only by his dashing away to do movie jobs, radio appearances, and recording sessions, after which he dashed back to rejoin his band on the road. It was in September 1937, when the band was on a swing through the Southeast, that Armstrong was stopped in his busy tracks.

It was a warm afternoon in Savannah, and Armstrong was taking a walk before his band played for a dance that evening. He stopped to buy some vegetables from an old man with a pushcart. As the peddler turned to him, Louis saw his face, and he realized that he was looking at what was left of Joe Oliver. He was toothless now, and his eyes were scaled with cataracts. The baddest sumbitch in New Orleans had become a ragged ghost. On impulse, Louis reached for his wallet. He had $150 on him, and he gave it to Oliver, urging him to buy a suit.

Oliver reluctantly took the money and, even more reluctantly, told Louis his story. He had spent the mid-'30s scraping up dates around the Southeast, trying to keep a band together and a bus running well enough to get them to the next small-town dance. His health and his playing deteriorated, and he hit bottom in Spartanburg, South Carolina. His bus was beyond repair, and his band deserted him. He called a Savannah promoter, Frank Dilworth, Jr., for help, and Dilworth drove to Spartanburg to get him. It was obvious that Oliver's playing days were over, so there was nothing that Dilworth could do for him except get him a doctor and a place to stay. He found Oliver a room in a boarding house at 508 Montgomery Street, in Savannah, and he often came by to check on him. If Oliver felt up to it, Dilworth would take him to listen to the rehearsals of a local group, Milton's Brass Band. When his health improved, Oliver began pushing a vegetable wagon.

Louis took up a collection among his band members, and when Oliver arrived at the dance, he was presented with their donations. The King stood in the wings, beaming in his new suit, as he listened to Louis for the last time. Oliver spent the winter working as a janitor in Connie's Billiard Hall and Grill, on West Broad Street. He died of a cerebral hemorrhage as he slept in his boardinghouse room on April 10, 1938. Frank Dilworth called Armstrong with the news, and Louis sobbed when he heard it.

To Louis the moral of Oliver's story was, take it while you can get it. *If* Oliver had not waited so long to come to New York, *if* he had not turned down the Cotton Club engagement, *if* he had broadened his repertoire while he had the Victor contract . . . there would be no ifs for Louis. He would go where he was wanted, and he would play what people wanted to hear.

Louis finally divorced Lil in September 1938, and on October 11 he married Alpha Smith. Soon after his marriage he took a job at the new (downtown) Cotton Club, at Forty-eighth and Broadway, co-starring with his performing idol, Bill Robinson, in the floor show. At the Cotton Club he met a shy chorus girl named Lucille Wilson, who was billed as "Brown Sugar." Their attraction to each other was immediate, and his marriage to the free-spending, flirtatious Alpha was in trouble before it began.

Armstrong was back on Broadway in late November 1939, in a musical version of *A Midsummer Night's Dream*. It was called *Swingin' the Dream*, and the production was an odd mixture of the grandiose and the low-down. Shakespeare's story was transplanted to New Orleans in the 1890s, and Armstrong played Bottom. Butterfly McQueen was Puck, and Moms Mabley was Quince. The Benny Goodman Sextet was thrown in for good measure, but nothing could overcome the awkwardness of *Swingin' the Dream*. Despite the Walt Disney sets, a book by Gilbert Seldes, and songs by Jimmy Van Heusen, the show was not successful. It lasted thirteen performances at the Rockefeller Center Theatre.

As Louis toured and recorded with the Luis Russell band in the early 1940s, some of his old New Orleans numbers began to creep back into his repertoire. "Save It, Pretty Mama," "Wolverine Blues," and "West End Blues" were among the tunes that appeared as B sides of his pop records for Decca. The American Federation of Musicians ban on recordings, which began in August 1942, cut off his studio activities (along with every other band's) and made it impossible to tell Louis's degree of interest in his earlier material. There would be no more Armstrong recordings until January 1945.

Armstrong rode out the recording ban by stepping up his work in movies and radio. In 1942 he made four "soundies" (three-minute musical films, which were shown in diners on a kind of visual jukebox), and these led to his being cast in the 1943 film version of *Cabin in the Sky*. Much of his role—including his big song, "Ain't It the Truth?"—was left in the cutting room, but he oozed mischief as an assistant devil to Rex Ingram's Lucifer. Louis and his orchestra had feature numbers in two 1944 films, *Atlantic City* and *Jam Session*.

Alpha left him for a drummer in the Charlie Barnet band, and Louis divorced her in October 1942. A few days after the divorce was final, he married Lucille Wilson. She was his fourth wife, and although she may have looked like another showgirl fling, Lucille was the one who figured out how to maintain a marriage to Louis Armstrong. She didn't like living on the road, so she seldom traveled with him. He was getting a bit tired of hotel rooms himself, so in early 1943 he delegated her to buy a house for them. When he returned to New York after his winter tour, he caught a cab at Penn Station and gave the driver the address of the place he had never seen: 34-56 107th Street, in Corona, Queens. It was a plain, three-story house in a middle-class neighborhood, and Louis was instantly at home there. There would be hundreds of hotel rooms in Louis' future, but, for the rest of his life, for however many weeks a year he could be there, he would enjoy time with Lucille in the Corona house. It was the only home he ever owned.

A new kind of jazz began to emerge in the 1940s, when bop arose as a reaction to, and the antithesis of, big-band swing. Bop was different, all right—so different that it evoked endless arguments about its sound and its musical validity. Armstrong was drawn into the debate by jazz journalists, who took a let's-you-and-him-fight approach to their interviews with him. Although he hardly typified the big-band era, he became the spokesman for swing because he didn't understand bop and didn't mind saying so. In his complaints, he aligned himself with the "moldy figs" (traditionalists), and in doing so, he conferred a fogeyness on himself that he didn't deserve.

Magazines ran lists of things Louis didn't like about bop: too many odd tunes; he couldn't find the melody; you couldn't dance to it. He thought it wrong for musicians to turn their backs on the people who had paid cover charges to hear them, and he especially hated the sound that bop trumpeters made: the thin tones of their open horns and the dry buzzing of their mutes. They didn't play full, he said, "they skated." Armstrong had never knocked anybody's music before, so it was considered news by the jazz press.

The flap was defused by the boppers themselves. They had no quarrel with Armstrong, and they refused to let him make one. They knew what they owed him, and they would not disavow him despite his peevish remarks. Miles Davis and Dizzy Gillespie, who, because they were trumpeters, were the worst offenders in Louis's book, never wavered in their admiration for him. Even though he disapproved of Louis's onstage antics, Davis admitted, "You can't play anything on the horn that Louis hasn't played—even modern." And Gillespie simply said, "No him, no me." Louis was happy with the detente that settled over the matter in the 1950s, and he became a good friend of Dizzy Gillespie's. The boppers went their way, and he went his.

Armstrong's elevation to patron saint of jazz began in the late 1940s. He had been in the public eye for twenty-plus years by then, and he was busier than ever. Audiences knew that nobody loved them like Louis, and that no one worked harder to please them. Honors came to him from various places. In 1947 he was the subject of an adulatory (but poorly written) book called *Horn of Plenty* by the Belgian jazz critic Robert Goffin. On February 21, 1949, he became the first jazz player to make the cover of *Time*. A week after the *Time* cover, he was in New Orleans for Mardi Gras as the guest of the Zulu Social Aid and Pleasure Club. He was there to lead their parade, which parodied the pomp of the white krewes of New Orleans. Louis painted on the ancient mask of the King of the Zulus—blackface, with huge white circles around the eyes and mouth—and made a triumphant ride along the Zulus' erratic, and traditionally unannounced, route through the city.

For three years in the late '40s, Louis was heard on the Broadway stage again, in a 1927 recording. Tallulah Bankhead had signed a run-of-the-play contract to appear in Noel Coward's *Private Lives*, and she insisted that Armstrong's "Potato Head Blues" be used as background music in one of the scenes. When it was suggested that this was unlikely music for a drawing-room comedy, she said she didn't care, it was keeping her sane during a seemingly interminable run.

In 1947 Armstrong appeared with Billie Holiday (another Glaser client) in a film called *New Orleans*. This was supposed to be the first movie about the history of jazz, but it went off course and turned its subject into "atmosphere" for a sappy love story. The following year Louis was featured in a Danny Kaye film, *A Song Is Born*, in which several music professors decided to study jazz. Their fieldwork involved listening to Armstrong's band, as well as those of Tommy Dorsey, Benny Goodman, and Charlie Barnet.

In September 1949 Decca teamed Louis with Gordon Jenkins's Orchestra and Choir, and the result was a record with a hit on both sides. One song was a new one, "That Lucky Old Sun," a workingman's meditation; the other was "Blueberry Hill," a simpleminded tune written in 1940 for a Gene Autry movie. Neither is much of a song, but Armstrong made each into something profound. With the sincerity of his singing, he lent his own character to these songs that had none.

Armstrong did two concerts in 1947 that set him on the musical course that he would follow for the rest of his life. The first was at Carnegie Hall on February 8, when he sat in with Edmond Hall's sextet for the first half of the evening and led his own sixteen-piece band in the second half. Hall was a New Orleans–born clarinetist who was sparking the revival of traditional jazz in New York from his home base at Cafe Society Uptown, playing the kind of music that Louis used to play. Although Louis had left small-band jazz long before, Hall wanted his presence (and his name) at this important concert. Against Joe Glaser's advice, Louis accepted Hall's invitation. When he tore into the old parade-band repertoire with Hall and his men that night, something awoke in him. He was transported, and he played furiously. He drove the band hard and fast, with a passion he had not called on for years. The second half of the evening—the Armstrong orchestra concert—was a letdown, for Louis and for the audience, after the excitement of the first.

Ernest Anderson, a jazz fan and sometime promoter, wanted to present an evening in which Louis could do more of his old hot stuff. Anderson had had to do an end run around Fats Waller's manager, Ed Kirkeby, to produce Waller's 1942 Carnegie Hall concert, and he knew there would be similar trouble with Joe Glaser. Glaser wouldn't permit any monkeying with his packaging of Louis—as a crossover artist, a singer of current pop material with a big band behind him—and it was unimaginable that he would cooperate in a plan to produce him in an evening of old-fashioned small-band jazz. Anderson knew that he could speak to Glaser only in Glaser's language: with money. He confronted the beast in his office, waving a check for $1,000 for Louis's services— without his band. Since this was more than Glaser was getting for a one-nighter with the band, he took the check. It was agreed that Louis would do a midnight concert at Town Hall on May 17, with a small band of Anderson's choosing.

The concert featured Armstrong and a five-piece band in an impromptu program of what Louis called "the good old good ones." The

New Orleans and Chicago classics poured out—"Muskrat Ramble," "Royal Garden Blues," "A Monday Date," "Big Butter and Egg Man"— and to show that he still had the chops, Armstrong played a blazing "Cornet Chop Suey." He sang a better "Rockin' Chair" with Jack Teagarden than he had sung with Hoagy Carmichael in 1929. Both Louis and the audience found it all delicious. Armstrong had come back to the music that brought the best out in him, and neither he nor the music was clichéd. He was reinventing it, as he was reinventing himself. It was the old New Orleans sound—loose and tight at the same time— but there was freshness in it. And Louis wasn't just standing in front of a wall of musicians; his trumpet was talking to his sidemen, and they were talking back. It was perfect, and even Joe Glaser had to admit it. The experiment was repeated in August 1947 at a Los Angeles club called Billy Berg's, with the same roaring success. In November Louis and His All Stars—as the group was now known—conquered Carnegie Hall, and by February 1948 they were in France, at the Nice Jazz Festival, the first of many international appearances.

Some of the All Stars ensembles actually had stars in them. Jack Teagarden was a charter member, and he stayed as trombonist and vocal foil to Louis for about seven years. Barney Bigard was a stalwart, and Earl Hines played in an early edition of the band. Besides the stars, who drifted in and out, there was a core of old reliables, like Edmond Hall and trombonists Trummy Young and Tyree Glenn. And there were many young musicians who took their first steps into the big time with Louis (such as pianist Billy Kyle, bassist Arvell Shaw, and drummers Danny Barcelona and Barrett Deems). The band's female vocalist for thirteen years was Velma Middleton, a huge, baby-voiced woman who was a perfect vaudeville partner for duets with Armstrong.

For twenty years the All Stars stayed at it, and there was nothing on the road exactly like them. Several 1940s bands survived into the 1950s and 1960s—the Dorsey brothers, Benny Goodman, a Glenn Miller band—playing the old arrangements of their old hits. But the All Stars didn't deal in hits, their own or anybody else's. And they were not like the revivalist Dixieland bands of their time, in repertoire or sound. They brought a parade band's zest to pop songs and a swing band's polish to traditional numbers. As musical styles came and went, the All Stars remained unaffected by them all. The band's last recordings sound much like their first, and there is no hint in them that bop, cool, rhythm and blues, or rock ever happened. The All Stars were the sleigh on which Louis Armstrong rode around the world, and his presence made them unique.

The return to his roots with the All Stars brought Louis full circle, and it changed the subject of his interviews in the jazz press. Instead of trying to provoke him about bop, writers wanted to know about the old days. He was an elder statesman now, someone who was present at the creation. He had known legends before he became a legend himself, and he loved to talk about them. Louis decided to get it all down in a book—and to write it himself this time—and in 1954 Prentice-Hall published his memoir, *Satchmo: My Life in New Orleans*. Although it takes him only into his twenty-second year, it is one of the most valuable documents in jazz history because of its point of view.

Armstrong's vantage point was that of the street, and his memories counterbalance those of Jelly Roll Morton, who spent his musical adolescence indoors, in fancy whorehouses and cabarets. Because he was poorer and blacker than Morton, and because he played the cornet rather than the piano, Armstrong was shaped by outdoor music: music he heard at parades, picnics, and Sunday excursions. *Satchmo* describes it all in detail: the playing styles of his boyhood idols, the poverty, the affection among the members of his hard-pressed family. It is a generous book, and Armstrong's spirit and his voice are on every page.

Hollywood still did not know what to do with Armstrong in the 1950s, but he was in demand for films all the same. He had small roles in *The Strip* and *Here Comes the Groom* (both in 1951) and in *Glory Alley* (1952). He had a bit more to do in *The Glenn Miller Story* (1953), and Cole Porter wrote two numbers for him in *High Society* (1956). The first, "High Society Calypso," is sung to his All Stars by a dapper Satch, wielding a cigarette holder, on the band bus as they head for Newport to play at a wedding. The second, "Now You Has Jazz," pairs him with Bing Crosby to introduce jazz—and the All Stars—to the wedding guests. Louis and the All Stars were featured at the real Newport in 1958, and they were an important part of the documentary film about that year's festival, *Jazz on a Summer's Day*. In 1959 Louis sang his "Someday You'll

Be Sorry" in *The Beat Generation*, and he appeared as himself in *The Five Pennies*, a film biography of Red Nichols, which starred Danny Kaye.

The film that was most important to Armstrong during this period was *Satchmo the Great*, an hourlong documentary produced for CBS-TV by Edward R. Murrow and Fred Friendly. The project began in May 1956 when Murrow sent a camera crew to follow Louis and the All Stars on a State Department tour to make a segment for his *See It Now* series. As they followed Armstrong to grand European concert halls and to makeshift stages in Africa, it became obvious to the producers that he was not just a master showman, he was a phenomenon whose appeal crossed all cultural and language barriers. A few days after playing to high-toned audiences in Paris, Armstrong drew more than one hundred thousand people at an open-air concert in Ghana, some of them driving wagons and many of them walking miles in hundred-degree heat to see him. Murrow and Friendly ran the story of the tour on *See It Now*, and the show was expanded to make *Satchmo the Great*. These two programs let America see Armstrong as the world saw him, as an artist of international importance.

The All Stars' sound energized Louis in the recording studio, as well as on stage. He made some of his best records in the mid-1950s, most of them with his own band. In 1954, they recorded eleven W. C. Handy songs for a Columbia LP, and the following year they paid tribute to Fats Waller on Columbia's *Satch Plays Fats*. In 1957 Decca released a four-LP set, *Satchmo: A Musical Autobiography*. Such an album could have easily been made by choosing from his backlog of classic Deccas, but this one wasn't. In a massive burst of creativity, Armstrong and the All Stars played forty-two of his old numbers, with Louis reworking—not just copying—his old solos. (He took several of them an octave higher than he did on their original recordings.) On the pop songs, the All Stars provided better backing than Louis had had the first time around. In September 1955 he made his first million-selling single, "Mack the Knife."

In August 1956 Louis was given his biggest challenge as a singer. Norman Granz had that year created a new record label, Verve, and he asked Louis to make a vocal album with Ella Fitzgerald. Louis and Ella had recorded together ten years earlier, doing two throwaway pop songs

("You Won't Be Satisfied" and "Frim Fram Sauce") for Decca. But, because of Granz, this was a different Ella from the one Louis had sung with in 1946. Granz had refashioned her image from that of a novelty singer—of such ephemera as "The Dipsy Doodle," "A -Tisket A-Tasket," and "Chew-Chew-Chew Your Bubble Gum"—into that of an interpreter of the best popular songwriting. Ella took a major step in her transformation in February 1956 with the recording of her two-volume *Cole Porter Songbook*, and now Louis was to take the next step with her. He might play a little trumpet, but the emphasis was to be on the singing. He was meeting a world-class singer on her turf, and the spare accompaniment, a quartet led by the pianist Oscar Peterson, left no place to hide. This was not like horsing around with Velma Middleton. This was serious.

Granz chose eleven ballads for the *Ella and Louis* album, several of them harmonically complex—"Moonlight in Vermont," "April in Paris," "Can't We Be Friends?"—and all of them in either slow or medium tempos. Louis and Ella complement each other perfectly, her smoothness floating over his roughness as each of them sings with absolute authority. There is intense *listening* going on between them, and each responds to the other's subtlest lyric or rhythmic urges. Louis occasionally adds some gentle scat to Ella's lines, and his trumpet playing is pensive and subdued.

A year after *Ella and Louis*, they made *Ella and Louis Again*, which added some up-tempo tunes and outright swingers (such as "Stompin' at the Savoy," "I've Got My Love to Keep Me Warm," and "Gee, Baby, Ain't I Good to You?") to the ballads ("Autumn in New York" and "Love Is Here to Stay"). And one afternoon in August 1957, they sang—and Louis played—with an orchestra to make an album of songs from *Porgy and Bess*. Taken together, the three Armstrong-Fitzgerald LPs represent the pinnacle of popular singing.

Soon after the *Porgy and Bess* session, Louis and the All Stars were back on the road, playing dates in the Northwest. On September 19 Louis was resting backstage before a concert in Grand Forks, North Dakota. He had promised an interview to a high school student who was a stringer for the local newspaper, and before the young man arrived, Louis turned on the evening news. What he saw horrified him. He watched nine black children walking toward the door of Central High

School in Little Rock, Arkansas, as a crowd of white adults cursed and spat at them. When they got to the door, it was blocked by a phalanx of National Guardsmen, who had been sent to keep order but who were actually blocking their way. His anger boiled over, and when his teenage interviewer arrived, he erupted. He said that President Eisenhower was gutless, that he was letting Governor Faubus, "an uneducated plowboy," run the country. He thought that the Guardsmen's presence was a publicity stunt "led by the greatest of all publicity hounds" (Eisenhower). He said, "The way they are treating my people in the South, the government can go to hell." The young reporter took it all down and went back to file his copy.

The editor couldn't believe that Louis had said such things, so he typed up the interviewer's notes and sent them to Armstrong to verify. Louis wrote "Solid!" at the end of the text and signed his name. The wire services picked up the story, and all hell broke loose. The State Department canceled his scheduled tour. Disc jockeys stopped playing his records. Syndicated columnists assailed him, and several prominent black entertainers hastened to separate themselves from his remarks. Joe Glaser's office tried to smooth it over with the press, but Louis wouldn't have it. He meant what he said, and he kept saying it. When Eisenhower finally ended the chaos by sending federal troops to Central High, Louis sent him a telegram of support.

The calming of the crisis in Little Rock didn't mollify Armstrong, however. He stopped performing in the South, making an exception only for military bases. He included his hometown in his boycott, and he did not play in New Orleans for ten years. If he wouldn't play the South, he would play everywhere else, and he did. There was no shortage of bookings after he had spoken his piece, and Joe Glaser, true to form, took as many as he could schedule.

Armstrong knew the old trouper's secret, which is to save one's energy in order to come fully alive at showtime. He did nothing more strenuous than typing letters and listening to records during the day, and he liked an afternoon nap. His regimen included a daily dose of Swiss Kriss (an herbal laxative that he swore by), a few applications of the lip salve made for him by a German trombonist named Franz Schuritz, some red beans and rice—when he could find them on a hotel menu—

and several marijuana cigarettes. His preparation for performance was inviolate: he rubbed his chest and throat with Heet before he dressed, then gargled a little glycerine and honey "to wash out the pipes," then put some Sweet Spirits of Nitre on his face and lips. After he was anointed and attired, Armstrong took his mouthpiece out of his back pocket— where he kept it safe from germs— and plugged it into his trumpet so he could run a little bit of "Cavalleria Rusticana." Then he strode on stage, beaming his thousand-watt smile. He would be there for the next two hours.

Some complained that Louis's repertoire became routine in the late 1950s, that he played the same two dozen tunes over and over. It didn't bother All Star trombonist Trummy Young. He told *Metronome* in 1961:

> It's amazing to me the beauty he can put into those numbers night after night, always keeping that same beautiful feeling . . . Here's a man, sixty years old, hitting those high ones every night, all night . . . When he's right, you can forget about him playing the same program because he's making it and it's a wonderful thing.

Trummy obviously believed that if you have seen one Monet water lily, you have not seen them all.

The All Stars loved traveling with him. He was good company, on stage and on the band bus. Bud Freeman said, "Some people put him down as an entertainer, but to me, Louis swings more telling a joke than most others do playing a horn." When he was accused of coasting musically, Louis replied, "If I'm out of style now, I was a flying cat when I was in—so to hell with it now. That's the way I can enjoy life. I don't sigh for nothing."

The first sign that Armstrong was mortal came on June 23, 1959, during an All Stars tour of Italy. He collapsed in his hotel room in Spoleto, and he was rushed to a hospital. When he was told that he had had a heart attack, he simply denied it. He spent a week in the hospital, then returned to America. By July 4 he was well enough to play half a set at a Lewisohn Stadium concert. Still telling himself that the episode in Italy was a severe attack of gas, he added Maalox to his daily regimen and took to the road again.

In early April 1960 Bob Thiele, an A&R man at Roulette Records, had a dream come true. His musical idols were Louis Armstrong and Duke Ellington, and he had always wanted to produce an Armstrong-Ellington album. He knew that it was unlikely that they would record for his small label, but he asked his boss, Morris Levy, to put the proposal to Joe Glaser, who was managing both Louis and Duke. Glaser surprised Levy and Thiele by saying yes, and he even called Louis in from the road to make the recordings. It was decided that the material would be Ellington songs, performed by Louis and four of his All Stars, with Ellington as pianist. It was unknown territory for both men: Armstrong was not familiar with the Ellington songbook, and Ellington had never played with the likes of the All Stars. In their two sessions the odd couple made enough tunes for two albums, and, as had happened with the Louis-Ella LPs, the stripped-down format provided a fresh look at familiar talents. With the composer's tasty piano underpinning his vocals, Armstrong immersed himself in Ellingtonia, giving especially fine readings to "Solitude" and "Azalea." (The following year, Armstrong appeared in the film *Paris Blues*, which was scored by Ellington.)

Louis and the All Stars went into the studio in December 1963 to make demos of a couple of show tunes that Joe Glaser had found for him. One was "A Lot of Living to Do," a three-year-old song from *Bye Bye Birdie*, and the other was a new number, the title song of a musical that was set to open in January. The new song was Jerry Herman's "Hello, Dolly," and Louis didn't think much of it. He quickly learned it, recorded it, and forgot it. After the recording session, Glaser added a banjo track to "Dolly" and began to peddle it. The record was picked up by Jack Kapp, who issued it on his new Kapp label. The record and the show promoted each other, and in early May 1964 Louis Armstrong's "Hello, Dolly" broke the Beatles' fourteen-week stranglehold on the Number 1 position in the pop charts. The record sold in the millions, and it was Armstrong's biggest hit.

Armstrong was more than a legend now; he was a legend with a hit record, and, as such, he was all over the place in the mid-1960s. Everyone wanted Louis, and Joe Glaser saw that everyone got him. He made the rounds of TV variety shows, he chatted with disc jockeys, he took "Dolly" everywhere. It even revitalized his film career. In 1965 he and the All Stars appeared in *When the Boys Meet the Girls*, a souped-up version of the Gershwins' *Girl Crazy*. Louis also had a supporting part in a 1966 film, *A Man Called Adam*. He played an aging trumpeter, and it was the closest he would ever come to an acting role.

In 1967 Bob Thiele brought him a song he had written called "What a Wonderful World." Louis liked it enough to record it for minimum scale ($250), but, for some reason, ABC-Paramount Records balked at spending anything to promote it. It caught on in England, outselling the Rolling Stones and the Beatles for thirteen weeks, but it bombed in the United States. It would eventually find its way onto American pop charts in 1989, as the highlight of the soundtrack of a Barry Levinson film, *Good Morning, Vietnam*.

There was another health scare in September 1968. Armstrong's doctor hospitalized him briefly and warned him he would have to stop playing the trumpet. He let the horn alone for a few weeks, but as soon as he felt better, he began sneaking away from Lucille to practice. In February 1969 he was back in Beth Israel Hospital. Unbeknownst to him, Joe Glaser had suffered a stroke, and he lay dying in a bed down the hall. The news of Glaser's death shattered Louis.

If he didn't have Glaser, Louis still had his work. And if he couldn't play any more, then he would sing. It was expected that he would be added to the cast of the 1969 film version of *Hello, Dolly*, and he was. He sang one chorus of the title song to Barbra Streisand. (Louis was a great admirer of Streisand. When a fan heard him praising her, he reminded Louis that she was not really a jazz singer. Satch replied, "Say what you like, Daddy, but she's outswinging every ass this year.") And he sang "All the Time in the World" over the credits of the 1969 James Bond film, *On Her Majesty's Secret Service*.

Honors flowed to Armstrong now. In 1970 he received two huge birthday tributes, one in Hollywood—attended by sixty-seven hundred fans and hosted by Hoagy Carmichael—the other at the Newport Jazz Festival, where he sang "Mack the Knife." He granted a long "birthday" interview to the *New York Times*. Duke Ellington paid his respects with the "Portrait of Louis" in his *New Orleans Suite*. *Down Beat* devoted an entire issue to him in July.

Louis made his last two albums in 1970, one a collection of country songs and the other a hodgepodge of special material written about him

LOUIS ARMSTRONG AND MILES DAVIS.

("Boy from New Orleans" and "This Black Cat Has Nine Lives") and contemporary songs (such as "Everybody's Talkin'" and "His Father Wore Long Hair"). Singing Lennon and McCartney's "Give Peace a Chance," he ad libs, "Give me a little ol' peace, dear."

Louis didn't stop performing because he couldn't. In September 1970 he played a two-week gig in Las Vegas, *with* his horn and with the All Stars. In late October he sang at a charity event in London, and December found him back in Vegas for another two weeks. He appeared on television with Bing Crosby early in 1971 to sing "Pennies from Heaven," and on February 26 he made his last recording, a reading of "The Night before Christmas." In March he played two weeks at the Waldorf-Astoria's Empire Room. Louis got bad reviews, and he was disheartened by them. He fell ill before the engagement ended, but he finished his stint there. He had had another heart attack, and he underwent a tracheotomy at Beth Israel. There was a death watch by the press for several weeks, but Louis rallied enough for Lucille to take him back to

Queens. On July 4 he gave television interviews at his home in Corona. He said he was feeling better and that he would be working with his band again soon. In the early morning of July 6, 1971, the day that he was to meet his All Stars for rehearsal, he died.

At Lucille's request, Louis's funeral on July 9 at the small Corona Congregational Church was simple and brief. Billy Taylor spoke, as did the radio personality Fred Robbins. Peggy Lee sang "The Lord's Prayer," and Al Hibbler sang "Nobody Knows the Trouble I've Seen" and "When the Saints Go Marching In." Many jazz players attended the service, but there was no jazz played.

The New Orleans Jazz Club thought Louis deserved a better send-off, so it planned a proper memorial service for 6 P.M. on Sunday, July 11. It engaged the Olympia Brass Band, the Onward Brass Band, and the Fairview Baptist Church Christian Band to assemble at different sites and march toward Duncan Square, a large grassy area adjoining City Hall, at 5:30. Mayor Moon Landrieu, who had just returned from the New York funeral, would be there to offer a welcome and introduce the speakers, including Richard Allen (the curator of the Tulane University jazz archives), the pastor of the First African Baptist Church, and a representative of the Zulu Social Aid and Pleasure Club.

What the Jazz Club should have reckoned on, but did not, was the effect of street music on a New Orleans crowd. The Olympia and the Onward started from their positions on Basin Street, and the Christian Band led off from Union Station. As the bands moved along, people did not just watch them go by, they went with them. Young men began to strut, children pranced alongside the marchers, and couples started to dance.

As the bands neared City Hall, they had collected far more people than had been expected to attend. There were about ten thousand there, and they were not in a mood for mourning. They overflowed Duncan Square, and they crowded onto the speaker's platform near the entrance to City Hall. Mayor Landrieu made a few brief remarks and turned the podium over to Richard Allen, who was to give a summary of Armstrong's life. Allen had just about gotten him into the Waif's Home when a man stepped out of the crowd, grabbed the microphone, and shouted, "Louis Armstrong isn't dead!" The crowd roared its approval, and, as Allen tried to continue, someone yelled, "Louis Armstrong was the greatest!" This brought more cheering from the crowd. Allen cut it short and yielded the podium to Ernest J. Wright from the Zulu Social Club. There were so many shouted interruptions that he lost his place in his speech and retreated. Reverend E. W. Henry seized the microphone and said, "If you're willing to listen, I have a eulogy to give." They weren't, and he didn't.

A trumpeter named Teddy Riley was there to end the ceremony by playing Louis's old cornet, and he thought it was time. He played "Taps," swinging it a little. When he finished, one of the bands struck up "Saints," and people started dancing again. They stayed for an hour or so, and when the band drifted away, the people did, too. It was still early, and there was plenty of time to find some more music.

SELECT BIBLIOGRAPHY

Armstrong, Louis. *Satchmo: My Life in New Orleans*. New York: Prentice-Hall, 1954.

———. *Swing That Music*. New York: Longmans, Green, 1936.

Asbury, Herbert. *The French Quarter*. New York: Alfred A. Knopf, 1936.

Badger, Reid. J*ames Reese Europe: A Life in Ragtime*. New York: Oxford University Press, 1995.

Bergreen, Laurence. *Louis Armstrong*. New York: Broadway Books, 1997.

Berlin, Edward. *King of Ragtime: Scott Joplin and His Era*. New York: Oxford University Press, 1994.

Berrett, Joshua, ed. *The Louis Armstrong Companion*. New York: Schirmer Books, 1999.

Blesh, Rudi, and Harriet Janis. *They All Played Ragtime*. 4th edition. New York: Oak Publications, 1971.

Blumenthal, Ralph. "Digging Deeply at Satchmo's Early Roots," *New York Times* (August 15, 2000).

Boardman, Gerald. *American Musical Theatre*. New York: Oxford University Press, 1978.

Brothers, Thomas, ed. *Louis Armstrong, in His Own Words*. New York: Oxford University Press, 1999.

Brown, Scott E. *James P. Johnson*. Metuchen, NJ: Scarecrow Press, 1986.

Charters, Samuel B. *Jazz: New Orleans 1885–1963*. New York: Oak Publications, 1963.

Condon, Eddie. *We Called It Music*. New York: Henry Holt & Co., 1947.

Curtis, Susan. *Dancing to a Black Man's Tune: A Life of Scott Joplin*. Columbia: University of Missouri Press, 1994.

Dance, Stanley. *The World of Earl Hines*. New York: Scribner's, 1977.

Dapogny, James. *Ferdinand "Jelly Roll" Morton: The Collected Piano Music*. Washington, DC: Smithsonian Institution Press, 1982.

Davin, Tom. "Conversations with James P. Johnson," *Jazz Review* (June–July, 1959).

Fletcher, Tom. *100 Years of the Negro in Show Business*. New York: Burdge, 1954.

Giddins, Gary. *Satchmo*. New York: Doubleday, 1988.

Godrich, John, and Robert M. W. Dixon. *Blues and Gospel Records, 1902–1942*. Chigwell, England: Storyville, 1969.

Gushee, Lawrence. "A Preliminary Chronology of the Early Career of Ferd 'Jelly Roll' Morton," *American Music* (winter 1985).

Handy, W. C. "I Would Not Play Jazz If I Could," *Down Beat* (September 1938).

Harris, Sheldon. *Blues Who's Who*. New Rochelle, NY: Arlington House, 1979.

Hornstein, Julius. *The Sites and Sounds of Savannah Jazz*. Savannah, GA: Gaston Street Press, 1994.

Jasen, David A. *Recorded Ragtime 1897–1958*. Hamden, CT: Archon, 1973.

———. *Tin Pan Alley*. New York: Donald I. Fine, 1988.

Jasen, David A., and Gene Jones. *Spreadin' Rhythm Around*. New York: Schirmer Books, 1998.

———. *That American Rag.* New York: Schirmer Books, 2000.

Jasen, David A., and Trebor Tichenor. *Rags and Ragtime.* New York: Seabury Press, 1978.

Jepsen, Jorgen Grunnet. *Jazz Records, 1942–1965.* Copenhagen, Denmark: Knudsen, 1970.

Jones, Gene. "Tom Turpin: His Life and Music." Savannah, GA: Tom Turpin Ragtime Festival Press, 1995.

Jones, Max, and John Chilton. *Louis: The Louis Armstrong Story.* Boston: Little, Brown, 1971.

Keith, Don Lee. "Two Bands to Pay Final Tribute to Satchmo, a Man and His Music." *New Orleans Times-Picayune* (July 11, 1971).

Kennedy, Rick. *Jelly Roll, Bix, and Hoagy.* Bloomington: Indiana University Press, 1994.

Kimball, Robert, and William Bolcom. *Reminiscing with Sissle and Blake.* New York: Viking Press, 1972.

Kirkeby, Ed. *Ain't Misbehavin': The Story of Fats Waller.* New York: Dodd, Mead & Co., 1966.

Kramer, Karl. "Jelly Roll in Chicago; the Missing Chapter." *The Ragtimer* (April 1967).

Lomax, Alan. *Mister Jelly Roll.* New York: Duell, Sloan, & Pearce, 1950.

Lord, Tom. *Clarence Williams.* Chigwell, England: Storyville, 1976.

Marquis, Donald M. *In Search of Buddy Bolden.* Baton Rouge: Louisiana State University Press, 1978.

Meryman, Richard. *Louis Armstrong—A Self-Portrait.* York: Eakins Press, 1971.

Morton, Jelly Roll. "Jelly Roll Says That He Was the First to Play Jazz," *Down Beat* (September 1938).

Nolan, Bruce. "Thousands Attend Memorial Services Given for Satchmo." *New Orleans Times-Picayune* (July 12, 1971).

Record Changer. New York, 1942–1957.

Rose, Al. *Eubie Blake.* New York: Schirmer Books, 1979.

———. *Storyville, New Orleans.* Tuscaloosa, AL: University of Alabama Press, 1974.

Rose, Al, and Edmond Souchon. *New Orleans Jazz: A Family Album.* Baton Rouge: Louisiana State University Press, 1967.

Russell, William, comp. *Oh, Mister Jelly*. Copenhagen, Denmark: JazzMediaApS, 1999.

Rust, Brian. *Jazz Records, 1897–1942*. 2 vols. New Rochelle, NY: Arlington, 1978.

Shapiro, Nat, and Nat Hentoff. *Hear Me Talkin' to Ya: The Story of Jazz by the Men Who Made It*. New York: Rinehart, 1955.

Smith, Willie the Lion, and George Hoefer. *Music on My Mind*. Garden City, NY: Doubleday, 1964.

Southern, Eileen. *Biographical Dictionary of African-American and African Musicians*. Westport, CT: Greenwood Press, 1982.

Waller, Maurice, and Anthony Calabrese. *Fats Waller*. New York: Schirmer Books, 1977.

Whitburn, Joel. *Pop Memories, 1890–1954*. Menomonee Falls, WI: Record Research, Inc., 1986.

Wright, Laurie. *Fats in Fact*. Chigwell, England: Storyville, 1992.

———. *Mr. Jelly Lord*. Chigwell, England: Storyville, 1980.

INDEX OF MUSIC TITLES

GENERAL INDEX

ABOUT THE AUTHORS

DAVID A. JASEN is an internationally recognized authority on ragtime, early jazz, and popular song. He is the author of numerous books, including *Tin Pan Alley* and *Recorded Ragtime, 1897–1958*. With Gene Jones, he is co-author of *Spreadin' Rhythm Around* (a study of black popular songwriters, which received the ASCAP–Deems Taylor Award in 1999) and *That American Rag*. He has edited several collections of ragtime-

era sheet music and produced many CD reissues of early pop song and ragtime recordings. A recent winner of the Scott Joplin Award, he is Professor of Media Arts at the C.W. Post campus of Long Island University.

GENE JONES, from Olla, Louisiana, is an actor and music historian. Besides co-writing three books with David Jasen, he is the author of *Fables in Slang*, a ragtime revue based on the humor of George Ade. *Fables* was produced off-Broadway in 1999. He has appeared in Broadway and off-Broadway shows, and in major regional theater productions. His voice is heard in several of Ken Burns's epic documentaries, including *The Civil War*, *The West*, and *Lewis and Clark*.